University of Oklahoma Press : Norman and London

THE WESTERN

PEACE OFFICER

A Legacy of Law and Order

Library of Congress Cataloging in Publication Data
Prassel, Frank Richard, 1937–
      The Western peace officer.
      Bibliography: p. 291
      1. Peace officers—The West—History.   2. Law
enforcement—The West—History.   I. Title.
   HV8138.P7   363.2'0978   71–39627
ISBN: 0–8061–1694–3

5   6   7   8   9   10   11   12   13   14

Preface

SOMEWHERE deep within the folklore of America may be found a figure of heroic stature. Surrounded by legends created through generations of poor reporting, fictional misrepresentations, and myth masquerading as history, his true identity is now virtually unknown. Yet images of his past flicker before tens of millions of Americans every day. This vast audience has a clear awareness of a presence somehow strangely blended by a bygone era and of today. While the countless viewers are conscious of a basis in reality, they know the current representations are beclouded by artificial dramatization and false portrayal. But few can divine the limits of fact and the borders of fiction. Although particular characteristics and individual traits may be lacking in common knowledge, the dim outlines of the figure remain clearly drawn. Against a background of almost limitless expanse he is found in silhouette. In the public mind he sits at ease astride a horse, wearing a broad-brimmed hat. While his face is shadowed, the eyes glint with a peculiar light of hard finality. Perhaps most clearly identified are the six-shooter at his side and, caught in the rays of the sun, the shining badge upon his chest.

This is the western peace officer, engraved into the hearts of

Americans and others throughout the world by books, comic strips, motion pictures, radio, television, and virtually every other known means of mass communication. In various portrayals the peace officer may be called sheriff, marshal, ranger, or by some other designation. He may be in Montana, Arizona, Oregon, Kansas, Texas, or elsewhere in the West. The details are varied and subject to endless combination. At times the peace officer may even be villainous, but he is usually fearless and deadly. It is widely accepted that he played a major part in bringing order to a lawless frontier during the last half of the nineteenth century. But as to how this unique task was supposedly accomplished and by what agencies, the answers are not apparent.

Recent decades have witnessed a truly incredible outpouring of materials on different aspects of law enforcement on the frontier. With few exceptions these products deal with individuals and are of a quality ranging from indifferent to dreadful. Although numerous they tend to be repetitious and based on dim but highly colored recollections. To seek the true nature of the western peace officer one must go beyond the superficial portrayals so readily obtained. To attempt a valid evaluation of a contribution to social order requires perspective; it also demands a certain amount of sympathetic understanding. To grasp the significance of the frontier lawman's role and image in America demands an interpretation of his problems and their attempted solution. Any effort to accomplish these goals must, of course, begin with the conditions which led to the existence of the western peace officer. It must begin beyond the Mississippi, with frontier America.

Acknowledgments

I wish to express sincere gratitude to Professors Joe B. Frantz, William H. Goetzmann, Robert A. Divine, and Dean Page Keeton of The University of Texas at Austin for their assistance in the preparation of this book.

Representatives of many police agencies, record centers, historical societies, university libraries, and governmental archives throughout the West provided co-operation and hospitality in the course of research. Appreciation should additionally be extended to hundreds of peace officers from private, city, county, state, federal, and military agencies whom the author has had as students of law enforcement. So long as their quest for professional improvement continues, the frontier of inquiry also endures.

Ultimately, the deepest felt thanks must go to my wife Ann for her patience, understanding, and assistance.

FRANK RICHARD PRASSEL

Contents

Illustrations

THE WESTERN PEACE OFFICER

"Wild and Unsettled Portions of Our Territories"

I

HOW lawless was the "wild" West? Most readers and many writers assume that the closing American frontier existed as a vast arena filled with violent crime. Cattle rustling, stage robbery, shootings, jail breaks—these are the violations that fill endless popular and fictional accounts. Of course, no one would presume to accept such portrayals as fully accurate, but the degree of variation from actual conditions is an open question.

The issue cannot be approached without some clarification of scope. For the purpose of this book the geographic scene is largely restricted to the regions now occupied by the seventeen contiguous states lying west of, but not bordering upon, the Mississippi River. This somewhat arbitrary line of demarcation corresponds closely to the 95°, west longitude, and divides the forty-eight conjoined states into roughly equal halves. It defines a West which matches to some degree that of the popular mind and forms a huge area of more than 1.7 million square miles. Reaching from the plains of Kansas to the forests of Oregon, it encompasses a diverse collection of mountain ranges, deserts, plateaus, and valleys, including many of the geologic wonders of the earth.

This sweeping panorama witnessed escapades of the most renowned outlaws in American history—Joaquin Murieta, Billy the Kid, Sam Bass, Black Bart, John Wesley Hardin, Butch Cassidy, the Daltons, and others of equal fame. As distinctive figures of a unique regional heritage they have few comparisons. But as examples reflecting widespread social conditions their legends are of use today only as yardsticks for the measurement of distorted memory.

Prevalent crime, as a characteristic of the West, has nevertheless stamped the region with an enduring reputation. A sound foundation for a heritage of lawlessness, however, existed many generations before settlement from the East. The early Spanish colonization in New Mexico had as one of its bases a thinly disguised system of illegal slavery. Forbidden in the New World by royal decree in 1532, the slave trade flourished in the Santa Fe region by the seventeenth century. This illicit market in humanity continued throughout the period of Spanish rule and into the brief era of Mexican control, despite efforts of *audiencias* in the South to eradicate the slave trade. Even when one is willing to regard the usual struggles with Indian tribes as conflict between competing societies, little doubt remains that the isolated Spanish settlements in the Southwest were frequently the locale for a wide range of criminal activity. In one instance, for example, adultery and murder led to a veritable civil war between clerical and secular groups in New Mexico.[1]

The appearance of great numbers of predominantly Anglo-Saxon colonists moving toward the Pacific and the eventual assertion of authority by the United States brought many changes to social conditions in the West. But the widespread occurrence of criminal activity continued without diminution. Rather, the newcomers only modified and introduced new forms of illegality. Land itself became a major cause of criminal design. Whisky and arms trade with the Indians served as another lucrative source of illicit profit. The variety of villainy covered almost every type of forbidden conduct known to man, from armed robbery to prostitution and horse theft. Lawlessness extended into the very agencies designed to cope with the problem. Judges sometimes required armed guards, while the courtrooms and legislative assemblies were themselves occasionally the sites of armed assaults and even murders.

Such conditions naturally led to alarm among the citizenry and prompted their spokesmen to comment upon existing problems. John J. Gosper, acting governor of Arizona in 1881, described the situation in these frank terms:

There is another side of the affairs of this Territory, connected with the history of the year named [1881], not so pleasant to consider. Crime, everywhere present in our common country, is far more frequent and appalling in the Territories than elsewhere, because of the less regard generally paid to virtue and the rights of property, but more generally because of the fact that criminals—fugitives from justice—from thickly settled sections of the East, flee to the wild and unsettled portions of our Territories, where they can form in bands for mutual protection against arrest and punishment.

Within the limits of this Territory there have existed companies or bands of outlaws, commonly called "cow-boys," who, the past year have committed many murders, and have stolen thousands of dollars' worth of stock and other property. Many times the stages carrying the United States mails, passengers, and the usual express, have been suddenly stopped by armed, masked men, who have rifled the mails, robbed the express, and deprived the passengers of all their valuables; and not unfrequently, they have committed murder in connection with these robberies—always where resistance has been offered.[2]

One Texas judge, writing to the state adjutant general, expressed the prevalent attitude more succinctly: "If the governor don't help us, I am going to bushwhacking."[3]

By the close of the nineteenth century a pattern of lawlessness represented the West, at least in the popular mind. It has been suggested that the frontier experience left a residue in the form of criminal traditions which today still have a severe impact on modern American society.[4] Regardless of specific effect, a heritage of violence etched itself deeply into the culture.

These conditions of social disorder had both causes and effects. They did not spring full blown from the uninhabited portions of the West, but developed with the arrival of settlers, one byproduct of a great and dramatic conflict of cultures. Resistance

5

of Indian groups lent to the American frontier a fundamental coloring of danger and violence that has never been fully dispelled. The indigenous tribes, representing a wide range of social advancement, fought a hopeless battle against the Spanish, French, English, and Americans. Such opposition, continuing for a period of nearly four hundred years and lasting until the early twentieth century in North America, developed in those of European heritage certain patterns of brutality and force which may yet be encountered as national and regional characteristics.

Apart from this highly significant background of societies in collision, the newcomers themselves contributed a leavening of unrest and individual deviance. Several years before the real opening of the West an alert observer, significantly investigating penal reforms in America, commented:

> Social condition is commonly the result of circumstances, sometimes of laws, oftener still of these two causes united; but when once established, it may justly be considered as itself the source of almost all the laws, the usages, and the ideas which regulate the conduct of nations; whatever it does not produce, it modifies.[5]

The first of these elements, that of circumstance, found many thousands of unusual personalities drifting westward across the Mississippi in the middle and later years of the nineteenth century. By their very willingness to move into the frontier, they were proven adventuresome, self-reliant, and courageous. Many went a step beyond these admirable traits and could justly be termed both wild and foolhardy. A smaller proportion would have to be classified in still another way. They were the sociopaths with a distrust, and sometimes an open dislike, for the complex cultural creations of men. Eccentric and maladjusted people, unable to find a satisfying position in the East, migrated to the newly opened lands of the frontier.[6] Thus the West, as had other regions in earlier eras, became a refuge for the potentially violent and the lawless.

Social misfits fighting a barbaric foe became a basic equation for disorder. The remarkably heterogeneous population of the new territories and a widespread impatience with formal authority as a means for local control contributed to a complex formula culminating in turbulence and crime. Indeed, at times they served to create conditions wherein citizens rejected ordinary social values and substituted frontier standards. As a consequence, the lawbreaker and the fugitive at times became the subject of general sympathy and support, with effects often not so disastrous as might be anticipated in a more complex and technologically advanced culture.

Such were the circumstances which some hundreds of thousands of Americans either found or created for themselves in the West. But, as has been indicated earlier, the general social conditions of lawlessness cannot be divorced from the statutes by which they are necessarily measured. Nearly a century ago a legal scholar and later eminent member of the Supreme Court, Oliver Wendell Holmes, caught the essence of the crucial process. "The first requirement of a sound body of law," he wrote, "is that it should correspond with the actual feelings and demands of the community, whether right or wrong."[7] Unfortunately, the written law and the usual silent demands of society on the frontier did not always neatly parallel. On occasion they came into outright opposition. More often, the disharmony existed below a surface of conformity.

While the frontier society may appear to have functioned with many violations of formal law, it sometimes more truly reflected community customs in conflict with superficial and at times alien standards. In time, of course, this struggle resulted in compromise and settlement by modification, but it originally contributed to an atmosphere of chronic unrest.

Crime in the West, however unique in quality and quantity, always reflected the social conditions in which it thrived. A limited insight into such patterns may be gathered by looking at the selected statistics in Table 1 of Appendix A. In 1880 western towns reflected a liberal attitude toward the sporting life. San Francisco reported no less than 8,694 saloons, while Boston, with half again the population, had only 2,347. Leadville, Colorado, calmly indicated an astonishing one hundred houses of prostitution, or one for every 148 residents. Although not all communities in the West displayed such tendencies, they generally indicated the influence of the passing frontier on attitudes toward sex and liquor. It should, nevertheless, be noted that New York and New Orleans, respectively, led the nation in total numbers of bars and bordellos.

The traditional lawlessness of the West, however, is usually associated with regions of sparse population instead of cities. Small isolated towns and the open range are the popularized backgrounds for frontier crime. These normally inaccurate fictional versions of violence have cast an unfortunate light on the early settlements which still confuses analyses of actual conditions. A few communities may have been under the temporary control of professional criminals, but the more common circumstance was that of sympathetic understanding, without direct connivance, for those in violation of penal statutes. Most western areas were really very peaceful when compared with urban centers in the East.

Nevertheless, the vivid and dramatic episodes depicted by popular writers do have foundation in fact. Cowboys shooting up a town, train and bank robberies, rustling of livestock—such exciting crimes constituted major problems, usually with very human complications. Every violation, particularly those against the person, involved strong individual feelings, a characteristic often lost in routine reports and dry statistics. Occasionally the personal drama found in every crime penetrates through the formalities, as in this letter from an undersheriff of Sandoval County, New Mexico Territory:

Juan Isidro Chije the Governor of the Zia Pueblo has been missing from the Pueblo for 23 days, it is quite likely that he has been made away with, he had trouble with his wife and on the morning the 14th [of April, 1909] he left the Pueblo to irrigate a field, telling his wife (this is her story) that as soon as he had irrigated he would journey to Naciemento, he took his rifle with him, nothing has since been seen or heard of or from him. No one saw him leave, his wife says that they trailed him several miles in the direction he said he was going, there is nothing to verify it.

Mr. Spader was at the Pueblo the other day and looked into the matter, he states that considerable jealousy existed between him and his wife. It is his opinion that he was murdered, the school teaher [sic] there is of similar opinion.[8]

An Indian governor's disappearance from a Pueblo serves as an example of the peculiar nature of crime in the West. It also, of course, illustrates the marked degree of social differentiation which marked groups on the frontier.

The geographical and cultural isolation of segments of the population gave rise to another peculiar type of crime problem —the bandit gang. In the vast wilderness areas of the West organized groups of outlaws sought refuge from ordinary law enforcement. Marauding bands might, for years, operate in a relative vacuum of population and control, although the identity of member outlaws acquired widespread fame. Fragmented social groups could, of course, also flourish in cultural isolation, such as those sometimes encountered in an urban setting. The West also developed gangs of this sort, particularly the Chinese fighting "tongs" of the late nineteenth and early twentieth centuries. By capitalizing on the gulf that existed before assimilation between the subcultural mores and the states' laws, these "highbinder" associations exploited a minority's social separation.[9]

Just as the existence of large foreign populations led to certain conditions of lawlessness, so did the existence of peculiar economic activities. In the West a unique institutional aspect served as one basis for the development of crime. Special patterns of lawlessness developed with the great herds of cattle and sheep which came to dominate the lives of so many settlers.

While illegal conduct involving livestock began with the unauthorized entry of animals, usually cattle, on reserved lands, trouble also arose over the passage of possibly diseased herds. Later, the most serious problems evolved with the gradual closing of the open range. Homesteaders and small ranchers came into conflict with major cattle companies over the issue of fencing. The disputes resulted in a series of bloody clashes across the sparsely populated territories in the years following the Civil

9

War. These controversies over the use and misuse of barbed wire, illegal fence cutting, and related activities became items of major political significance in the West. Before the difficulties could be resolved, state laws had to be rewritten, Congress moved to provide aid, federal troops marched into the fray, and one territorial governor, George W. Baxter of Wyoming, found himself removed from office.[10]

Even more durable and violent than the wars over fencing were those between the sheepmen and the cattlemen. The struggle culminated in some of the West's most famous feuds and gunfights. It also led to the passage of special statutes designed to prevent the continuance of violence which, in turn, only resulted in technical means of evasion. These measures did not meet with immediate success; conflict continued between sheep and cattle interests well into the twentieth century.

Conditions on the range, however, only served as one underlying cause of disorder. The more immediate provocations were identical to those involved in contemporary crimes of violence—women, liquor, gambling, and firearms. As instigations to disorder, of course, the four cannot be totally divorced from one another. Women eventually served as a basic stabilizing influence in the West. They were, in fact, desperately needed, a condition which probably contributed directly to their early receipt of political equality. But in the early days their relative rarity provoked many violent encounters. The affections of a female, regardless of her place in life, often unfortunately sparked hostility and sometimes released the latent sexual destructivity of men on the frontier.

Across the vast frontier women also constituted a commodity of real significance in organized houses of prostitution. These bordellos sometimes reflected an opulence and luxury rare in the undeveloped territories; more usually, the bawdyhouses served as centers of violent crime, corruption, and disease.

As "white slavery" flourished, so did the traffic in illegal alcohol and the activities associated with forbidden gambling. Liquor and wagering, often in violation of the formal codes, endured as highly significant problems for frontier communities. Regardless of the restrictions imposed on forms of vice, a goodly proportion of the populace had little difficulty in satisfying their desires.[11] Whether or not legally condemned, liquor and gambling clearly contributed to an atmosphere of unrestraint. With both present in abundance, they became companions to crimes against person, property, morality, and public welfare.

No symbol is more commonly representative of the West than the pistol. The availability of firearms to ordinary citizens was perhaps never so prevalent as along the American frontier, contributing immeasurably to an already tense environment. Consequently, events which normally might lead to a common disagreement and perhaps a simple assault could be rapidly transformed into a deadly encounter. Firearms were a necessary tool in the development of the new lands, but they remained to create social havoc. Efforts to control the use of concealable devices such as pistols and knives came soon after the establishment of formal authority, but these measures usually ended in failure. By avoidance, lack of enforcement, or outright misuse, the laws sometimes seemed totally ineffectual. "In 1875 the carrying of deadly weapons without special permission was forbidden in San Francisco; since which time hundreds of applications for such permission have been made and granted. It has been questioned whether under this law the safety of the citizen or of the robber is the better secured."[12]

Restrictions on firearms extended from simple prohibition, through specific exclusion and enhancement of punishment, to special defenses for those slaying armed parties. The result in most jurisdictions endures as a complex patchwork of regulations made worse by the addition of grotesque provisions designed to curb a soaring crime rate. However involved the efforts, firearms and other dangerous weapons in the hands of evildoers continued to plague the West. Such lethal devices as pistols, knives, and dirks, of course, were not themselves a direct causative factor; they only constituted one element in the equation of prevalent lawlessness.

No analysis of crime can be fully divorced from the instrumentalities by which it is normally determined and measured— the courts. In the early days of the frontier, organs of formal criminal justice were rudimentary in structure and crude in operation. These conditions, however, soon gave way to institutional systems comparable in many instances to those of today. The courts of the West reflected the problems of a frontier society and the weaknesses of pronounced local political control.

In general, the actual administration of justice was not favorably regarded by the populace on the frontier. This attitude did not come about because of any pronounced resistance to the presence and duties of the courts, but developed in disapproval of the policies and functioning of judicial bodies. Many citizens felt that widespread inefficiency and corruption subverted the ends of justice. Demoralized communities witnessed examples of great political and economic influence routinely exercised on magistrates at all judicial levels. In the administration of criminal cases, a common attitude viewed the courts as too slow, too lenient, and too often inclined toward the release of the guilty —opinions still prevalent today. Thus, each of the three primary principles of punishment as a deterrent—celerity, severity, and certainty—encountered frustration by the very agencies established to represent the law.

While the majority of judges in the West did their best to uphold high standards, enough doubtful activity occurred to cloud the reputation of many courts. Some magistrates remained on the bench for long periods despite desperate efforts at removal by embittered citizens.[13] To some, such legal tribunals seemed only to aggravate conditions of crime and disorder.

Courts of law were in bad repute in those days. Venality and corruption sat upon the bench in the form of duelling, drinking, fist fighting, and licentious judges. Where the people looked for justice, they found too often jokes and jeers. It was not uncommon to see a judge appear upon the bench in a state of intoxication, and make no scruple to attack with fist, cane, or revolver any who offended him. Two prominent [California] magistrates bore the significant sobriquets of

Mammon and Gammon. The universal absence of restraint and indifference to conventionalisms were as conspicuously apparent in the supreme court of the state as elsewhere.[14]

Criticisms of formal justice extended to other arms of the legal process; it did not end with judges. In many jurisdictions, for example, juries were notoriously lax, debauched, or openly corruptible. In postsentence stages a low level of conduct continued. A convicted party, unsuccessful in efforts to escape pronouncement of punishment by efforts before or during trial, might avail himself of various measures to avoid any actual correctional imposition. The most popular of these means probably existed through the purchased pardon. For a sum, executives of different jurisdictions could often be convinced of the wisdom of granting a release. As one citizen of Colorado, Joseph Bailey, stated in 1887: "There are too many pardons granted criminals in this state. Why, a large number of pardoned criminals who have got out of the penitentiary during the past year are now back in jail again."[15]

Complaints based upon the failure of courts to convict and punish, perhaps apart from direct charges of graft, stemmed from actual conditions. In the Republic of Texas, less than ten per cent of indictments for serious crimes of personal violence resulted in successful prosecutions.[16] Nor did later eras witness any rapid improvement on this low rate of conviction.

Not unique was the February, 1883, term for the federal district court at Santa Fe, New Mexico Territory. During this continuing session a total of twenty-three cases, involving such diverse charges as selling liquor to Indians, embezzlement, and "uttering counterfeit notes" came to a conclusion by clearance from the docket. Seven of the cases were ordered discontinued, the prosecutor withdrew by *nolle prosequi* in two causes, the judge ordered dismissal in two more actions, and the court received eleven verdicts of not guilty. Of the twenty-three initial charges, only one resulted in the passing of sentence—"30 days" for violation of election laws.[17] Typically, none of the cases involved a crime against the person.

Ironically, much of the discontent with court operations stemmed from social pressures and outright control. The tribunals of the West, however inefficient, were clearly products of their human environment. Distrust of those in official position, a traditional American trait, increased among frontiersmen and extended to attitudes concerning magistrates. Local control of judges could best be asserted by popular election, a means first utilized on a comprehensive scale in Mississippi about 1832.[18] This expression of provincial sovereignty proved quite popular in the West and left an enduring legacy. While only slightly more than half of all the states, including several in the South and Midwest, elect judges of district courts, twelve of the seventeen western states do so. Most of these naturally elect appellate justices as well. Only Nebraska, Kansas, Colorado, Utah, and California use some form of routine executive appointment for their primary trial judges in courts of record.[19]

The strong assertion of social control included more than the selection of magistrates. Many jurisdictions on the frontier utilized some form of jury sentencing, rather than the traditional judge-fixed punishments, in criminal cases. At least four of the western states (Montana, Oklahoma, Texas, and North Dakota) still provide under statute for certain types of venire-determined penalties.[20] Even more unusual was Colorado's short-lived experiment with popular recall of judicial opinions, a technique struck down by the state supreme court in 1921.[21]

Elected judges, jury sentencing, recall of court decisions—these were expressions of a desire to correlate closely court practices with community demands. They helped to create a situation wherein justice could be directly tied to public wishes. With them came certain strong protections of local self-government, but they also incorporated a tendency for political considerations to outweigh requirements of equity.

Courts on the western frontier also came under the influence of another and more obvious form of social pressure. In an era preceding the entertainment provided by mass communication, criminal trials served as a source of local amusement. Citizens attended court sessions as intensely interested spectators and the course of a notable case might hold popular attention for many days. At times the social gatherings surrounding important trials became a significant factor on the administration of justice. Some judges turned their courts into theaters to accommodate the demands of the electorate audiences, with disastrous effects on the dignity of the judicial system and the fairness with which it might operate.[22]

Before these tribunals paraded the criminal cases upon which much of the West's lawless reputation is based. The validity of such fame, however, remains subject to question. Was crime in the newly opened territories significantly more common than in the East? Also, to what degree have conditions really changed with the formal passing of the frontier? Unfortunately, no recourse is available to detailed and reliable statistics on lawlessness in the present, much less in the past.[23] If, as previously noted, the early western social environment created a climate conducive to disorder and violence, traces might still indicate how distinctive a crime rate truly existed.

Currently, the most complete system of reporting on national crime deals with major index offenses. These include murder, robbery, burglary, aggravated assault, etc., but exclude lesser violations against property and public morality. Present statistics indicate a very wide regional variation in degrees of lawlessness. The rate of reported index crimes per one million population extends from a low of 124.2 in the East South-Central states (Alabama, Kentucky, Mississippi, and Tennessee) to a high of 291.4 in the Pacific region (Alaska, California, Hawaii, Oregon, and Washington). Dividing the nation into three primary areas, the Federal Bureau of Investigation indicated for 1967 the following overall annual frequency of index violations, adjusted to estimated population:[24]

United States—total	192.2
Northeast	203.2
South	163.9
West	267.9

While these general reports are indicative of conditions, they must be approached with caution. Such statistics originate with voluntary notices from local agencies and remain subject to distortion. The regional variation, furthermore, is not so marked as that involving density of population. Throughout the nation, the spatial concentration of people correlates quite consistently with an increased frequency of index crime. In cities of over one million population, for example, the rate in 1967 reached 417.4.[25] This pattern clearly transcends state boundaries and makes any conclusion on the significance of regional variation subject to doubt.

Although in general the West does report the highest degree of serious crime in the United States, this is largely the statistical result of extensively urbanized areas along parts of the Pacific Coast. California leads the nation in major offenses with a rate of 320.8. But in sparsely populated Idaho, with a rate of only 98.5, crime is less than one-third as likely. Mississippi, by tradition a center of disorder, reported only 57.5 index violations per million inhabitants during the year, the lowest in the country. But North Dakota, also a state with relatively little urbanization, approached this progressive nadir with a rate of only 59.6.[26]

Before accepting the existence of a high degree of serious crime in the West, one should note that a wide variation in types of offenses contributes to the overall index rates. Generally, the great frequency of property crimes, which nationally compose approximately 87 per cent of all violations, accounts for an extremely disproportionate element in western statistics. And, as noted, these offenses are heavily concentrated in urban areas. It is, then, not so much the recent frontier regions that provide high rates of violent crime, but the great cities of the new West that must be blamed for excessive violation of property rights.

It is impossible to state categorically that the greater degree of apparent lawlessness in the West results from traditions of long standing. For many years the South seemed to reflect unusually marked rates of violence, a tendency still encountered in recent reports. If any conclusion can be drawn from recent crime statistics, it must be that the last great frontier left no significant heritage of offenses against the person, relative to other sections of the country.

Any attempt to determine the extent of actual disorder must turn to the limited and questionable records of the past. Unfortunately, many of the files and ledgers kept by agencies of criminal justice have either been lost or destroyed. Those which still exist, however, can serve to illuminate certain of the processes of law enforcement so often beclouded by fiction and false assumption.

Surprisingly, arrest rates, adjusted for population growth, reveal a sharp decrease in the number of people placed in custody over the last century. In 1880, however, the West tended to require more than its share of police activity. Certain port, mining, and trail communities, particularly in Texas, reported unusually large numbers of homicides and arrests, but other towns, including Virginia City, Nevada, and Salt Lake City, were quite orderly. One must, however, remain aware that no western region compared in the amount or rate of crime demonstrated by New York and other urban areas of the East. Table 2 of Appendix A summarizes certain police reports for selected cities in 1880.

Total arrest statistics, of course, tell little about the actual character of crime. Some indication of the situation can be gathered from typical records. The police of Denver, Colorado, for August, 1886, a normal month, reported 489 arrests. Of those taken in custody, 202 (41 per cent) were charged with drunkenness and 106 (21 per cent) more with public disturbances or disorderly conduct. Forty-four women composed nine per cent of the formally detained.[27] For comparative purposes, the current proportions of similar categories are approximately 33 per cent (drunkenness), ten per cent (disorderly conduct), and thirteen per cent (women).[28] At least in these respects, Denver in 1886 did not vary greatly from urban centers of the present, although juvenile delinquency was notably less frequent.

This, however, is not meant to indicate that conditions peculiar

17

to the frontier had little influence on types of crime committed. Half of the total extraditions issued on fugitives in one year by the New Mexico Territory, for example, resulted from charges of horse or cattle theft.[29] But in the main, at least in larger communities, arrests in the West resembled those in other times and regions.

Not all persons placed under restraint or taken into custody ever came to trial. Probably half of all adults arrested do not reach the stage of formal accusation or arraignment. Those finally entering the judicial system, therefore, have never represented more than a small fraction of all offenses reported. Of legal proceedings actually undertaken, the overwhelming majority have always occurred in lower tribunals. The Denver police docket may serve to indicate the variety of cases and their subsequent dispositions in one western town in 1873. While charges included such routine violations as vagrancy, "immoderate riding," discharging firearms, selling liquor without a license, and breach of peace, some 80 per cent of the defendants were accused either of ordinary drunkenness or of being an "inmate of a house of ill fame." Approximately 90 per cent of those tried pled guilty, a proportion almost identical with the present. The general verdicts and sentences handed down were as follows:

	Per cent
Dismissed	6
Not Guilty	4
Fined	48
Jailed	40
Appealed	2

Most of those convicted received institutionalized punishments of "5 and 8," or a fine of $5 with court costs of $8. Drunks often could not pay and had to serve out their penalty at the rate of $2 a day, but prostitutes invariably managed to provide the cash necessary to secure an immediate release.[30] The conclusion of anyone acquainted with current machinations of justice is obvious. The last century has brought no real modification, improvement, or alteration. Three generations have apparently been unable either to devise or effectuate any significant changes in our lower courts.

City magistrates and justices of the peace heard the over-whelming majority of criminal cases brought to trial. Only the more serious charges, plus a few matters on appeal, found their way onto the dockets of the various courts of formal record. Here one might expect to have found a parade of those violent and dangerous outlaws around whom the legends of the "wild" West revolve. Such, however, was not the actual situation. The criminal district courts normally decided cases not involving indictments of murder, aggravated assault, or armed robbery. Most of the dockets were consumed with charges involving nonviolent violations against property, public morality, and order—in approximately the same proportion as found in modern jurisdictions. For every crime against the person resulting in a trial, there were often at least four other and less dramatic offenses at the same stage in the judicial process.

In the various federal district courts, which heard most major cases in the territories, a great variety of violations could routinely be found on the docket. A session might include accusations of embezzlement, incest, perjury, making false affidavits, false entry, assault, mailing obscene letters, conspiracy to defraud, and contempt. Certain jurisdictions did, of course, have considerable numbers of offenses peculiar to their location, such as the introduction or disposition of intoxicants in the Indian Territory.[31] Other examples could be found in the abuse of the land by those accused of preventing surveys, unlawfully cutting timber, and improper fencing. Interference with the mails provided other fairly widespread problems, and some areas did have notably frequent charges of assault or affray. But these crimes relating to particular times and circumstances normally occupied only a small part of the court's work. Infinitely more common were simple charges of larceny, often of livestock, and, significantly, offenses against public morality. An astonishing number of indictments charged adultery, fornication, bigamy, and seduction. Of the first twenty-six cases docketed with the U.S. District Court at Roswell, New Mexico, in 1890, no less than seventeen dealt with adultery and five with fornication.[32] The West's lawless element obviously had something on its mind other than bank robbery and cattle theft. Perhaps the pioneers had an unconscious desire to help alleviate the scarcity of population. Surely they were making an effort to relieve any feelings of loneliness or boredom.

Of those cases tried in courts of record for all offenses, roughly one-half ended in some type of exoneration. It might be by *nolle prosequi*, dismissal, or verdict of not guilty, but those accused clearly enjoyed an excellent opportunity to obtain a successful defense against more serious charges. For those convicted, sentences approximated those of the present day for similar crimes. While the courts did not have the benefit of advanced systems of probation and juvenile correction, many managed to utilize some form of suspended punishment. After pronouncing a sentence of two years in the penitentiary for attempted robbery of a post office, one judge at Santa Fe in 1903, for example, suspended incarceration "during good behavior and absence from the territory."[33]

Having examined records of arrests and trials, still another possible measure of the diversity and extent of crime can be gathered from statistics of correctional institutions. Local jails held the most mixed group of accused persons, for they received both accused felons and misdemeanants serving time. During 1882, the lockup of Arapahoe County, Colorado, recorded a total of 780 inmates. The more interesting offenses, in decreasing order of numerical representation, were as follows:[34]

Petty larceny	206
Grand larceny	114
Vagrancy	112
Assault and battery	74
Carrying concealed weapons	26
Mischief	20
Burglary	18
Murder	14

Forgery	14
Arson	11

Present jails contain the same types of offenders. One can easily note the high proportion of property crimes relative to those involving some form of violence. Offenses against the person presently compose only about 13 per cent of all violations; there is little evidence that the portion could have been significantly different in the old West.[35]

Prison statistics reflect only the more serious or repeating and convicted offenders; they should never be taken as a valid indication of the overall crime rate. Rates of incarceration remain a direct product of such variables as enforcement, prosecution, conviction, and sentencing. However, the records of correctional institutions do provide a concrete and reliable means of regional and jurisdictional comparison. Table 3 of Appendix A reflects the changing rates of imprisonment in several jurisdictions. The frontier states and territories never indicated any consistent pattern of large penal populations compared to the nation as a whole. Indeed, they tended to show an increase with the development of cities and rapid means of transportation. By 1880 the more populated areas of the West already had large prison systems; Texas reported 3,162 inmates, while California held 2,647. But Arizona, the Dakotas, Idaho, and New Mexico had a combined prison population of less than two hundred.[36] It would appear that, in the American West, crime may have been more closely related to the developing urban environment than the former existence of a frontier. So far as prison populations are concerned, the entire nation has shown a slow but fairly steady relative growth.

Unfortunately, no available statistics for past or present, whether dealing with reports of violations, arrests, trials, or imprisonment, reflect actual rates of crime. The evidence which may be obtained, however, indicates that the dubious reputation of the West is somewhat lacking in foundation. Of course, certain areas and communities did have unusually high rates of lawlessness, but these neither were nor are restricted to frontier regions. While it cannot be definitely documented, the Westerner of the late nineteenth century probably enjoyed greater security in both person and property than did his contemporary in the urban centers of the East.

The early settlements of the frontier, while small and isolated, usually demonstrated public peace and order. Violence existed more as a by-product of the era and environment than as a demonstration of true lawlessness. People had to look elsewhere for news of murder, rape, and armed robbery. In the small camps, villages, and towns of the West, the most exciting crime for many months might be a claim jumping or petty pilfering.[37] It was, perhaps, because of the general absence of disorder that the exploits of occasional outlaws and bandits received special notoriety. The majority of the settlers came to build a new life in the West, not to kill and pillage. As a consequence, they wanted to make their villages as orderly and peaceful as possible. As has been noted, gambling, drinking, and prostitution were commonplace, but they ordinarily took place with the same general complacency as currently exists.

In the main, the crimes of the old West comprised primarily the same violations most common in modern America—drunkenness, disorderly conduct, and petty larceny. Most citizens lived peacefully and without great fear of personal attack. The cowboy's revolver, when worn, proved far more useful against snakes than rustlers. In many communities people rarely felt the need to put locks on their doors, while local saloons and gambling parlors made a sincere effort to exclude women and minors.[38] Courts quickly appeared in most settlements, but the early judicial bodies rarely heard serious criminal charges.

As a place of wild lawlessness the frontier's spectacular reputation is, therefore, largely without substantiation. It is true that a band of daring outlaws, enraged over "land theft" might sweep down from their mountain stronghold to terrorize an isolated village, take command of a courthouse, and shoot or capture local peace officers. But these events did not occur in the distant past, they took place in 1967.[39] While a stage passenger going through Nevada during the 1860s might certainly have been in some danger of hijacking, he probably enjoyed greater security than his counterpart flying over Florida in a jet airliner a century later. A pioneer of the old West surely may have had his property taken in the dead of night or even been physically assaulted at noon on a main street, but these offenses also occur with appalling regularity in every modern American metropolitan area, usually with far less public attention than would have greeted a similar violation on the frontier.

In retrospect, it appears that the West did not, after all, attract extreme numbers of the lawless and deviant. Most settlers displayed a hardy and self-sufficient character which, while not prone to the acceptance of centralized authority, desired the creation of a peaceful society. "By far the larger part were order-loving men of pronounced morals and integrity."[40] Crime, to be sure, existed along the frontier, and it often reflected a violent heritage. Considering the factors present, however, it is perhaps surprising that even more murders, assaults, and robberies did not occur.

"A Duty to Maintain Public Order"

II

Confronted with instances of crime and disorder, the pioneers of the far West turned to members of their communities and charged them with the responsibility of law enforcement. Against a background of social instability and supported by courts of somewhat limited utility, the western peace officer came into being. While clearly reflecting the conditions which he sought to control, he also echoed traditions extending back many thousands of years.

Some form of police system, of course, reaches into man's dimmest recollections. In the thousands of years before written history, tribal systems probably relied upon group sanctions to enforce codes of behavior. And in later periods the leaders of clans and primitive cultures surely themselves served to maintain community peace and order. After the passage of many generations such functions became delegated powers and simple systems of formalized law enforcement emerged as one cohesive factor in the complex fabric of society.

By the reign of Hammurabi, king of Babylonia some two thousand years before the birth of Christ, agents of the ruler had certainly been charged with the specific duty of carrying out the famous dictates of early legal codes. There is little doubt that the civilizations of China, Egypt, and Greece also utilized types of police organization. But the Roman Empire, with its renowned statutory codifications, is the oldest culture with historically well-recognized means of law enforcement. Apparently, military units had responsibility for the maintenance of social order among the Romans. The legions and cohorts carried out various functions of peace keeping in cities and rural areas. Caesar Augustus, the first Roman emperor, created a Praetorian Guard to protect the royal person and property. He also formed a force of citizenry known as the *Vigiles* to maintain the internal security of Rome. These units operated on military principles and had as their primary duties the prevention of harm and the elimination of danger to the ruling powers. It is still possible, of course, to analyze the police function in the same framework of pragmatic utility.

The early Middle Ages in Europe witnessed a sharp decline in the sophistication of formal law enforcement. The nobility and clergy relied upon their supporters to preserve order. As the continental nation-states developed, centralization slowly brought with it stronger, well-organized systems of social control. Although actual derivation is difficult to determine fully, such words as "marshal," "patrol," and "police" apparently came from this era of gradually increasing authority and continue to illustrate the significance of expanding political power. Throughout the gradual establishment of central control and acceptance of customs, symbols, and usages, the tendency of law enforcement to parallel developments in the military can be noted. Marshal, patrol, and police, for example, have different but closely related connotations reflecting their mutual ancestry in the two systems.

While interpretations vary with changing concepts of social thought and philosophy, the fundamental functions of internal law enforcement and external defense continue to be similar and often, by necessity, closely related. Both are institutional arms of government operated for social protection, and both rely on the ultimate threat of physical violence to accomplish their objectives. In most instances, both are armed, uniformed, entrusted with special powers and privileges, and can be used for either democratic or despotic purposes. The police and the military are structurally based on a chain leading through concepts of authority, power, and force. And, to a great but often unrecognized extent, the two systems are mutually interdependent.

Such fundamental patterns, of course, did not reach the American West in pure or easily deciphered form. The organization, techniques, and heritage of the police evolved over several centuries and predominantly reflected deeply entrenched Anglo-Saxon and Norman traditions. Medieval England served as the background for many of the offices and functions which continue to dominate formal law enforcement. The early Anglo-Saxon era featured largely self-governing towns scattered in relative isolation throughout the countryside. These small villages provided their own citizen-police, centering around the ancient "hue and cry" by which the able-bodied could be summoned to lend assistance and take the wrongdoer into custody. By the ninth century royal power had been established over much of the land, but it remained for Alfred the Great to organize a system of central control over the various counties, or shires. In order to prepare for defense against the Danes and Celts and provide a dependable source of revenue, he devised a system to maintain the peace and to supervise taxation. This scheme involved the appointment of powerful nobles to offices combining enforcement and judicial functions and carrying the title of reeve. By the tenth century these figures, known as "shire-reeves," had obtained positions of significant political power in their respective counties. The name was eventually combined and shortened to the familiar "sheriff," but the duties endured with little change for hundreds of years.

William the Conqueror, victorious at Hastings in 1066, brought with him to England many Norman customs and offices. He strengthened the shire-reeves and permitted the introduction of a lower rank in the hierarchy of control. The baronies of France had long used "constables," from *comes stabuli* or "man of the stable," to raise and maintain mounted companies. In England officers with the same title were appointed primarily in rural districts to maintain order and collect revenues for the crown.

Within a few generations after the Norman invasion the basic pattern of local law enforcement, originating in centralized demands for efficient taxation, had been established in England. Over each county a sheriff exercised authority; beneath him, in districts or precincts, the constable held sway. Their offices and general duties, outdated even before the discovery of America, were imported to the colonies and still serve as common anachronisms throughout most of the modern United States.

By the close of the twelfth century, during the legendary era of Robin Hood, other enduring titles appeared. To preserve and protect unsettled areas from poachers and outlaws, the crown appointed special officers called foresters and rangers to patrol the reaches of the kingdom. By 1285, however, England had undergone considerable growth in urban population. Certain cities, particularly the London area, could no longer operate successfully with the rudimentary systems of law enforcement then extant. Edward I, in an effort to provide more security for such troubled sections, declared a kind of curfew and turned to an old Anglo-Saxon system of citizen patrol. Known as the watch (for night) and ward (for day), groups of men guarded the town gates and maintained order within the walls. Householders had to perform these duties, equipped with lanterns and staffs. In the smaller villages a citizen might be required to provide himself with a breastplate, sword, and horse to preserve the king's peace by answering an official call to arms.[1]

During this same era the early beginnings of many police procedures may be noted. Edward I created regular marching watches to patrol given districts in cities and ordered a register of local prostitutes maintained to permit simplified social regulation. Furthermore, a system to identify strangers to the community was devised utilizing court bailiffs and sergeants of mace. Edward's grandson, Edward III, also significantly strengthened law enforcement by the appointment of powerful justices of the peace, originally combining police and judicial functions.

From the fifteenth into the eighteenth centuries these basic patterns of formal control endured and underwent very gradual modification. Several other types of peace officers, however, grew up around the established structure. With the expansion of mercantile activity in centers of commerce, the inability of the citizen patrols to protect property became evident. Businessmen, traders, and bankers turned to employment on a large scale of special police agencies, usually with private support and official recognition. These merchant policemen came to play a great part in the evolution of public agencies in later years. Quite specialized by the era following the Glorious Revolution of 1688, they eventually spawned relatively advanced governmental forces for the protection of docks, rivers, and markets in the greater London area.

Religious groups, faced with security problems similar to those of merchants, also formed law enforcement units. The parochial police, at first voluntarily composed of parishioners, later utilized special constables to protect lives and property. Like their commercial counterparts, the church-connected officers had specific and limited authority with quasi-public status.

Another kind of police consisted of detachments from the regular military forces. With a heritage extending back to King Arthur's era, troops guarded the post roads and royal properties throughout the kingdom. This system culminated during the Cromwellian Protectorate when England and Wales endured division into several large districts controlled by provosts marshal who exercised command through some six thousand mounted military policemen.

In the eighteenth century several radical innovations appeared. For the first time local authorities obtained permission to tax for purposes of hiring peace officers. New decrees prescribed equipment and definite duties for city watchmen. And a local magistrate named Henry Fielding, incidentally the author of *Tom*

Jones, began work on a highly significant study of crime and the municipal police. The resulting suggestions led, with strong support from his brother John, to a greatly strengthened system of patrol along the streets and highroads between 1750 and 1780. Together the Fieldings also created one of history's oldest and most famous detective forces, the Bow Street Runners. Actually a rather sophisticated group of commercial bounty hunters, the "Thief Takers" of London's Bow Street station earned a dubious reputation for both efficiency and somewhat ruthless tactics.

The agencies of police developed in England prior to the nineteenth century served as obvious examples and models for the American colonies along the North Atlantic seaboard. A parish constable was appointed for Jamestown in 1607, the first peace officer in England's new lands.[2] Throughout the next several generations the colonists adopted with slight modification familiar titles and methods. In general, the New England region focused on the traditional citizens' patrol for their townships, while the areas to the south emphasized the old office of county sheriff. Constables operated at the precinct level, but no formal police agencies of major consequence appeared in either the few urban or wide rural districts. Larger communities such as New Amsterdam–New York, Boston, and Philadelphia depended upon various forms of either volunteer or conscripted watchmen, supplied with rattles for communication, and left them under local control.

Originally, sheriffs and high constables attained their office by crown appointment. With the passage of time and the dramatic consequences of the American Revolution, this method of selection changed to a matter of popular politics. Prior to the development of large cities, ordinary property and personal crime never posed really serious problems in the colonial and early national periods. By 1800, with the increasing urbanization of a new century, the rudimentary police systems utilized in the United States had passed into predominant local political control. Despite social change of vast scope and profound depth, to a very great extent this pattern has been geographically extended and temporally perpetuated with notable consequences for the American system of criminal justice.

The opening of the West continued a long and little-changed heritage of law enforcement. Many of the titles and primary duties of peace officers had endured for hundreds of years and crossed the Atlantic to spread gradually across the continent with the pioneers. Aside from growing local control, no major innovations had appeared. The earliest western settlements, of course, preceded establishment of any system of formal police. While this usually very brief period has been greatly exaggerated by popularized representations, the frontiersmen in many areas did provide their own simple forms of social code enforcement before ordinary local means existed. Most notably among booming mining camps, some communities adopted sets of rules and means of selecting leaders without providing for any formal scheme of enforcement.[3] The laws enacted naturally were to be executed and even administered by everyone's adhering to the standards of behavior imposed. Before ordinary systems of government could be imported, local leaders had to serve as policemen and judges, usually without compensation. These officers often were compelled to accept and then serve in a responsible capacity because of community demand rather than through any marked political ambition or qualification. Nevertheless, such men became the clear forerunners of police agencies soon to be organized. Their essentially disinterested nature, self-reliance, and locally independent quality left a clear imprint on later imagery surrounding the western peace officer. Serving in a simplified system of significant isolation, they began a tradition of freedom and resolution quite rare in the history of law enforcement.

More traditional methods of administering justice soon appeared to displace the temporary utilization of ordinary citizens. It is clear, however, that preservation of the peace continued to be regarded as a duty of the public and not merely the special responsibility of particular governmental agencies. In the early territories of the West, crime could not easily be made the sole concern of professional peace officers and conveniently located courts; the general lack of such facilities found implied recognition in the written laws of the frontier areas. As Idaho declared: "Public offenses may be prevented by the intervention of the officers of justice: First, By requiring surety to keep the peace. Second, By forming a police in cities and towns, and requiring their attendance in exposed places. Third, By suppressing riots."[4] The ultimate duty, of course, remained with the ordinary citizen.

With the growth of stable and centralized government, the distinction and identification of those charged with law enforcement functions became clear. Those normally recognized as peace officers included the traditional county, precinct, and community positions of English origin. In some states, such as Utah and Idaho,[5] the basic and formal limitation of those qualified to carry the title has remained unchanged for generations. But the statutes of other jurisdictions have clearly indicated the advancing complexity of a technical civilization. When first organized as a territory, for example, Nevada followed the usual language of criminal procedure stating: "Peace officers are Sheriffs of counties, and Constables, Marshals, and policemen of cities and towns respectively."[6] In 1967, reflecting numerous additions to this simple statement, the statutory definition directly descended from the above read as follows:

Peace officers are the bailiff of the supreme court, sheriffs of counties, constables, members of the Nevada state police, personnel of the Nevada highway patrol when exercising the police powers specified in N[evada] R[evised] S[tatutes] 181.150 and 481.180, the inspector or field agents of the motor carrier division of the department of motor vehicles when exercising the police power specified in NRS 481.049, special investigators employed by the office of any district attorney or the attorney general, marshals and policemen of cities and towns respectively, arson investigators for fire departments specially designated by the appointing authority, and members of the University of Nevada police department.[7]

Obviously the variety of those given powers as officers of the peace expanded greatly during the last century. At least one western jurisdiction, Montana, has simply given up the task of listing particular offices and now states: " 'Peace Officer' means any person who by virtue of his office or public employment is vested by law with a duty to maintain public order or to make arrests for offenses while acting within the scope of his authority."[8] Defining the position in terms of its authority, however, is something of a legal subterfuge since the usual need is one of determining the claim to proper power, not its mere existence. The issue can be further confused by the variety of justified claimants to the title. At one time, for example, a single jurisdiction recognized as peace officers those acting in such diverse capacities as sextons of cemeteries, game and fish wardens, labor inspectors, agricultural sealers, and election judges.[9]

The present situation remains highly involved. By formal definition, those on duty as coroners, parole officers, and investigators for medical examiners and boards of pharmacy, osteopathy, and chiropracty are titled peace officers by California.[10] For purposes of transporting prisoners, certain employees of correctional institutions from other jurisdictions may even be included within the designated category.

There are, in many areas, at least two primary categories of actual peace officers. Those falling under the original governmental distinction of being associated with a local sheriff, constable, or community police agency, comprise only one. A vast assortment of special and private forces, including authorization of those in charge of any graveyard, agents of humane associations, members of school district security patrols, mine inspectors and foresters are recognized by statute in different western sections of the country.[11] One observer has noted the existence of more than eighty different types officially termed peace officers in California alone.[12] Such a great variety of those involved in diverse law enforcement functions is not uncommon. Many occupy specific positions with particular duties but, because of their designation, also with wide authority. Typical of these are the agents of alcohol and narcotics units, arson and district attorneys' investigators, toll takers on public roads, police designated to serve for the protection of harbors, capitol grounds, parks, state schools, and a host of additional government-related facilities. The very wide legal application of the title of peace officer is neither unusual nor a recent development. It does, however, greatly complicate any accurate analysis of those carrying such an official designation.

The difficulty of restricting application of the peace officer title serves merely as one example of the complexity encountered by any study of American law enforcement functions. There is a truly astonishing lack of concrete information, despite marked public interest, about police agencies. For example, it is impossible to give a definitive total for the number of actual officers throughout the nation. The most reliable estimates available indicated the presence in 1965 of approximately 370,000 sworn individuals in some 40,000 agencies; in addition, perhaps 50,000 civilian employees supported these units.[13] Such statistics include both full and part-time workers, but exclude hundreds of thousands under private and military auspices, even though they often serve in direct law enforcement capacities.

A highly complex situation has existed for many years and the difficulty of developing valid interpretations for the structure in the West is by no means unique. Adopting the various definitions for peace officer and police now utilized in the different jurisdictions, one can roughly estimate the total number of persons presently so designated in the seventeen-state region as at least 100,000. This number would include federal agents not in military service, but is limited to employees both recognized and paid by governmental units. Most reserve and honorary personnel would, therefore, be excluded along with those having authority derived entirely from private rather than public sources. It must be stressed that these designations vary with different definitions necessarily adopted. A judge, for example, is technically a peace officer in Texas, but not in Arizona.

Perhaps 80 per cent of our somewhat arbitrary total estimate of 100,000 are employed by local, as distinguished from state or federal, agencies. And most of these, naturally, are concentrated in the larger urban areas of the plains, mountains, and Pacific

Coast regions. The complexity of the system becomes obvious if one accepts the realization that more than one thousand independent countywide units operate in the West alone. The total of agencies at the precinct, township, and municipal levels is perhaps ten times this number.

Assuming reasonable accuracy for present statistics, the scope of historical background is obviously enormous. Probably more than 400,000 individuals have been classified, using formal definitions, as peace officers in the western states. At least 25,000 different sheriffs must have served during the last century in this vast area. The intricacies of the picture are not a recent development. In 1903, for example, Los Angeles County, California, contained thirty local law enforcement agencies, with several quasi-official units also in operation.[14]

The variety of separate titles applied to peace officers is equally staggering. To give one instance of this entanglement, in the period of World War I Arizona counties utilized at least twenty-five distinct appellatives for their law enforcement positions. These included such unique titles as "Ranger Sheriff," "Railroad Livestock Inspector," "Lady Deputy Sheriff," "Night Jailer," "County Ranger," and a host of others. Other officers, at work in the same area, carried such designations as "Immigration Service Chinese Inspector," "Railroad Train Rider," and "U.S. Marshal's Field Deputy."[15]

What sort of men and, on occasion, women filled such positions? Were they the fast-drawing, quick-shooting heroes beloved by writers of popular fiction? Or, were they the bullies and braggarts also frequently portrayed? Did they conduct their offices with courage and honor, or did they routinely resort to connivance and conspiracy against the public welfare? As much of the following material will illustrate, some fell into each category. When dealing with hundreds of thousands of individuals, one can anticipate the presence of every possible virtue and flaw of character. Among the western peace officers, these elements came in close and dramatic proximity, often being encountered within the same personality.

Some of those occupying positions in law enforcement themselves eventually turned to lives of crime. But most, with varying degrees of success, attempted to carry out their assigned duties with both honor and efficiency. One noted scholar has observed that an outstanding peace officer must possess three virtues: bravery, intelligence, and honesty.[16] Unfortunately, such qualities cannot be either made mandatory by legislation or determined by formal examination. The jurisdictions of the West found no simple way to instill character and courage among peace officers. Instead, they finally resorted to enforceable qualifications designed to strengthen provincial control and establish minimal standards.

In those states which have attempted to legislate basic requirements for peace officers, the most frequently encountered prescription is still probably that of residence established within the jurisdiction. Emerging in legal reform movements toward the close of the nineteenth century, such laws today often serve as a severe restriction on effective recruitment. Also common are provisions requiring those serving in police capacities to possess a written appointment, or commission, which may involve both a sworn oath of office and posting a bond to insure liability. States may also preclude employment of those with criminal records, normally interpreted as one or more felony convictions. Interestingly, California has modified such limitations so that the restriction does not apply to deputies appointed "in time of disaster caused by flood, fire, pestilence, or similar public calamity."[17]

As will be discovered, the peace officers of the West brought with them a variety of backgrounds and aptitudes. Their positions, as today, were highly sensitive and demanded both personal ability and political skill. A successful lawman had to possess an aura of authority and still maintain proper relations with those of influence. Initial achievement and retention of office ultimately depended upon these nebulous but essential characteristics. Whether elected or appointed—and many individuals eventually utilized both means—the peace officer could never rely on simple force to accomplish his goal. Without support from the public and its leadership, law enforcement turned into oppression or chaos. The numerous fictional versions of the old West have left far too strong an impression of violence and conflict. Any policeman, in any area or time, must depend upon co-operation to carry out his assignment, and those serving on the far frontier operated in a social structure basically similar to that of the present. These significant considerations are illustrated by a letter, typical of the time and setting, concerning an applicant for a position with one of the federal services.

My Dear Governor [George Curry, New Mexico Territory]:
    I return herewith letter addressed to you from W. D. Wood [of] Douglas, Arizona, in reference to an endorsement from you to the Collector of Customs at Nogales, Arizona, for the position of Mounted Inspector of Customs in that district.
    W. D. Wood was a member of your troop in the Rough Riders and his record as a soldier was good. After the Spanish-American war, he went to Arizona and there followed gambling for a livelihood, but since gambling has been abolished in that territory Wood has, I believe followed mining. He came originally from Colfax county New Mexico and has a good many friends there. I enclose also a letter from Deputy United States Marshal Jack Foster of Bisbee, Arizona, to whom I had written about Wood. I can see no reason why Wood would not make a good mounted inspector, as I believe that should he be appointed he would arise to its responsibilities. Everybody in the troop liked him and I know of nothing in his character that would prevent you from endorsing him should you so desire.
Very respectfully,

[Fred Fornoff]

Captain N.M. Mounted Police
P.S. Wood got into a shooting scrape at Tombstone a few years ago but was acquitted.[18]

With officers widely divergent from one another in background, character, and authority, conflict within the realm of law enforcement might well have been anticipated. If so, the reality must surely have exceeded the expectation. While representatives from different agencies normally co-operated, disputes and open hostility between officers frequently enlivened the scene. Disagreement and competition went so far, on occasion, to include accusation, false arrest, assault, and even murder. But these conflicts, while occasionally very bitter and dramatic, rarely took precedence over the daily routines of ordinary law enforcement.

For the most part the problems faced by the peace officers of the West were the same as those still encountered by their contemporary counterparts. Ordinary duties and routines often produced dissatisfaction and drove many into other types of employment. Continuing danger, though greatly exaggerated in popular fiction, probably actually caused a much smaller disaffection from the ranks of lawmen. Then as now, the ever present possibility of sudden and violent encounter served as a unique inducement to those seeking action and adventure. In the absence of reliable and detailed information from earlier times, it may be worth noting that of the 411 officers killed in line of duty between 1960 and 1967 inclusive, 76 died in the western states. During the same period, by comparison, the South lost 179.[19]

The primary difficulties of those in frontier law enforcement seldom involved excitement or overt conflict. Their basic problems will be immediately recognized by those in comparable positions today—lack of public interest, absence of political support, co-operation of the press, and the desirability of obtaining reduced rates or adequate compensation when traveling on official business.[20]

For comparative purposes it is interesting to note some of the major regional variations directly relating to general law enforcement. While statistics are only available for recent times, it is still possible to detect distinctive operational differences. Analysis of annual numbers of arrests per officer, divided into sections of the country reveals the following:[21]

	Drunkenness and Disorderly Conduct	Other Criminal Arrests	Traffic Citations
Northeast	3.2	6.5	119
North Central	6.2	14.2	166
South	16.2	18.8	190
West	11.9	21.4	235

As may be noted, the law enforcement officer of the present West is either somewhat harder working or more efficient than his counterparts in other regions of the United States. This is, perhaps, understandable in view of generally better pay and facilities for higher education found among police agencies along the Pacific Coast. While possible technical competence of peace officers in the modern West has not produced any significantly reduced rate of indicated crime, conclusions based upon such comparisons should be highly qualified. There is, for example, reason to believe that any efficient police operation will result in sharply increased rates of reported violations along with additional clearances by arrest. Neither may be a valid test of actual criminality.

Violence, theft, and disorder create a need for the peace officer. His actual duties in regard to offenses and regulatory action, however, are scattered throughout involved statutes of penal law and criminal procedure. Those so titled are normally required to preserve the peace by taking into custody anyone committing either felonies or, with knowledge, common misdemeanors. In addition, they are usually instructed by law to suppress any public disorder and to execute proper warrants issued by a magistrate or court. Beyond these broad but general duties, specific statutory instructions vary enormously in different jurisdictions.

In many western states peace officers are still given broad authority under various provisions passed to prevent or eradicate "criminal syndicalism and sabotage." Led by Idaho and Minnesota in 1917, most jurisdictions, at the urging of strong local industrial and agricultural interests, passed such laws to aid in the struggle against unionization.[22] Justified originally by a stated fear of sabotage to war industries, and utilized erratically and with wide discretion during the early 1920s, such vague and general statutes have endured with rare later use in several western areas.[23]

Aside from such general duties, officers in many states continue to be formally responsible for the enforcement of an incredible assortment of peculiar statutory provisions. In Nevada all those charged with preserving the peace must also prevent the improper harvesting of pine cones; lawmen in Oregon are required to implement all regulations affecting log load binders; Oklahoma peace officers have, by statute, the responsibility of reporting prize fights.[24] And, in North Dakota: "Every officer who has the duty of enforcing the laws of this state shall be charged with the enforcement of the provisions of this chapter [dealing solely with licensing for the dispensation of imitation ice cream], and for failure to enforce the same shall be subject to removal from office."[25]

Perhaps no other state has imposed such a unique variety of duties upon its peace officers as Colorado. In that jurisdiction lawmen not only must continue to prevent any public display of the "red flag," but they are also required to seize and report any "defective prophylactics" discovered within the jurisdiction! Additionally, all Colorado peace officers have the potentially intriguing duty of taking into their custody ". . . girls habitually wandering around the streets or public places."[26] Obviously, such provisions are not subject to rigid enforcement. Charged with the technical duty of enforcing thousands of strange laws, many sworn officers remain simply unaware of their existence. The original passage and statutory endurance of such odd provisions can, of course, usually be traced to the power structure and lethargy of most state political systems. While laws of this nature are seldom a practical problem, some continue as potentially dangerous anachronisms open to the threat of discretionary application.

In order to accomplish both routine and unusual duties with which he may be entrusted, the police officer is given special powers. These normally include extraordinary authority to carry weapons, summon aid, make arrests both with and without warrant, search and seize property, execute process, and otherwise enforce the laws. The peculiarities of such powers and privileges, however, are as varied and remarkable as the duties to which they are related. Authority to forcibly enter buildings or rooms, for example, is usually qualified with respect to the purpose and the existence of probable cause. Consequently, peace officers in Montana possess a special right to break in where some form of gaming is believed to be in progress.[27] In Nebraska: "It shall be lawful for any sheriff, constable, chief of police or any policeman or city marshal . . . to enter any house of ill fame to search for any child [a female under eighteen] allowed, kept, or harbored therein."[28]

Peculiarities of outdated legislation relative to law enforcement agents are by no means limited to those of search. They relate to restrictions on arrest, preventing breaches of the peace, or the service of legal process. The power to call for assistance in performance of duty, while commonly extended but rarely utilized, endures in highly antiquated style in the codes of certain jurisdictions. In New Mexico, for example, the relevant statute has continued to read without modification for more than a century as follows: "In all cases when, by the common law or a statute of this state, any officer is authorized to execute any process, he may call to his aid all free, white inhabitants, above the age of twenty-one years, in the county in which the officer is authorized to act."[29]

Special privileges in regard to carrying firearms and other prohibited weapons are also normally given lawmen. Such authority, however, may take rather strange form. In Oregon, where retired officers are privileged to carry machine guns upon their persons or in their vehicles,[30] a statute reads:

Any person who places, throws, uncorks, opens, breaks or who maliciously attempts to place, throw, uncork, open or break any stink bomb . . . shall be punished upon conviction by a fine . . . or by imprisonment in the penitentiary for a period of not more than two years, or both . . . this section shall not apply to peace officers in the performance of their duties.[31]

Authority of those enforcing the law is, however, more extensive than dramatic provisions permitting forceable entry, summoning aid, carrying weapons, or throwing bombs. Some are of a primarily economic nature. The conflict between officers, particularly over rewards, led to the passage of statutes designed to provide special protection from interference. A relevant Montana act, still in force, provides a suitable example:

Any sheriff or other officer who shall have arrested any prisoner or prisoners, may pass over, across and through any county or counties that may be in the ordinary route of travel from the place where such prisoner shall have been arrested, to the place where he is to be conveyed and delivered; and such prisoner or prisoners so conveyed, and the officers having them in custody, shall not be liable to arrest or civil process while passing through such county or counties.[32]

Rivalry among lawmen also existed on less dramatic levels. In Texas, where the struggle became quite intense, a statute provides that any railroad granting a free pass to any sheriff, constable, or marshal must do the same for all others with such titles.[33]

The broad duties and powers assigned to peace officers in many jurisdictions are not given without qualification. Some states impose limitations on various authorities of peculiar and historic significance. The traditionally extended privilege of possessing prohibited weapons has, since 1890, been technically very restricted in Oklahoma, where

Public officers while in the discharge of their duties or while going from their homes to their place of duty, or returning therefrom, shall be permitted to carry arms, but at no other time and under no other circumstances: Provided, However, that if any public officer be found carrying such arms while under the influence of intoxicating drinks, he shall be deemed guilty of a violation of this article as though he were a private person.[34]

In the present era, when many law enforcement agencies require their representatives to be armed at all times, such acts are, naturally, subject to something less than rigid enforcement.

Arrest, the power perhaps most popularly related to peace officers, may also be sharply restricted. Texas, in a peculiar statute, limits custody occasioned by credible reports of serious crimes to instances where the felon is actually about to escape. The same jurisdiction imposes very strict qualifications on the defense of justification in homicide by those in law enforcement. Escaped convicts, for example, cannot be killed having once actually gotten away; in such cases only ordinary means of routine arrest may be employed. Texas also closely restricts the killing of burglars and thieves. At night the taking of their lives is quite legal, but in the day the same homicide could be murder.

Western jurisdictions often impose special penal sanctions, applicable only to peace officers, upon those found guilty of taking bribes, tormenting prisoners, preventing attorneys from counseling those in custody, declining to execute process, refusing to arrest for offenses known to occur, drunkenness, or permitting escapes. In one state it is even possible for a lawman to be fined up to $100 upon failure to report by sworn oath vagrants within the community.[35]

New Mexico goes so far as to prohibit peace officers from entering any election booth "except to assist in preserving the peace," although those with state, as distinguished from local, commissions possess a complete right at any time to visit "polling places." The same jurisdiction, recognizing a very real problem, prohibits employment of any officer whose compensation may be dependent upon fines paid by traffic violators. Drivers stopped by those so rewarded, as well as by law enforcement representatives not in uniform, are accorded a valid defense to resulting charges.[36]

It is readily apparent that neither a conclusive definition of "peace officer" nor an explanation of his duties can be easily accomplished. The West adapted an already involved system of law enforcement, utilizing agencies and functions of long historical significance. From simple police organizations a highly complex structure slowly developed. Unfortunately, no sincere and comprehensive legal effort has been made to clarify or standardize the many different titles and responsibilities involved.

Individual jurisdictions continue to vary enormously in their technical construction of police powers and limitations. In practice, of course, the differences are not immediately apparent. Many of the peculiar statutes indicated above, while perhaps of interesting and valid origin, have become archaic in form and function. The majority of peace officers in the West remain unaware of their existence and a goodly number of magistrates would be loathe to give them harsh application. Rarely subject to judicial interpretation, such laws endure because of the lethargy and inefficiency personified in many state legislatures. While police agencies and courts find methods of ignoring, avoiding, or circumventing provisions of this kind, a need exists for clear and logical statements both of those with special law enforcement duties and of the reasonable extent of powers conferred. Statutes now in force can, however, serve to illuminate the combination of popularity and fear with which the western peace officer continues to be regarded. This odd equation of admiration and suspicion greatly influenced the development of law enforcement agencies on the closing American frontier. It continues to cloud important issues concerning the police of present times.

"The Marshal Shall Be Chief of Police"

III

Earp, Hickok, Masterson—such names are synonymous with the image of the western town marshal. Their legend is one of a tall lone figure, striding down a dusty street in the dim direction of public order and immortality. It is a myth, yet one based on a slim foundation of truth.

The towns of the frontier West did not long remain without some sort of police agency. Many communities found that the county sheriff or constable could supply the necessities of formal law and order. Demand for a strictly local peace officer often did not emerge until the population reached a thousand or more. In many instances settlements developed considerable size before agitation for a community police began.

Village law enforcement among settlers moving across the Mississippi into the West first appeared in Texas. During the 1820s assorted emigrants from the United States had begun colonization of large land grants which later became the seedbed for revolution against Mexico. The Mexican government provided early East Texas with nothing in the form of police. Colonists consequently established their own law enforcement agencies. Within a very few years local *comisarios* of police, such as James

B. Patrick in the Gonzales district, began working toward regulation of gambling and other activities. By 1831 the town of San Felipe de Austin established a community patrol to maintain order and warn of approaching danger. Formed at the suggestion of an attorney from Georgia named Robert McAlpin Williamson (locally dubbed "Three-Legged Willie") and placed under the command of Captain Thomas Gay, the force probably comprised the first actually operating local police agency of the English-speaking West. Within a short time the guard required the passage of formal rules and regulations by the village governing council.[1] The patrols at San Felipe de Austin, well before the Texas Revolution, did not constitute more than a semiformal organization, but they reflected an established tradition of citizen police and demonstrated both the elemental needs and basic solutions to law enforcement on the frontier.

In later years countless communities throughout the West faced essentially the same conditions as had confronted the early Texans. Subsequently, developing areas normally operated under general but clearly drawn statutory authority for the creation of local law enforcement. Some legislatures, such as that of Kansas, originally provided for the popular election of town constables.[2] More frequently, the term "marshal" was employed, with power of appointment given to the community's mayor and council. Within given formal limits the actual duties of these local peace officers could be prescribed by governing authorities for the village. In later years the title "chief of police" often replaced "constable" or "marshal" to designate law enforcement personnel, but most states still utilize a legislative framework originated in frontier days.

What kinds of men filled these offices? In some villages they came from the ranks of local toughs, on the theory that such persons would most easily gain the fearful respect of the region's criminal element. Occasionally personnel of such dubious qualifications were the only volunteers willing to undertake the work. Unfortunate results, of course, often followed this method of selection. Some local marshals had to flee the community when made to appear cowardly; others resigned after disgraceful public performances caused by drink and gross abuses of office.

With the passage of time and the growth of population, most villages developed functioning police forces, although the old titles tended to remain. Long before the end of the nineteenth century growing communities in the West established local agencies of considerable sophistication and close interrelationships with existing political structures. By 1866, for example, Chief of Police W. S. Edwards of Virginia City, Nevada, directed a sizable and well-paid force with the advice of a standing committee composed of interested citizens. With the considerable monthly salary of $215 as an attraction, Edwards' appointment depended upon harmonious relations with both local officials and a generally satisfied electorate. The structured agency at his command rarely resorted to firearms. Their primary tasks consisted of arresting those found drunk and disorderly, sleeping on the street, or fighting in public.[3]

The legal authority of town peace officers naturally varied with the provisions of state law. In Kansas they were given, and still possess, the technical power of county sheriffs; in Utah the rights granted are those accorded constables.[4] More typically the legislatures assigned the general authority of community officers in such language as:

> The marshal shall be chief of police, and shall at all times have power to make, or order an arrest, with proper process, for any offense against the laws of the State, or of the city, and bring the offender for trial before the proper officer of the city, and to arrest without process, in all cases where any such offense shall be committed, or attempted to be committed in his presence.[5]

In addition, local lawmen have taken on specific duties of attending and serving warrants of corporation courts, quelling riots, and otherwise protecting property and the public peace.

Local marshals encountered a variety of routine tasks in the towns of the frontier West. In some communities they had to prevent bathers from using convenient rivers, or keep the streets clear of obstruction and congestion. In larger towns their duties could be delegated to the lower ranks of town deputies or police-men. Leadville, Colorado, a booming mining camp in 1880, had a sizable but still typical organization:

The members of the police force are elected annually by the city council. The force is governed by the mayor, and its chief executive officer is the city marshal . . . he receives a salary of $180 per month. The rest of the force consists of a captain, with a salary of $125 per month, 2 sergeants and 18 patrolmen, with salaries of $100 per month each. They wear navy-blue uniforms with brass buttons, and each provides his own. They carry clubs and navy revolvers. They serve 8 hours per day each winter and 12 in summer, and patrol about 6 blocks. In 1880 there were 4,320 arrests, the principal causes being intoxication and disturbance of the peace. The mayor may appoint as special policemen without pay any persons of suitable character. . . . The yearly cost of the force is about $30,000.[6]

Community lawmen, regarded as a necessary evil, rarely enjoyed public favor. Doing a job few diligently sought, they seldom reflected the heroic romanticism portrayed so frequently in fiction. While the town marshals courted political support, their patrolmen maintained a watchful eye on local activities. Violence occurred, of course, but it usually came in sudden and unexpected form. The empty street, the deadly gunmen, and the structured duel have little foundation in fact. One study has revealed that in the period from 1870 to 1885 the supposedly roaring trail towns of Abilene, Caldwell, Dodge City, Ellsworth, and Wichita experienced a combined total of 45 homicides, only sixteen of which could be construed as the result of law enforcement. The effective presence of local peace officers could actually reduce violence, and many later very famous marshals never killed anyone in performance of duty.[7]

When lawmen occasionally found themselves engaged in fatal encounters, such combat usually resulted from arrests for routine offenses. An incident in Braggs, Wyoming, in 1912, is quite representative of such episodes. Called from his supper table by the mayor, the town marshal proceeded to the Davis Saloon, a noted focal point of social activity in Carbon County. There he found John Bowen and others in a somewhat intoxicated state "hollering" about the tavern. After following the rowdy group to the Elkhorn Hotel, the marshal placed Bowen and another under arrest. On the way to jail a fight occurred in which the lawman apparently received bruises and a broken nose, but he managed to fire several shots during the struggle. Bowen died as a result and the town marshal, long before claims of police brutality, found himself convicted of second-degree murder. The Supreme Court of Wyoming eventually reversed the case on an issue of self-defense, but not without stating that ordinary arrest for misdemeanors carries no authority for peace officers either to kill or maim.[8]

Local lawmen obviously enjoyed no special privileges from criminal charges. Indeed, judges and juries along the frontier displayed a remarkable tendency both to try and convict peace officers upon circumstances which at present would rarely pass either to or through the indictment stage. A clear desire to carefully restrict those overstepping legal powers lingered on in smaller communities for many years.

Many other problems plagued the town marshal. He had to be careful in remaining within his designated authority. Beyond his geographic jurisdiction he possessed no special power as a lawman, and within it the courts required him to act under strict color of office. The law could hardly be termed sympathetic to the troubles of a local marshal. In an era when juries would sometimes demand payment of their fees before rendering a verdict, no officer could anticipate special treatment. Courts, usually reflecting community attitudes, gave little consideration to the lawman's unique situation and routine travail. Some marshals discovered this difficulty when attempting to recover the rewards which had been offered to stimulate effort in special cases.

Despite legal authority to summon aid, officers sometimes found themselves quite alone in times of immediate need. Without local support, they often could do little to control the disorderly:

There was usually but one lone police-man at Austin [in 1867] who was unable to enforce one order. In many cases young men from the country seemed to exhibit a desire to imitate the dress and bearing of the Mexican ranchers. Some of them appeared to affect the embroidered jacket, the goat-skin breeches, red sash, broad brimmed hat, and loud, jingling spurs. This class of young men usually came to town on a raw day, fully equipped with six-shooter conspicuously displayed, riding a Spanish pony that pitched and snorted like unto its rider. One or two drinks of whiskey seemed to fill them with what the new version describes as hades.[9]

The hundreds of thousands of individuals who served in local western law enforcement encompassed all kinds of personalities. They have, at times, been portrayed as corrupt bullies. These representations have some basis in fact. A few community peace officers, as mentioned earlier, came from the ranks of outlaw and desperado groups. One member of the famed "Billy the Kid" gang, for example, drifted into Kansas to become marshal of Caldwell. Along with a deputy, his police career ended by being caught and lynched after an aborted bank robbery. Other local lawmen simply departed their jurisdictions when confronted with difficult situations. Billy Brooks of Dodge City, Kansas, and Ben Sippy of Tombstone, Arizona, were but two of those who rather hurriedly left their posts in time of stress.

Some town marshals were selected according to their association with and support of local vice interests. At times those active in gambling, prostitution, and liquor played a major role in appointment of police officials. Of course, this pattern is by no means unknown to the modern municipal scene. In the West, at any rate, it occasionally resulted in close co-operation between law enforcement and commercialized vice. Officers with such connections quite naturally tended toward open corruption and debauchery.

Impossible to divorce fully from this legacy of impropriety are the truly legendary figures of western town law enforcement. The two names most immediately recognized as connected with this phase of police activity have today become almost synonymous with the fighting peace officer—"Wild Bill" Hickok and Wyatt Earp. Around these personalities countless novels, motion pictures, and television series create enduring clouds of romanticism

49

and glory. Yet the true characters of both men remain open to discussion and argument. Strangely, their different careers reveal several similarities.

Although separated by eleven years, the births of James Butler "Wild Bill" Hickok and Wyatt Earp took place only some one hundred miles apart in frontier Illinois. Reared on farms, both boys entered law enforcement through guard work for stage companies. Hickok, following a successful scouting career in the Civil War, and Earp, having wandered throughout the West for several years, followed trails which eventually brought them to the cowtowns of Kansas in the 1870s. By a peculiar coincidence of local conditions and national publicity, both attained a fame which still places them, along with Sheriff Pat Garrett, in the forefront of western peace officers.

Hickok primarily gained his reputation as marshal of Abilene in 1871. Earp's notoriety really commenced while serving in a comparable position at Dodge City between 1877 and 1879. Each had acquired some early experience in law enforcement at other Kansas rail stations. The two marshals were tall, slender, had blue eyes and light hair. While the validity of their epic adventures falls outside the scope of this inquiry, both were obviously men of physical courage and capable of proven efficiency with firearms. However, they did not earn their enduring fame by taking unnecessary risks for the sake of law and order. Hickok and Earp were semiprofessional lawmen who carefully weighed the odds before engaging in mortal combat. They apparently enjoyed their risky occupation and often ensconced themselves within saloons and gambling centers. Indeed, each added to his monthly salary of $150 and $250, respectively, by close connections with such local establishments. Neither Hickok at Abilene nor Earp at Dodge City really brought law and order to their towns. It already existed to a large extent before they arrived on the scene. Both men relied upon their deputies, such as Earp's friend W. B. "Bat" Masterson. What violence and crime did exist continued as the primary concern of each community's usual police agency after the departure of the famous marshals.

After Kansas, the careers of the two men were widely divergent. Hickok, discharged from his post of marshal, joined the "Buffalo Bill" show for a time. In 1876, in Deadwood, Jack McCall murdered him in a saloon. Earp resigned his similar position and traveled to Arizona where within a few years he further contributed to the legend of the frontier lawman. Actually, the performance of the two while at work as local peace officers did not by any standard earn the prestige which followed.

Hickok and Earp are hardly representative of the western town marshal. They happened to be selected for unique fame through colorful publicity and a remarkably receptive audience. Consequently, their romanticized personalities have become so closely connected with local frontier law enforcement that one has difficulty in isolating reality from legend. Armed conflict, so frequently, portrayed in fiction and popular history, clearly stands as the most thoroughly integrated element in the legend of the community peace officer in the West. While countless writers have subjected that segment to enormous distortion, a slight foundation of truth cannot be denied.

A few town marshals were selected in part because of their reputations as expert gunmen and killers. This dubious distinction could be accorded two better-known Texas peace officers of the 1880s closing frontier—Ben Thompson of Austin and Dallas Stoudenmire of El Paso. To men of this type, rather than more celebrated figures, the image of death with a badge can properly be related. Thompson, originally from Nova Scotia, earned a fearsome reputation before finally winning election as marshal in 1882. His history included at least one prison term and some fifteen different indictments on charges of homicide.[10] Stoudenmire, born in Alabama, drifted westward after the Civil War to receive his El Paso commission in 1880. During one authenticated fight he alone killed three men. Neither Thompson nor Stoudenmire enjoyed long careers as lawmen. While each apparently maintained considerable tranquility in his respective community, both eventually died in the kind of vicious gunbattle which had originally brought them public attention.

Even in the era of Ben Thompson and Dallas Stoudenmire the true gunfighter-marshal could be considered a rarity. Most communities, logically enough, preferred local and dependable citizens as their peace officers. Towns with greater problems often turned to men with already well-established records in law enforcement. The agencies supplying such generally reliable marshals were numerous. Thomas J. Smith, who maintained order in Abilene with fists instead of guns, gained his experience on the Bowery with the police of New York City. Bill Tilghman, the chief officer for several Kansas and Oklahoma towns, came from the ranks of deputy federal marshals. James B. Gillett, who replaced Stoudenmire at El Paso in 1882 and later became a well-known rancher, had served for six years with the Texas Rangers. They are typical of a more successful but usually less acclaimed kind of local officer. With a penchant for stopping trouble before it began, using words instead of firearms, and substituting judgment for bravado, such lawmen maintained the peace by hard work and a minimum of violence.

The majority of village police, of course, never shot at anyone. A few moved from one community to another, following both a shifting need and improved opportunities. W. J. "Jesse" Benton, for example, served throughout the central Rockies between 1869 and 1886 as marshal at Laramie, Silver City, Las Vegas, Ouray, Kit Carson, and Denver. But most local lawmen, like William R. Schnitger of Wyoming and Martin Duggan of Colorado, remained in close association with their communities. Schnitger, the well-educated son of a former territorial marshal, earned a reputation for efficiency, gentlemanly conduct, and impartiality while upholding the law in frontier Cheyenne. He eventually served in Wyoming's Senate and as its Secretary of State. Duggan represented quite a different background. An Irish immigrant and Rocky Mountain miner, he found himself suddenly selected marshal of Leadville in 1878 following the murder of George Conners. With no prior experience, Duggan kept peace in the rough mining camp by protecting rather than taking lives and later turned to operating a livery stable.[11]

Wild Bill Hickock, 1871. Courtesy of the Dickinson County Historical Society, Kansas.

The Dodge City Peace Commission in 1870. Top row, left to right: W. H. Harris, Luke Short, Bat Masterson. Seated: C. Bassett, Wyatt Earp, Frank McClane, Neal Brown. Courtesy Western History Collections, University of Oklahoma Library.

Tom Horn. Courtesy Western History Collections, University of Oklahoma Library.

Three sheriffs of Lincoln County, New Mexico. Left to right: Pat Garrett, John W. Poe, James Brent. Courtesy Western History Collections, University of Oklahoma Library.

Dallas Stoudenmire, city marshal of El Paso, Texas, in 1881. Courtesy Western History Collections, University of Oklahoma Library.

John Slaughter. Courtesy Arizona Pioneers' Historical Society Library.

Frank M. Canton. Courtesy Western History Research Center, University of Wyoming.

Indian police (above) at Oklahoma City in 1889 and (below) at Anadarko, c. 1894. Courtesy Oklahoma Historical Society.

Indian agent John P. Clum with his Apache bodyguard. Courtesy Western History Collections, University of Oklahoma Library.

Judge Roy Bean posed on horseback before his saloon, courtroom, and billiard parlor. Courtesy Western History Collections, University of Oklahoma Library.

Judge Isaac C. Parker. Courtesy Western History Collections, University of Oklahoma Library.

The hanging of William Gay, Helena, Montana, 1896. Courtesy University of Washington Library.

The last local hanging in California, at Santa Barbara, 1891. Courtesy Santa Barbara Historical Society.

Execution in the Choctaw Nation, 1894. Courtesy Oklahoma Historical Society.

Whipping a cattle thief in Oklahoma, 1901. Courtesy Oklahoma Historical Society.

Colonel Emilio Kosterlitzky. Courtesy Arizona Pioneers' Historical Society Library.

Union Pacific Railroad posse. Left to right: George Hiatt, T. T. Kelliher, Joe Le Fors, H. Davis, Si Funk, Jeff Carr. Courtesy Western History Research Center, University of Wyoming.

Thomas Jefferson Carr. Courtesy Wyoming State Archives and Historical Department.

There is a tendency to assume that the era of the town marshal ended with the passing of the frontier. Such is not the case. The West still contains several hundred one-man police forces, many of which continue to carry the title of marshal. There are additional thousands of small departments and with the individual incorporation of many suburban areas the total numbers of these units are probably increasing. While chartered villages may not be required by law to have police forces, as in Texas where another peace officer can be utilized,[12] many communities seem anxious to gain a local force of their own, if only composed of volunteers.

Small town law enforcement has actually changed very little in the West during the last century. There are, of course, somewhat more immediate ties with county and state police agencies. Many local officers, for example, now utilize radio equipment providing direct communication with wider or peripheral jurisdictions. But actual control and operation is nearly always maintained at the community level. Unfortunately, some towns do not really desire objective law enforcement. They want, instead, a combination security guard and source of revenue. Victims of certain "speed traps," which do appear to be diminishing in number, can attest to this enduring tendency. Unfortunately, the antiquated laws of some states, which even preclude the payment of a salary to certain officers, only serve to perpetuate the problem. In some regions, particularly through use of county departments in California, the contract system has developed support. This method, wherein smaller incorporated governments pay a larger unit for law enforcement has come to enjoy great popularity in Canada, but in most of the United States no pronounced trend toward adoption is apparent. Despite the advantages of a larger and better-equipped force, most communities seem loathe to sacrifice any local autonomy.

In several respects this attitude is unfortunate. With the exception of certain wealthy suburbs, small towns simply cannot support an expensive police operation. Forces with less than six officers are usually unable to provide 24-hour protective service and must therefore rely on part-time and volunteer personnel. The problem is particularly magnified in some sparsely populated western regions by a complete lack of lawmen with precinct, county, or state jurisdiction to occupy a vacuum of patrol. Inevitably the overall result is lack of co-ordination between isolated and virtually forgotten agencies. Generally poor pay in smaller communities leads to low personnel qualifications, little or no training, abuse of office, and a negative public attitude which only tends to extend the cycle of inadequate protection.

A few states have minimum standards for lawmen, but even these legislative provisions include only rudimentary limitations on the employable. Montana, for example, requires town policemen to be at least 21 years of age, able to speak English, and possess U.S. citizenship. The same jurisdiction also demands a minimum monthly salary, recently set at $400.[13] Such restrictions, however, are not typical and many states have no functioning standards for officers. As a consequence, former convicts, illiterates, and those not yet eighteen may still be found as policemen.

While the situation has probably improved somewhat in the past generation, the elevation of standards has been far less than might be imagined. The small town is not alone in perpetuating problems in police personnel, but the difficulties encountered therein are among the most serious. In some parts of the country sincere efforts have been made to improve opportunities for interagency co-operation and centralized training. Programs such as those conducted through the University of Wyoming have opened the door for units actively seeking improvement. But agencies most in need of raised standards consistently demonstrate the least interest in betterment.

In the continuing deluge of popular history and fiction concerning the western lawman, one is likely to associate frontier disorder with the village. By contrast, attention to current conditions is directed almost entirely to urban police problems. Both emphases are misleading and, to a surprising degree, uninformed. While the small town of today is usually ignored, law enforcement in the cities of the old West has been virtually forgotten.

Any perspective on the development of urban police forces in the United States demands a comprehension of conditions in England at the close of the eighteenth century. Since the reign of Edward I larger towns in Britain had relied with little success upon combinations of informal watches and various government constables. The Act of 1774 for the City of Westminster, an experimental effort to co-ordinate police activities, proved a dismal failure. Attempts to remedy the situation by legislative patchwork continued, however, into the nineteenth century. By 1828 Greater London possessed nine official and distinct police organizations.[14] With crime rampant, Parliament finally chose to adopt a revolutionary program to centralize and greatly elevate standards for law enforcement officers. Designed by Sir Charles Rowan, a distinguished army colonel, and promoted by the energetic Sir Robert Peel, the scheme culminated in 1829 with passage of the Metropolitan Police Act. The opening phrases of this statute heralded a radical departure from prior means of crime control:

Be it therefore enacted, that it shall be lawful for his majesty to cause a new police office to be established in the city of Westminster. . . . The whole of the city and liberties . . . shall be constituted, for the purpose of this act, into one district, to be called "the metropolitan police district"; and a sufficient number of fit and able men shall from time to time, by the directions of one of his majesty's principal secretaries of state, be appointed as a police force for the whole of such district, who shall be sworn in by one of the said justices to act as constables for preserving the peace, and preventing robberies and other felonies, and apprehending offenders against the peace.[15]

Under the act a new kind of constabulary with crown supervision came into being for Greater London. Rowan, commissioner of the force from 1829 to 1840, created sixteen divisions and companies. While the organizational structure closely paralleled army systems, these units avoided military connotations. One precedent-setting decision rejected any routine authorization of firearms. Uniforms were determined to be essential, but the color blue was chosen instead of the originally proposed red and gold to prevent association with the royal regiments.[16]

71

The most significant innovations of Rowan and Peel dealt with personnel. New constables had to meet rigid standards of selection and they served a challenging period of probation. Careful records of performance along with demands for control of temper, good appearance, and overall efficiency constituted essential elements of the system. The first few years of operation for the new Metropolitan Police found a personnel turnover, by discharge and resignation, of several times force size, but within a decade the major goals were accomplished. The people accepted the constable as a reliable friend and true protector of the peace. The old image of a corrupt agent of oppression disintegrated as the determined policemen, nicknamed "Bobbies" after Sir Robert Peel, made their rounds.

Imaginative English police experimentation did not go unheeded in the United States. Many American cities had utilized citizenry patrolling at night since early colonial days. But it was not until the 1830s and 1840s that major innovations appeared. Relying upon British successes and made possible by the estate of a wealthy philanthropist, Philadelphia in 1833 organized a small force of paid officers for the day and a sizable company for night protection. In 1838 serious riots forced Boston to disband its paid but informal watch of fifteen years' standing and adopt a "special city police."[17] These early steps toward comprehensive municipal law enforcement culminated in 1844 with the creation of a consolidated agency for New York City. With state authority and funds, the metropolis established shifts for police assignment and placed operations under a superintendent appointed by the mayor.

New York clearly emulated certain features of the British system and its police organization in turn served as a model throughout the nation. Within less than twenty years Chicago, Cincinnati, New Orleans, and other cities created forces on the same principles. Interestingly, however, America carefully avoided some of the most obvious and favorable features of the English police. Uniforms, for example, did not come into general use in the

United States until shortly before the Civil War, the color blue being taken from both the British lawmen and the U.S. military. No effort was ever made to avoid general carrying and use of firearms. Perhaps most significant, American cities permitted their police to remain under close political domination with results still obvious.

Confronted by pronounced corruption in local law enforcement and obvious interaction with existing power structures, various jurisdictions tried to establish independent agencies. Several related and overlapping stages beginning in the latter half of the nineteenth century may be noted. First came delegation of supervisory authority either to the city council or to groups of commissioners, elected or appointed. The next phase saw intervention by the states in municipal matters through legislation removing the police from strictly local control. Such measures typically required the governor to appoint, with limitations, police board members with different political affiliations. Early state provisions sometimes took unusual form. Nebraska and New Mexico established maximum permissible salaries for local officers instead of setting minimum rates; in Dakota, technical jurisdiction might be extended considerably beyond city limits.[18] The final major trend in attempted reform concerns the imposition by state legislatures of standards for municipal lawmen. Such steps have most notably included civil service requirements, usually starting with larger urban areas followed by coverage gradually extended to smaller communities. These measures often included provisions for police pensions, minimum salaries, and insistence upon uniforms furnished by cities.

Each of these popular waves helped shape the modern municipal agency; vestiges of the commission system and state appointment remain. Civil service, not yet accepted in certain regions, is currently being reinforced elsewhere by minimum state standards for all peace officers; and federal aid may well open the pathway to a still higher level of influence. Despite these efforts and some progress, the typical police force in the United States remains under considerable and continuing political pressure. Reform efforts have in large measure merely shifted the center of power or introduced new interest groups into the scene.

Cities in the West naturally benefited from prior experimentation in England and the East. Urban areas did not spring full-born into the land, and during their expansion and development reform efforts had pronounced impact. A typical community soon outgrew a single marshal for law enforcement purposes and established a police force along well-determined lines. These agencies functioned with an appearance and procedures somewhat resembling those of today. Operations at Omaha in 1880 can serve as a suitable example.

The police force is appointed by the mayor, with the consent of the city marshal. He receives a salary of $1,200 per annum. He has the direction and control of the police force while on duty. The rest of the force consists of a deputy marshal and 8 patrolmen, who receive $840 per annum each. Their uniform consists of a double breasted frock coat of blue cloth and a blue cap. The men provide their own uniform. Each man carries a billy, a revolver, and Phillip's patent police nippers. Each serves 12 hours a day and patrols four blocks, about 400 feet square. In 1880 there were 867 arrests, the principal causes being drunkenness, larceny, assault and battery, disorderly conduct, and prostitution. . . . Special policemen are appointed by the mayor and council at the request of any firm or corporation to do service in or about the business or premises of such firm or corporation. They have the powers of regular police in the discharge of their duties. In 1880 the force cost about $10,000. . . .[19]

The appointment of special officers, as noted in the above report from Nebraska, deserves some attention. To hold operating costs at a minimum and to permit the exercise of private interests, cities very frequently commissioned private policemen. Today such personnel can still be found in "auxiliary," "voluntary," "honorary," or "reserve" categories and are probably as numerous as ordinary lawmen. Their authority varies greatly according to state provision and local custom. In Kansas, mayors of first-class cities (generally defined as those of 15,000 or more population) retain full discretion to appoint and dismiss special officers. The same state gives chiefs of police power to commission recreation personnel as deputies.[20] In Texas, "Whenever the mayor deems it necessary, in order to enforce the laws of the city, or to avert danger, or to protect life or property...he shall summon into service as a special police force, all or as many citizens as in his judgment may be necessary."[21] North Dakota allows electors to petition for appointment of salaried nightwatchmen, while in Oregon, city officials can commission police for specific duties, such as preserving the purity of the water supply.[22] Quite obviously, the special town officer is still a duly constituted lawman of considerable significance.

Every city experienced a slightly different pattern in the development of its police organization. No single community could possibly be representative of all the influences and modifications affecting municipal law enforcement over more than a century. It is, therefore, advisable to survey the early periods of expansion in several departments representing different problems and regions. For this purpose three distinctive western cities can outline conditions and attitudes during representative phases of development in more populous urban settings—San Francisco, Denver, and San Antonio.

The history of the San Francisco police is unique in all the world; no other municipality demonstrated such a leading involvement by the local citizenry in actual law enforcement. Before the Gold Rush, when the community consisted of only a few thousand persons living on the bay, six undisciplined and largely ineffective constables served as the only peace officers. In just a few months, however, conditions of lawlessness became serious. With miners flocking toward the interior, ships disgorging passengers, and sailors and whalers deserting in unprecedented numbers, disorder threatened the continued existence of the community. On July 16, 1849, the citizens of San Francisco held a mass meeting and formed a special police force of 230 men with W. E. Spofford as its chief.[23] Under the new city marshal the simple and poorly paid organization began operations, but it was probably the first functioning municipal unit of consequence in the West.

Within a month the committee on police recommended salaries ranging from $300 a month for an assistant captain to $6 a day for patrolmen. They obtained the brig *Euphemia* for use as a temporary prison and had her moored to a convenient wharf.[24] By the middle of 1850 the police had San Francisco divided into three districts, each under a captain with an assistant, first and second sergeants, and detachments of patrolmen varying in number according to area. Total regular police strength stood at fifty; thus did the municipal agency dawn with the very opening of the far western frontier.

It required only a few months for San Francisco law enforcement to become deeply involved in the political and social conflict raging in the city. A sizable element in the community originally regarded its peace officers favorably. A local newspaper reported: "In point of efficiency we hesitate not to say that the police department of San Francisco is equal to the police of any city in the world. It would be difficult to find a set of men their superiors as regards gentlemanly conduct and intelligence . . . such men should be well paid for their services. . . ."[25]

But growing public disorder soon prompted formation, in 1851, of the first of two famous vigilance committees. For several months the citizenry simply took over law enforcement. With ordinary policemen resigning for lack of pay and departing for the gold fields, San Franciscans created a volunteer force of considerable sophistication and delegated authority. "Beside the regular police there was a water police, of which Ned Wakeman was chief. The regular police were paid, but often members were detailed for police duty who drew no pay. The city was districted, and a committee appointed to oversee the affairs of each district. The water police were stationed along the city front to keep an eye on ships and sailors, and to watch for thieves accustomed to enter from beneath stores built over the water."[26]

Eventually the regular police once more took over control of law enforcement. The force expanded in size to about sixty, but while official monthly pay for patrolmen rose to $165, the officers sometimes waited long periods without actual salary disbursements. In 1854 the men were distributed as follows: two under direct control of the mayor, eight to the city marshal's office for service of warrants and attachments, one to the recorder to aid in procuring witnesses, five to Mission Dolores to maintain a small jail and generally preserve order, one to the tax collector, and one to the office of the street commissioner to serve citations and enforce appropriate ordinances. In addition to the approximately thirty left for routine patrol, two officers served as interpreters capable of rendering assistance in Spanish, French, Chinese, Portuguese, and Malay. Finally, San Francisco relied upon ". . . 33 watchmen in the city hired and paid by individuals and neighborhoods, who are sworn and have the same powers as the regulars and are subject like them to the orders of the marshals."[27]

Despite the obvious advances in a short space of time, widespread dissatisfaction with the police made itself known. The force earned a reputation for corruption and stood accused of failing to carry out essential investigations under political pressure.

As a general thing, the selection of officers has been as good as could have been expected, where the fulfillment of political promises and the rewarding of favorites have been of paramount importance to the detention in power of experienced men. As a general thing, also, the officers have performed their duties with alacrity and courage; but, at the same time, the number of evil doers has not been diminished. . . .

There has not been one officer in the city government since its foundation, who has not been charged with unfaithfulness; and some on no salary at all, and some on a yearly salary—the whole of which has been spent in a month—have grown rich, and are men of standing in the community. Each day has its tale of depravity.[28]

Conditions within the city police contributed to renewed disorder and by 1856 to resurrection of citizen control through formation of the second major vigilance committee. Several executions and deportations gave the era a coloring of mob rule. In truth, the characteristics usually associated with vigilantes and lynching were quite absent. Most indications imply that the citizenry merely reasserted by violent means a rudimentary form

77

of democracy with primary emphasis on means of local law enforcement.

> The police force of the Committee [of Thirteen, 1856] was organized with a chief director and regular policemen. When complete it numbered two or three hundred men, some of whom were under pay. In their permanent quarters on Sacramento street a part of the building was set off from the military department [of forty companies]. The police had access to all parts of the building, which privilege members of the military had not. Mr. [G. B.] Watkins was made captain of police, and was assisted by Oscar Smith, and others, at first. "The force was not very large," says Mr. Watkins, "probably not more than ten or fifteen men, but we could at any time call any number of men to our aid in an emergency."
>
> Many of the regular city police resigned and joined the vigilant police. The city was patrolled night and day by foot and horse, and was never so well watched before or since. All the military companies except the Marion Rifles and the San Francisco Blues, composed chiefly of sporting men, abandoned their organizations and joined the committee. . . .[29]

This operation led directly to the Consolidation Act of 1856, which gave the city a larger and more formally structured law enforcement agency. The Vigilance Committee maintained influence by selecting James Curtis as San Francisco's chief of police from 1856 to 1858. Despite many shortcomings in the Consolidation Act, improved efficiency could not be doubted. Between 1855 and 1858 the number of persons convicted and punished in San Francisco rose by ten times; police and prisoner costs fell by approximately 75 per cent.[30]

Within ten years a thoroughly institutionalized department along usual lines developed in the city. Actual strength did not reach authorized totals and complaints of laxity and graft continued, but the day of active vigilantism had ended. Political influence still made itself quite evident with serious results to internal discipline. Some officers even refused to buy or wear a uniform, although the city had in 1855 been among the first in the nation to require such.[31] San Francisco continued to rely upon large numbers of private officers to enforce the law and preserve the peace; the regular force, however, slowly increased its position within the community.

Over the next generation the changing significance of the department can be illustrated through reference to its strength and general activity. The following summary illustrates San Francisco police expansion:[32]

Fiscal Year	Force Size	Arrests	Officer Arrest Rate
1865–66	84	9,240	110
1870–71	104	12,332	119
1875–76	150	20,108	141
1880–81	400	23,011	58
1885–86	406	26,587	66
1890–91	406	24,528	53

Most of the important modifications came about under a new police commission formed by the state legislature in 1876. Consisting of the mayor, police judge, chief of police, judge of the city criminal court, and a county judge, the supervisory body greatly increased force size within three years. However, the same period witnessed a sharp decline in the average number of arrests per officer.

By 1895 San Francisco, with a population of approximately 300,000, possessed the largest and most active police department in the West. In the fiscal year of 1894–95 it reported 25,960 arrests in 148 different categories for an officer arrest rate of fifty-four. Drunkenness alone accounted for 12,402 of those taken into custody, with vagrancy supplying 2,269 and disturbance of the peace 1,685. Fifteen individuals found themselves unexpectedly arrested for urinating in the streets, five for "giving indecent entertainment by phonograph," and five for "bathing undressed in proscribed limits." Some other charges giving indications of things to come included 104 listed as "visiting opium places" and 108 seized because of fast and reckless carriage driving.

The department received forty-eight complaints, all dismissed, against its men during the year and reported sixteen vacated positions—by death, resignation, retirement, and outright discharge. The total police force numbered 482, with 412 patrolmen, thirty-eight sergeants, and five captains. In modern terminology, this gave the city a police ratio (number of commissioned officers per 1,000 population) of 1.6, considerably under the larger urban areas of the East.[33] By way of comparison, San Francisco in the 1960s enjoyed a police ratio of about 2.5, still well below eastern centers.

In his report for the fiscal year 1894–95, Chief P. Crowley made several interesting recommendations. He proposed a small reserve force, centrally located, to aid in control of riotous mobs, and suggested that the mayor issue permits for any parades or public meetings. Furthermore, he urged formation of a mounted patrol for suburban areas and the purchase of five additional station-houses. The chief went on to propose prohibition of the sale and use of fireworks, the closing of saloons and open theaters at midnight, and the licensing of masked balls for, "They are scenes of debauchery, demoralizing to the youth of both sexes, and a disgrace to the city."[34]

Despite improvements in size and organization, charges of extreme corruption in the San Francisco police continued. One frequently assigned source of the problem had racial implications. According to some sources, Chinese criminals systematically bribed local officers. Disclosures revealed large payments to secure immunity for vice operations, particularly gambling and prostitution. These accusations sometimes involved a unique police unit, the China Town Squad. Organized in 1889 and colorfully equipped with hammers and axes to effectuate rapid entrance into opium dens, the detachment remained in operation for some eighty years. Scandals over inefficiency and graft culminated in 1908 with the mysterious disappearance from a police launch crossing the bay of Chief William T. Biggy. Although his body was found a week later, the death could never be satisfactorily explained and led to even greater suspicion about conditions within the department.[35]

Corruption could hardly be said to be limited to any single agency. Every large city probably experienced similar charges. While San Francisco undoubtedly had its share of political involvement and graft, the same problems endured as a continuing theme in police history at Denver, Colorado.

Originally a conglomerate of three communities, Denver received its first charter shortly before the Civil War. On December 21, 1859, Wilson A. Sisty became city marshal of the booming community. A Pennsylvanian and veteran of the Mexican War, he created a simple police force and soon returned to the hunt for gold. Under the newly organized Colorado Territory, Denver selected George E. Thornton as its first chief of police in 1861. Thornton, a New Yorker by birth, had considerable early experience as a member of New York City's precedent-setting police force; later, he served as warden of Colorado's penitentiary.[36]

During the next few years Denver experienced a rapid expansion in population. Between 1870 and 1880, the city grew from 4,759 to 35,629, with serious natural consequences for law enforcement. In 1873 the police docket indicated approximately ninety arrests per month, with about 60 per cent of these for drunkenness. Prostitution posed the second greatest problem, with breaches of the peace composing most of the remainder. Such routine offenses as "immoderate riding" and "obstructing the sidewalk," however, were also noted.[37]

After 1885 the police began a decade of modification and expansion under strong political influence. A new chief, Austin W. Hogle, attempted during his typically brief two-year tenure to bring military discipline to the department. This probably reflected his background with the Union Army and the Colorado National Guard. Under Hogle several lasting innovations occurred. An energetic detective named Sam Howe, already a veteran of twelve years in the department, began keeping a highly significant "rogues gallery" of photographs, perhaps the earliest of such systems in police history. Howe later became chief of detectives, earning fame with his unique museum of crime and a mascot cat named "Roxy" who by legend could distinguish any investigator from an ordinary citizen.[38]

During the 1880s the Denver department, already complaining of court decisions which hampered its activities, operated three regular "runs," or shifts of duty. The first extended from 4:00 A.M. to 1:00 P.M. A second and preferred shift then continued to 8:00 in the evening. The final and least desired "run" completed the system of 24-hour patrol. Each roll call witnessed an inspection by the officer in command with two men normally detailed to "house duty" at headquarters. Their primary functions at night consisted of listening to women complaining of abuses and providing free lodging for "sleepers" voluntarily wandering in from the streets.[39]

Anyone familiar with modern activities in a police department of equivalent size would have felt quite at home. The daily problems and ordinary solutions have really changed but little.

> There are many men in Denver and in every community who think police duty is "a soft snap." . . . They think that they have only to wear nice dark blue clothes with pretty bright buttons and then they walk slowly over a beat and drive accumulated boys from a street corner, help the ladies—the well-dressed ones—across the street where street cars or carriages are approaching, and grow fat; for it is a fact that very few men can remain upon a police force any length of time without growing fat. So these ambitious mortals "work" for their particular candidates for the Mayorality or for positions in the City Council. . . .
>
> The latest style now in arresting a man, whether intoxicated or in an abnormal state of sobriety, is to politely persuade him to a patrol box and then pull the signal. While the victim is arguing, the patrol wagon, with its dashing horses and its brilliant lights, comes to the place with a graceful curve and a cloud of dust or splatter of mud, and the prisoner is in the jail. . . .[40]

The next major reform phase came under Chief J. F. Farley, appointed in 1889. The former head of Thiel's Detective Service in Denver, he commenced a campaign which doubled departmental strength to alleviate many of the problems associated with a police ratio of only 0.3. An immigrant from Ireland, Farley tried diligently to rectify the department's badly marred reputation. His position was a difficult one, for the force had just seen its chief, Henry Brady, along with several other officers, resign under charges of blackmail. Wilson S. Swain, then chief of detectives, quit in the same period after committing a rather questionable homicide.

Farley's first administrative order to the department forbade the fifty uniformed patrolmen from smoking in uniform or entering saloons except in line of duty. He felt that an officer must be dignified to be effective, and he wanted his men to build a new police image in Denver. Within a year the force had a school of instruction with organized squad and company drill. Furthermore, the chief wanted a gymnasium and workhouse to replace outdated facilities.

By the summer of 1890, Farley directed eighty individuals, including at least three Negroes and one woman. Despite rapid expansion, the police were still relatively few in number for a city of approximately 125,000. Denver had some four mounted officers, four patrol-wagon drivers, two jailers, two lieutenants, two sergeants, and twelve detectives, but the great bulk of strength naturally remained in foot patrolmen.[41]

Most accusations of corruption and brutality concerned the detectives. In October, 1890, the *Daily News* of Denver reported charges of confessions extorted by cruelty and abuse, illegal arrests without warrant, and the need for citizens to offer rewards or bribes to get attention. The department as a whole appeared lax in rendering reports, showed partiality and favoritism, warped information at will in criminal cases, and maintained a jail with disgraceful conditions.[42]

In March, 1891, such a situation led to passage of the Metropolitan Police Bill by the state legislature. Under the new act the governor, with approval of the Colorado Senate, appointed a three-member commission to supervise department operations. As usual, the effort to remove the police from political control only shifted the source of authority and produced new kinds of abuse.

Denver's difficulties with the police board culminated within a few months. Davis H. "Bloody Bridles" Waite was elected governor of Colorado on the Populist ticket in 1892. His newly appointed commissioners soon faced charges of gambling protection and earned the bitter opposition of older peace officers in the city. Waite eventually called out the militia as citizens demanded aid from the U.S. Army.

Such drastic measures had no lasting effect on conditions of the police. The Denver department continued to experience serious charges of misconduct. One detective, Samuel Emrich, received a homicide sentence of from fourteen to sixteen years in 1904, while the new chief of police, Michael A. Delaney, stood accused of beating almost to death an aged and infirm ash handler.[43] These events led to another crisis in 1906. Judges Ben Lindsey and Frank Johnson charged the police with open corruption and deliberate failure to enforce the laws. The atmosphere became even more tense following a barroom brawl in which policeman Charles S. Secrest, a known troublemaker throughout the West, killed a man over a dice game and then resisted arrest. Late in February, 1906, approximately 150 citizens formed a Law and Order League to promote better conditions within the city.[44] Such a heritage left an imprint on the Denver police which has not yet been fully overcome, as indicated by scandals in recent years over officers operating burglary rings.

The history of the police in San Antonio illustrates a much older and perhaps more typical heritage than that of either Denver or San Francisco. Under Spanish and Mexican rule city law enforcement remained largely under control of regional governments. Before independence the chiefs of police in San Antonio often were appointed from the state capital in Mexico proper. The city council, however, exercised financial power over the agency and debated such issues as the necessity of reporting missing funds and supplying candles for the jail turnkey.

During the era of the Republic of Texas, San Antonio had only a town constable. With annexation to the United States the city faced greater problems of maintaining the peace, and in 1846 the council placed James Dunn in the dual posts of marshal and poundkeeper. In the same year the mayor obtained authority to organize a force of special policemen at a salary of $1.50 per day.[45]

The marshal's post was a political prize and frequent disagreements between councilmen and the chief local officer created highly unstable conditions for law enforcement. In the fourteen years following creation of the title, twenty city marshals served in San Antonio.

During the Civil War the police not only continued to exercise their usual duties but also collected special taxes imposed under the Confederacy. Conclusion of the conflict between North and South, however, left city law enforcement in limbo. The regular force simply evaporated before a military government took control. San Antonians, like their counterparts in other sections of Texas, organized temporary guard units to protect homes from thieves, arsonists, and suspected looters. Reconstruction brought many new problems to the community, including crucial issues relating to the police. Carpetbaggers and scalawags clashed bitterly with former Confederates. As one indication of hectic conditions, no less than six men served as chief marshal during the two years following surrender to Union forces.[46] Each city administration brought changes in personnel and claims of new efficiency. "Never was the city better policed or the peace better kept than by the present city administration [1867–68]. The standard of police service has been raised—men of worth and steady habits have been given the positions, men who have served their country in the United States Army or Navy, during the rebellion, have always been given the preference. Twelve good men now do the service well that was performed poorly [by twenty]."[47]

Despite the serious problems of a Reconstruction police, the basic routines of ordinary law enforcement continued, with drunkenness, disturbing the peace, and theft being typical charges.

When in 1875 conditions had largely returned to normal, the department underwent sweeping modifications. For the first time the city created a structured and fixed force with Chief Marshal John Dobbin, one assistant marshal, one detective, and twelve patrolmen.[48] This gave San Antonio a ratio of approximately one officer for every one thousand citizens. Such a figure has remained remarkably constant in the community for nearly a century; most expanding urban areas show a sharply increased police ratio with expansion in total population.

Another peculiar similarity ties the past and present. For fiscal year 1866–67, San Antonio city government expenditures totaled $96,494.30, with $21,389.62 (or 22.2 per cent) allocated directly to the police. Exactly one century later in fiscal year 1966–67, the comparative figures were $28,937,145 and $6,352,655 (or 22 per cent).[49] The proportionate appropriation for local law enforcement had remained the same, as had the police ratio. By almost any standard San Antonio in 1866–67, with an estimated population of 12,000, stood on the edge of the frontier. One hundred years later, with an estimated population of 700,000, it had not moved in the comparative significance accorded crime control.

The newly formed force of 1875 became, with the usual resistance from officers, uniformed. Double-breasted gray coats with matching caps were specified by the city council for general use. In summer months dark blue blouses and Panama hats could be substituted. While money for the uniforms came from the police fund, officers eventually had to repay the cost. This method of acquisition did not apply to badges, revolvers, communicating rattles, and clubs; the city continued its long-standing policy of making these available to officers without charge.

Uniforms of Confederate gray endured for a number of years in San Antonio, but the headgear soon changed to tall helmets of a matching color, in emulation of British and eastern styles. The city's few mounted officers, however, wore "ten gallon grey hats." Clubs carried by San Antonio's patrolmen of the era, incidentally, were made of mesquite, a highly unsuitable wood which tended to shatter upon contact. As a consequence, the police always had a supply of kindling for use in winter months.[50]

For many years after the Civil War the city had no wagon for transporting prisoners, posing a serious problem for officers. Working laborious twelve-hour shifts, they either had to drag unwilling drunks and disorderly cowboys many blocks to the notorious "Bat Cave" jail or secure some means of private conveyance. With considerable ingenuity, patrolmen resorted to hacks, express wagons, vegetable carts, wheelbarrows, and even a hearse. Often, of course, the lack of transport resulted in bloody encounters and contests of physical strength before recalcitrant prisoners could be jailed.

During the 1880s the San Antonio police department expanded and specialized operations. By 1885 the force totaled thirty-three, including a "poundmaster" with responsibility for livestock and pets found wandering the streets, a "sanitary policeman" to prevent violation of appropriate ordinances, a jailer, and a night clerk. Administrative duties fell upon City Marshal Phil Shardein, Assistant Marshal Juan T. Cardenas, and first and second assistants to them.[51] Although only three of the additional policemen were of Mexican descent, the custom of having a Latin-American serving as second in command had already begun; it endured in San Antonio for approximately fifty years.

Technological advances also brought changes in police methods. The department kept officers on constant duty at the new railway depots. Telephones provided a wonderful and immediate means of communication. Traffic conditions became so critical that the city council warned the police to stop driving the long overdue patrol wagon at high speeds. The marshal's force, however, remained trapped between the public and its leaders. Officers obtained their commissions through political patronage, while the grand jury, in turn, censured the police for failing to enforce the laws.

Shortly after the turn of the century San Antonio attracted considerable attention through experimentation with the "pill box" system. This consisted of eight very small patrol stations located throughout the city. One officer at each pill box maintained telephone communication with headquarters while his partner patrolled on horseback; every hour the men would rotate duties. During the same era the city made another unsuccessful effort to economize through abolition of the wagon. Attempts to transport inebriates by hired hack or by force to the accompaniment of large and appreciative crowds, along with occasional riots, led to abandonment of the scheme within a few years.[52] By 1910 the number of substations had fallen to six, but annual arrests totaled 7,429. Of those taken into custody only 179 were classified as juveniles, while police reported 3,909 charged with either drunkenness or vagrancy. In twelve months officers also picked up no less than 3,663 loose dogs on the public streets.[53]

The department made a notable acquisition in 1910, a magnificent air-cooled Franklin automobile equipped with a dashboard gong to attract attention. With four motorcycles received during the same year, the San Antonio police started to face problems created by self-propelled vehicles. While regular mounted officers continued in the city until late in the 1920s and a few "ropers" along with park patrolmen rode on until nearly World War II, the automobile quickly began to take its place in operational plans. The city police, incidentally, owned only draft animals; individual officers furnished their personal mounts for service in return for a monthly allotment to cover care and feeding. Similar policies may still be noted in many smaller agencies where officers continue to provide their own cars.

The automobile also brought the demise in 1928 of the pill boxes, as the city created twelve patrol districts for its new fleet of Fords and finally switched from two to three daily work shifts.[54] Cars created fully as many police problems as they provided solutions. In the decade between 1914 and 1924 arrests relating to automobile violations, among the total for all crimes, rose nearly tenfold in San Antonio, from approximately four per cent to 36 per cent. By comparison, the percentage of arrests for intoxication remained virtually unchanged, at slightly more than 30 per cent, despite passage of state and federal prohibition laws during intervening years.[55] The 1920s witnessed yet another significant change in local law enforcement. After some twenty years of interchangeable usage, the title "chief of police" at last replaced "city marshal."

Police history in San Francisco, Denver, and San Antonio during the transition from the frontier to a complex urban environment cannot be taken as fully representative of conditions, but it does illustrate typical patterns of development. Expansion in size, specialization of duties, improvement in equipment, and division by substation are but a few of the more obvious trends. These modifications occurred under close political control with the usual accompaniment of corruption and favoritism. Even more important is the continuation of basic techniques and problems; there is little evidence of major change in the basic social role and function of the town policeman.

Table 4 of Appendix A illustrates conditions of selected cities in 1890. As an easily identified frontier gradually faded away, the police underwent subtle transitions. The title of marshal, for example, showed remarkable tenacity in the West. And cities of that region, while not obviously far from a national average, were slightly underpoliced. This condition, furthermore, has not been alleviated in recent times; western communities continue to have fewer than ordinary numbers of policemen. Of course, urban areas reflect greater proportional force size and consequent activity, but cities undergoing rapid expansion normally have relatively smaller numbers of peace officers. Thus, in 1890, Lincoln, Nebraska, with a population of 55,154, had only sixteen policemen. Charleston, South Carolina, then a city of about the same size, employed a force of 89. It is worthy of note, however, that in many western communities peace officers averaged a hundred or more arrests annually, a rate rarely equaled in the larger eastern cities. Although dry statistics give some insight, they can never depict fully the vicissitudes and difficulties besetting the policeman of the western towns during the latter half of the nineteenth century. Besieged by the public courts and offenders alike, he faced an impossible but enduring task.

City officers throughout the country clearly did not enjoy public esteem or respect. In comparison with the firemen of the era, they came far behind in community popularity. In 1887 a distinguished observer commented:

The policemen of our American cities are a byword, a standing joke on justice. Composed mostly of the lower quality of our imported element, who, by attending at primaries and working for the successful candidate at the polls, have in their own opinions earned subsequent distinguished recognition, they sun themselves upon the streets, draw their salaries, and repose upon their luck and laurels. If wakened from their *dolce far niente* by the report of a pistol, and the offender rushes into their arms, they lead him off to prison, proud of their achievement. But he who expects from detectives that activity and keen enthusiasm in the ferreting out of criminals which the case seems to demand, without the stimulus of reward other than that of salary, is smiled upon for his simplicity. Go to the police-office of any of our cities and enter a complaint. If you want thorough and efficient action you must pay for it, and pay in proportion to the amount of work you want done. So long as politics is made a profession, and office is the reward of pre-election service, the people must expect, if they would have a thing well and quickly done, to do it themselves.[56]

Pronounced political control contributed greatly to the low status accorded the police in many western towns; efforts to remove forces from such influence encountered many obstacles.

Struggles for power also existed within the departments themselves and early efforts to provide job security only exacerbated unpleasant personal antagonisms. In 1898, for example, the city marshal of Houston attempted to discharge an officer who then demanded duty assignment under terms of the city charter. In a legal battle involving another special appointment by the mayor, the policeman eventually received a judgment for back salary.[57]

The extent of a lawman's authority frequently brought him into court, sometimes under strange circumstances. In one illustrative situation following the disastrous Galveston flood of 1900, the mayor ordered police to impress private horses to assist in removal of the dead. An officer seized a mount belonging to A. A. Brown and unfortunately worked it to death performing the trying task. Brown sued for his horse's value, but a Texas appellate court ruled against the claim, asserting that the policeman had acted outside the scope of his authority; the mayor could not properly issue such a command even in the immediacy of the emergency.[58]

Just as today, many powers of the police are poorly defined by statute and rarely clarified by the bench. City policemen, for example, might be restricted from carrying firearms outside their immediate jurisdiction. Any overstepping of authority could have dire results. In one case a uniformed Utah officer placed a man under arrest following a barroom knife fight. At the call box he escaped and when chased drew a pistol, fired, and killed the policeman. On appeal the Supreme Court of Utah reversed a conviction for murder, holding in part that the homicide might have been self-defense.[59]

Violence, of course, was part of the job. Any routine arrest might suddenly become a fight or an armed assault. While popular portrayals have exaggerated the danger, local officers would occasionally be involved in mortal combat. No more than four of every one thousand community peace officers lost their lives in line of duty and many of these deaths did not occur at the hands of criminals. Fatal accidents regularly took place, and with some frequency policemen killed one another either by mistake or design. Lawmen took several lives for each given and, at least in some communities, they killed more innocent people than did the criminals.[60]

Police departments in western cities did not lag in experimentation with new ideas and methods. Whether uniforms in San Francisco, photographic identification in Denver, or substations in San Antonio, developments equaled those in eastern areas. One example of innovation and change concerned the acceptance of women into the police. While jail matrons had served in New York as early as 1845, their primary function was that of guarding female inmates. Under pressure from women's groups other cities in the East utilized additional paid prison visitors in the 1870s. The first actual policewomen—usually termed matrons—appeared in the same era. Mrs. Sadie M. W. Likens of Denver was among the first of these precedent-setting ladies. Appointed about 1884, she served as a duly constituted peace officer for nearly a decade. Mrs. Likens subsequently became quite active in social and club work in the Denver area.[61] Other cities of the western states, such as San Antonio in 1900, appointed policewomen after petitions of local citizens.[62] The lady officers first achieved wide acceptance in southern California shortly before World War I, and in 1915 founded their national association at Los Angeles.

Most work for the early policewomen involved local jails, and no phase of law enforcement had greater need for their services. Community lockups were, and are, a national disgrace. As Omaha admitted in 1880, "Of the present quarters in the city prison . . . 'they are unfit to be the recipient of the vilest prisoner.' "[63] Early jails consisted of trees or logs to which those in custody could be chained. A few communities, such as San Francisco and Sacramento, utilized converted ships as places of incarceration. Most towns of consequence eventually modified existing structures or built simple facilities to house inmates. Usually filthy, often vermin infested, sometimes crowded, and rarely supervised, these jails served primarily as holding points for drunks and vagrants. In one unsuccessful case resulting from lockup conditions in Concordia, the Supreme Court of Kansas specified that in 1884:

> The city prison was an open building, set upon posts some two feet from the ground, with cracks in the building, rendering it cold, and that said building was not provided with any means of heating, and that during all of the time he [the complainant] was confined therein [for disturbing the peace] he was without any fire, and he was provided with no bedding by which he could keep warm; that during the time he was so confined the weather was severely cold, the thermometer showing some 10 degrees below zero.[64]

The jails of western towns contained prostitutes, thieves, juvenile delinquents, lunatics, robbers, sexual deviates, and wife beaters with only superficial efforts at segregation. Not all of those temporarily placed in local lockups, however, were suspected or convicted criminals. Some communities regularly placed runaway and lost children in their jails and police throughout the country accommodated vast numbers of "night lodgers" who simply wandered in from the streets in search of a place to sleep.

While the deplorable condition of most lockups could not be said to be directly caused by individual peace officers, local administrators often profited through inmates' discomfort. Some communities, for example, paid their lawmen according to the number of prisoners. By reduction of expenses many town marshals or chiefs managed to operate quite lucrative jails. Another possible source of income derived from work performed by those incarcerated. Since many early towns required prisoners to labor, the marshal might arrange for private employment at his personal profit. Usually, however, the inmates worked on public projects such as clearing new roads, digging ditches, or cleaning parks and streets. Many states held town peace officers responsible for supervising these tasks and protecting the laborers from abuse or public annoyance.

Still another source of income for local lawmen derived from provision of special services for those incarcerated, occasionally extending to outright connivance over escape. Flimsy and poorly guarded lockups often proved no serious barrier, "especially after the fetters were unlocked with money."[65] Inmates unable to arrange such timely releases still might derive other benefits, for town marshals sometimes adopted a benign attitude on holidays. They could, for example, allow the prisoners to join in a community celebration, returning them to the jail after completion of festivities. In other towns the custom yet continues of permitting minor misdemeanants an early release at Christmas.

Local lawmen of the western frontier faced problems and operated within structural systems not greatly different from those of today. Either in small villages or in large cities they functioned as the repressive arm of political institutions somewhat removed from public need. While much current attention is presently directed at the "image" of the police, status on the local level has clearly improved within the last century. Yet the actual routines and ordinary duties of community peace officers, apart from great technical innovation, display no fundamental alteration. The patrolman continues to make his rounds amid social situations highly resistant to change. Urban riots, disorderly youths, alcoholic vagrants, indescribable jail conditions—these patterns of individual and group disfunction remain. For the town policeman, the unpleasant side of society represents a significant part of reality as little known to the general public of today as that of yesterday.

Posse Comitatus

IV

In early England county law enforcement primarily depended upon sheriffs, as chief representatives of the crown, and local constables. Introduced in America during the seventeenth century, both officers followed traditional lines, with popular election supplanting executive appointment. Sheriffs became especially powerful in the rural South, while township and precinct constables gained greater significance in the village-oriented culture of the Northeast.

During the opening decades of the nineteenth century these positions of English origin were transported across the Mississippi River. Frontiersmen moving westward from the United States encountered similar functional agencies being utilized by those of Spanish heritage. San Antonio de Bexar, for example, had an *alcalde*, combining the powers of mayor and judge, who appointed a local *alguacil*, with duties roughly equivalent to those of a sheriff. The settlements led by Stephen F. Austin in East Texas combined features of both English and Spanish systems to handle routine problems of law enforcement. In 1823 and 1824 the colony at San Felipe de Austin provided each of the justices of the peace with a constable and created an appointed post of sheriff, predating town police agencies by several years.[1]

These positions found official recognition a few years later with adoption of a constitution for the Republic of Texas:

> There shall be appointed for each county, a convenient number of Justices of the Peace, one sheriff, one Coroner, and a sufficient number of Constables, who shall hold their offices for two years, to be elected by the qualified voters of the district or county, as Congress may direct. Justices of the Peace and Sheriffs shall be commissioned by the President [of the Republic].[2]

Under this provision the first legally qualified sheriffs of the American Far West took office. Apparently Dave Rusk, a veteran of San Jacinto and later ferryboat operator, received the first commission in 1837.[3] When Texas entered the Union the basic provisions affecting county peace officers remained largely unchanged in the state constitution. One significant addition, however, provided that "The Sheriff shall not be eligible more than four years in every six."[4]

Such laws endured in Texas for more than twenty years, lasting through the Civil War. But Reconstruction quickly transformed constitutional provisions regarding county lawmen. In 1866 the term of office for sheriffs and constables was increased from two to four years and eligibility for the former positions became "eight years in every twelve." Within three years Texas adopted yet another constitution and numerous charges of misconduct led to creation of a special provision making sheriffs subject to removal by district judges and eliminating eligibility limitations. Every county was to be divided into five justice-of-the-peace precincts with an appointed constable serving in each.[5]

In 1876 Texans seized the opportunity of rewriting the state constitution without the influence of a carpetbag government. The new law dropped requirements of formal commissioning by the governor and prepared the way for a reassertion of local control.

> There shall be elected by the qualified voters of each county a Sheriff, who shall hold his office for the term of four years, whose duties and prerequisites, and fees of office, shall be prescribed by the Legis-

lature, and vacancies in whose office shall be filled by the Commissioners Court until the next general election.[6]

Although the constitutional term of office became four years in 1954, the state legislature has with typical lethargy and inattention to detail never revised the statutory enactment which still would technically limit the sheriff to a two-year term; the 1876 constitution restored popular election of constables and specified that from four to eight precincts should exist in each county.[7]

In other regions, a slightly later frontier experience paralleled developments in Texas. Newcomers to California, for example, modified a similar *alcalde-alguacil* system and soon provided by law for the popular election of sheriffs and other county officers. Those sections without a well-defined Spanish system emulated the early office of territorial marshal or county law enforcement used in the East. In any case the normal pattern witnessed slowly increasing specificity with regard to duties and authorities. Jurisdictions throughout the West, however, closely adhered to popular control of local lawmen.

Even those isolated sections operating beyond the reach of state or territorial control had the equivalent of county peace officers. Popular representations of small towns on the frontier existing without functioning formal law are totally misleading. While procedures may have been simple and comparatively rare, the West had local systems of enforcement with the earliest of enduring settlement. Gilpin County, an independent mining district in the Colorado Rockies, for example, provided for the prompt election and bonding of a sheriff as "conservator of the peace" and specified his general duties.[8] Appendix B lists the fees of office which in 1861 this lawman had authority to charge.

With the assumption of authority by organized states and territories came somewhat more rigid formal means of acquiring office. But practices continued to be rather rudimentary for several years. In 1868, for example, the community of Cheyenne, Wyoming, organized a vigilante committee to exorcise local evildoers. A leader of the active citizenry, Nathaniel K. Boswell, temporarily assumed control at the scene. After several months the governor recognized "old Boz" by appointing him sheriff, but Wyoming had no official forms for such purposes. The territorial leader consequently took pen in hand on May 25, 1869, and wrote: "Know ye: That reposing special trust and confidence in the patriotism integrity and ability of N. K. Boswell, I John A. Campbell in persuance of and by virtue of authority vested in me do appoint him Sheriff of the county of Albany. . . ."[9] Under this simple but adequate commission the former vigilante became chief lawman of a vast region reaching from Colorado to Montana.

Technical legal provisions concerning county peace officers assumed a variety of forms throughout the West. Generally, constables were elected on a precinct basis along with local justices for whom they served processes, maintained order, and executed various warrants, attachments, and notices. Essential statutes regarding sheriffs invariably provided either two- or four-year terms as primary police agent for the organized government.

Intervening years have greatly complicated the picture of county agents with law enforcement functions. In several states, for example, the local coroner may act as sheriff under given circumstances, such as the latter's being himself jailed. Oregon allows county-fair boards to appoint "marshals or police as may be necessary to keep order and preserve the peace."[10] Texas permits an incredible array of special lawmen for a variety of functions. Water improvement, control, or supply districts can employ their own deputies. The commissioners of counties having five thousand or more sheep, goats, or cattle are privileged to appoint peace officers restricted to enforcement of livestock laws and paid at a rate not exceeding $5 per day.[11] Texas also permits independent employment, under the sheriff's direction, of special traffic personnel. "Such deputies shall be, whenever practicable, motorcycle riders . . ." with apparently limited authority emanating directly from the local commissioners.[12]

Some concept of the complexity of district law enforcement may be gained by looking at those persons regarded as county peace officers, for retirement purposes, in California. These include not only sheriffs, undersheriffs, constables, and their deputies, but all bailiffs, turnkeys, foresters, district attorneys' detectives and investigators, jailers, process servers, motorcycle officers, plus the fire wardens, apparatus engineers, prevention inspectors, patrolmen, observers, and the foremen of fire suppression crews together with forest firemen.[13]

Such statutory listings, however, do not by any means mark the totality of those treated by the courts as county lawmen. Part of the confusion arises over power to appoint citizens and empower them to preserve the peace or perform a specific function. Such authority ultimately derives from the ancient common-law right, originally restricted to the sheriff, of *posse comitatus*, or the "power of the county." This right, eventually extended by statute to most magistrates and peace officers, enables the summoning of aid in serious crimes. As imported and interpreted in the West,

When any felonious offense shall be committed, public notice thereof shall be immediately given in all public places near where the same was committed, and fresh pursuit shall forthwith be made after every person guilty thereof by sheriffs, coroners, constables, and all other persons who shall be by any of them commanded or summoned for that purpose.[14]

Either by statute or judicial interpretation, authority to commission citizens informally, descending from *posse comitatus*, reached many local officials. In many states, for example, a justice of the peace or district judge may designate with very wide discretion a private person as a peace officer to serve particular arrest warrants or *capias* writs. County attorneys and commissioners also possess generally broad authority to appoint special deputies and investigators.

Sheriffs in all western jurisdictions have authority to appoint deputies. In some states the scope of power is rather general, while in others it may be closely restricted. New Mexico orders that, "No person who may be under indictment or may be generally known as a notorious character, or as a disturber of the peace shall be eligible to serve as a deputy sheriff."[15] Arizona provides for appointment of special "ranger deputies" uniquely required to "provide and keep at his own expense a means of travel."[16] Although courts in other states have indicated a liberal construction of statutes establishing eligibility requirements for deputies, few approach the standards established in Texas. There, appellate judges upheld mere belief in service as a deputy and further created an incredible but artful distinction between officers *de facto* and *de jure*.[17]

County lawmen possessed all the powers of an ordinary peace officer. They could, therefore, arrest with or without warrant in certain situations as determined by state laws, although exercise of the right often led to bitter controversy. Strangely enough, the privilege of carrying firearms brought county peace officers into court with great frequency. Even more peculiar are the numbers of cases wherein local judges claimed the right to possess forbidden weapons. A typical situation involved a homicide committed by Justice of the Peace W. M. Patton of Karnes County, Texas. Attending a gay drinking party at a local dance hall, Patton discovered himself participating in a fist fight. Following one of his opponents to the "beer room," the magistrate then dared the doomed party to get his gun; a short time later, the man suddenly turned and shot. Although wounded, Patton returned the fire with deadly accuracy. The Court of Criminal Appeals, with considerable precedent, held that all magistrates in the state are conservators of the peace permitted to carry firearms and preserve public order. Perhaps most surprising is the date of the decision— 1935.[18] One does not toy with a Texas judge, especially at dances.

In addition to general powers of arrest and going armed, states gave county lawmen special and widely divergent privileges. They consequently permit the sheriff to call directly upon the national guard or militia for assistance. Wyoming specifies that he "shall not be charged rent for any building owned or controlled by the county" and used as a residence; New Mexico, considerably extending jurisdictional limits, permits the sheriff and his deputies to enter all counties of the state to perform an arrest with the concurrent right of *posse comitatus*.[19]

While the powers extended to county lawmen are broad, they may yet be subject to peculiar limitation. Texas has a totally ignored statute reading,

No Sheriff, Constable, or Deputy or [sic] either shall have authority to arrest or accost any person for driving a motor vehicle . . . in violation of the law . . . unless he is at the time wearing on his left breast on the outside of his garment so that it can be clearly seen a badge showing his title, and unless he is also wearing a cap, coat or blouse, and trousers of dark grey color, or dark blue, which cap and uniform shall be of the same color. Provided, if any person shall violate the provisions hereof, he shall be guilty of a misdemeanor and . . . shall be removed from office.[20]

Such a provision, fully enforced, would undoubtedly lead to the dismissal of nearly every county peace officer in the state attempting to supervise traffic.

The duties of sheriffs, constables, and their deputies are involved and multitudinous. Their primary law enforcement function, repeated in virtually identical wording throughout the West, reads as follows:

It shall be the duty of Sheriffs and of their deputies to keep and preserve the peace in their respective counties, and to quiet and suppress all affrays, riots, and insurrections, for which purpose, and for the service of process in civil or criminal cases, and in apprehending or securing any person for felony, or breach of the peace, they may call upon the power of their county. . . .[21]

Earlier and much later legislation reflect the basic premises and phrasing typical of this Nevada example. One should note the absence of a stated responsibility for arresting on simple misdemeanors without warrant.

As chief executive officer of the county the sheriff performed diverse duties. Many of these were of a routine clerical nature demanded for local operation. Because of his close association with local and district judges, states routinely passed laws requiring the sheriff both to maintain an office during regular hours at a county seat and to attend court sessions. In most instances, of course, deputies or clerks carried out such functions. But in the early days the sheriff himself might receive a note such as that from a justice of the peace in old California: "You will likewise summons a Jury of either six or twelve persons six I think would be enough for our small population however, I leave that to yourself not knowing how many people there is in your neighborhood but which ever number you may think proper I have two here Mr Wood & Mr Rhoades which you will please put on the jury list."[22]

Sheriffs served in many jurisdictions as the tax collector, a duty which at times appeared to occupy most of their time. And they could be called upon to carry out particular administrative tasks by state assignment. Along the early frontier, sheriffs administered punishment by flogging or banishment and even performed rather rustic executions by choking or other means.[23] The main tasks, however, remained the routine ones of serving process, making criminal and civil arrests, and preserving the generally peaceful conditions.

The county's primary law enforcement officer also had numerous other duties peculiar to his jurisdiction. Wyoming required him "to inspect the brands of all horses transported or driven out of the state," while New Mexico still specifies that the sheriff must "immediately trace and discover all livestock" reported as rustled. Somewhat less expected are laws ordering him to maintain the pound, fight forest and range fires, license canines, and eradicate prairie dogs.[24]

During the later part of the nineteenth century the sheriff occupied the foremost position in law enforcement throughout most of the West. Part of this significance derived from the rural conditions which naturally emphasized the role of an officer having a broad geographic jurisdiction. The great diversity of functions also related to the importance of the position. As a result of these conditions some of the most colorful and dramatic personalities ever to serve as American peace officers held the title of sheriff. James Butler "Wild Bill" Hickok, William B. "Bat" Masterson, Bill Tilghman, and most of the other famous frontier lawmen served at one time or another in the capacity.

Such well-known names, however, do not give an indication of the vast number and incredible variety of western sheriffs. It is quite impossible to select a few from the approximately 25,000 who served to represent fully such an assemblage. In order to survey superficially the types of men attracted to the office, however, one can briefly analyze the careers of four representative figures.

Many sheriffs came from the ranks of those with prior military or law enforcement experience, John C. Hays being one outstanding example. "Coffee Jack" came to Texas in 1836, fought in the revolution against Mexico, and served as an early leader of the Indian-fighting Rangers. Following a series of daring escapades during the Mexican War he moved westward through El Paso and opened a southern route to California. By 1850 Hays found himself in San Francisco, some 43 years of age, and upon short notice the independent candidate in the bitterly fought election for sheriff, the first to be regularly held in the county.

Against two ordinary political party nominees the former Ranger proved an exceptional campaigner. With the support of the local gambling crowd, Hays emphasized his reputation as a fearsome fighter and true man of the frontier. At one point backers of one opponent staged ". . . another grand display upon the plaza. . . . But in the midst of the excitement thus produced, Col. Hayes [sic] mounted upon a fiery black charger, suddenly appeared, exhibiting some of the finest specimens of horsemanship ever witnessed."[25] The dramatic lone rider from Texas triumphed at the polls as San Francisco County, California, elected its sheriff.

Hays occupied an office in town hall and began to organize his new law enforcement agency. During the next three years he helped form a local fire company and volunteer night patrol, recruited a cavalry unit to deal with possible Indian threats, and accepted subscriptions which eventually led to the construction of a new jail. The sheriff had difficulty finding deputies, gathering juries, and locating fugitives from the East. Although he managed to survive politically during the hectic days of the 1851

Vigilance Committee, Hays resigned in 1853. Three years later he emerged in open opposition to the vigilante element to serve as a captain of the largely unsuccessful "law and order" party. In later years the former sheriff gained a position of great influence as developer of Oakland and as Surveyor General of the United States. He remained active in California politics until shortly before his death in 1883.

Hays's responsibilities in early San Francisco hardly fit the popular image of the frontier sheriff. In some respects the work of Thomas Jefferson Carr in Wyoming more closely resembled the romanticized peace officer. Born in Pennsylvania in 1842, "Jeff" was the son of a river pilot. The future lawman was taken as a youth to Ohio, where he clerked and later taught school. After brief service with the Union Army, young Carr earned an accountant's diploma from Iron City College in Pittsburgh and proceeded westward to the Rockies. During the next few years Carr held several positions in Colorado as clerk, miner, and Central City policeman. Shortly after the Civil War an opportunity as a bank bookkeeper brought him to the raw railtown of Cheyenne. In 1869 the Wyoming legislature elected Carr, at the age of 27, sheriff of Laramie County, only to have the appointment declared illegal. The following year, however, he properly won the office in a regular election on the Democratic ticket. Within a year the new sheriff performed the territory's first legal execution, miraculously escaped a fierce gunbattle outside the town's most notorious bordello, and brought in several of Wyoming's most noted desperadoes.

Carr served as sheriff for three terms during the 1870s. Nicknamed "Red Cloud" by the Indians because of a flowing beard, he became a familiar figure throughout the region. As the chief lawman in Laramie County, Carr transported prisoners, served warrants, chased stage robbers, collected taxes, and maintained the detailed records of office. Defeated in a campaign for re-election, he obtained an appointment as city marshal at Cheyenne and held the post for three years. Carr then re-established a long-standing association with the Rocky Mountain Detective

Association. As detective and assistant superintendent for the Wyoming region, he maintained close ties with law enforcement for many years. Through real estate investment Carr also became a citizen of considerable financial substance in Cheyenne and continued an involvement in political affairs, serving as federal marshal for the entire territory under President Grover Cleveland.[26]

Hays and Carr both achieved considerable fame in their own communities, but neither has a reputation approaching the most famous of frontier lawmen—Patrick Floyd Garrett. Born in Alabama and raised in Louisiana, Garrett had by age 19 moved to Texas. He worked as a cowboy and hide hunter during Reconstruction and, about 1878, drifted westward once again. This time Garrett settled in New Mexico and involved himself in a race for sheriff of Lincoln County. With strong support from powerful cattle interests, the soft-spoken 6'4" giant won the election and soon began the now legendary chase after the "Billy the Kid" gang. After the sheriff killed William Bonney in 1881 and wrote a book to describe the event, his name became almost synonymous with western law enforcement.

The remainder of Pat Garrett's life can only be described as an unfortunate anticlimax. At the age of 31 he had first captured and later killed the frontier's most famous outlaw. While still serving in Lincoln County he came into conflict with the judiciary.[27] In 1889 John W. Poe defeated him in a contest for sheriff of Chavez County. Garrett then returned to Texas to operate an apparently unsuccessful horse ranch at Uvalde. In 1898 he switched political allegiance to the Republican party and served briefly as sheriff of Doña Ana County, New Mexico, followed by a four-year appointment as collector of federal customs at El Paso. By the age of 55 Garrett had become an embittered and somber figure. Troubled by financial and personal problems, he was killed under never satisfactorily explained circumstances near Las Cruces in 1908.

Despite his troubled later life, Garrett's reputation has remained, for one having disposed of a leading folk hero, remarkably free from attack. He has never been accused of representing the more bloodthirsty variety of lawman beloved by certain writers of fiction. Garrett has sometimes been identified as the last of the great western peace officers, but such assertions seem quite unjustified.

One of the most colorful and greatest sheriffs held office in the Arizona Territory as the frontier formally closed. John Horton Slaughter, born in Louisiana, served with the Confederate Army and briefly with the Texas Rangers. By 1879 he had driven a herd of cattle to the region south of Tucson and had begun to establish a great ranch reaching into Sonora. Slaughter scarcely resembled popular portraits of western lawmen; taciturn, slender, only 5'6" tall, his power relied on something more than mere appearance. Slaughter was crafty, tough, ruthless, and apparently capable of the sudden violence more often associated with the few actual gunfighter-marshals. In 1886, at the age of 45, he ran on the Democratic ticket and became sheriff of Cochise County. During the next few years Slaughter killed some twelve men while acting in an official capacity. Most of these deaths occurred in isolated areas, however, and neither public nor courts cared to question "Don Juan's" version of the events.

Countless stories can be told of John Slaughter. He usually drove a rig, for example, but kept his saddled horse tied behind. In cold weather the sheriff appeared curiously bundled in muffler and heavy coat, for he suffered severely from asthma. Slaughter appointed many relatives to office, a habit shared by most other lawmen, and routinely utilized his deputies to infiltrate criminal centers. He frequently changed announced plans without warning or apparent design—a trait which legend says repeatedly avoided ambush.

After two terms Slaughter retired to his nearby San Bernadine ranch; in 1895 the former sheriff received a deputy's commission which he retained for nearly thirty years. While the rancher and lawman certainly earned his reputation as a dangerous character, he also demonstrated traits of underlying compassion and sympathy, exemplified by his adoption of a little Apache girl. Feared and respected by Mexicans, Indians, and Americans, Slaughter eventually lost most of his land in a lengthy legal dispute with the federal government, but he remained an influential enigma along the border until his death in 1922.[28]

Hays, Carr, Garrett, and Slaughter exemplify only the best known of the West's early sheriffs. Despite the many grandiose claims, their terms of office brought no true end to lawlessness in the territories. But such men clearly forced criminal activity into more routine and tolerable channels. They also served as a strong foundation for the legend of the frontier sheriff—strong, silent, capable, and at times quite deadly.

There have been perhaps 100,000 county lawmen in the history of the West and many did not measure up to the dramatic standards of the famous few. Among these sheriffs, constables, and deputies were failures and occasional evildoers. Before one either praises or denounces, some comprehension of personality and character variation must be attempted. It is, above all, necessary to place the county lawmen in their proper political perspective. The axiom that a public deserves the police agency it supports cannot be ignored.

Henry Plummer of Montana holds the rare distinction of being removed from office by the expeditious procedure of lynching. Born in Connecticut in 1837, he moved into the Northwest shortly before the Civil War and, following one gunbattle, taught himself to shoot comfortably with his left hand. Convicted of murder while serving with one police force, he received a pardon and consequently won election as sheriff for the Bannack, Montana, mining district. Unable to obtain an appointment as deputy federal marshal, Plummer became the leader of a notorious band of road agents by 1862. His activity led eventually to formation of a vigilance committee which caught and hanged the sheriff-outlaw from his own gallows. Plummer is the best known of sheriffs directly involved in aggressive crime. John M. Larn of Shackleford County, Texas, also ended his career as a peace officer on a vigilante rope.

Only a few years after Larn's demise another Texas lawman,

Sheriff Dario Gonzales of Webb County was less violently removed from office because of an apparently too close association with a band of border rustlers known as "Forty Thieves." Misconduct, malfeasance, and incompetency led to dismissal of many others in the state. John J. Reeves of Titus County, for example, could not withstand charges of conspiracy and protection of bootleggers during prohibition; Troy C. Jones, a constable in Gregg County, failed to satisfactorily explain charges of swindling, false arrest, and holding prisoners to coerce confessions.[29]

Western lawmen frequently faced indictments for improper conduct. These typically included accusations of employing as deputies those serving terms of imprisonment, simple drunkenness and neglect of duty, overcharging on fees of office, indiscriminate use of firearms resulting in culpable homicide, and invasion of privacy without proper cause. An embarrassing matter involving Sheriff Neil Harr of Ottawa County, Oklahoma, serves as one example of overzealous enforcement. Upon the request of local citizens officers broke into a private home without warrant, to discover a couple in bed. Charging them with adultery, the sheriff placed the two, proven shortly to be man and wife, in jail. When confronted with the case the Supreme Court of Oklahoma defended the lady's social position with the code of the frontier:

. . . be her character as bad as the defendants [the sheriff and his deputy] would have painted it prior to such marriage, it is such acts as these on the part of officers that cause women to fall lower, when it should be the object of all good citizens, and particularly conservators of the peace, to help them rise above their former lives, and not by such acts as this drag them down to deeper infamy and shame.[30]

Disapproval of local lawmen did not always find expression in legal disputes. Newspapers often attacked less popular officers with an abandon extreme by current standards. One such vitriolic report in the Denver *World*, prompted by the escape of a noted desperado, states: "Sheriff [Fred] Cramer is a disgrace to his sex. He ought to be put into a petticoat. Himself and his gang of pusilanimous and idiotic deputies are not only bringing the authority of law into contempt, but they are running up an enormous bill of expenses on the county."[31]

A most interesting and neglected source of information on less successful western sheriffs, constables, and their deputies may be found in the numerous reports concerning damage suits on officers' surety bonds. Such cases could result from failure to safely transport prisoners, arrest without cause, or simple trespass. More alarming are those incidents where peace officers improperly opened fire on innocent parties or those suspected of minor violations.

Encounters with violence occasionally disrupted the routines of county law enforcement. At times they resembled the dramatic instances so often portrayed by writers of fiction. In 1882 the *Evening Review* of Albuquerque reported one such tragic occurrence:

> Yesterday news was received at Santa Fe that the Pueblo Indians of Taos Pueblo and the peace officers of Taos county had a fight in which Eduyigen Miera was killed and Deputy Sheriff Elfego Martinez was mortally wounded.
> It seems that some of the Pueblos had become drunk and were threatening to kill some Mexicans. They were arrested and put in jail, but by the help of the Pueblos managed to escape. Upon attempting to recapture them the sheriff and his deputies were shot by about fifty armed Pueblos and a fight took place with the above mentioned result.[32]

The working peace officer had to remain aware that an ordinary arrest or routine patrol might, however infrequently, become a deadly battle. These came about under circumstances not usually giving cause for prior alarm and they rarely resembled the fights presented by films and television series. Occasionally they took on aspects of a pitiful spectacle. In 1915, for example, Deputy Sheriff L. H. Mitchell of Wellston, Oklahoma, proceeded to the railroad station with a number of companions to intercept a Negro known in the community as "Kid" Henderson. On the platform the lawman and the suspected robber met, but reality this time served as no foundation for legend.

Instead of attempting to arrest Henderson, Mitchell walked by him fumbling at his trousers pocket in which he had a revolver; some one called out that Henderson was going to shoot, and the terror-stricken officer made a dash back to the depot into the negro waiting room, drew his revolver, reached around one of his friends who had followed him, fired through the open door of the waiting room, and killed James E. McLain, a member of his own party, who was standing on the platform of the depot.[33]

Deputy Mitchell's tragic performance, of course, should no more serve as a standard of judgment than the often-told escapades of the few famous county peace officers. Stories of Pat Garrett, Perry Owens, and William "Bucky" O'Neill have been retold many times and now carry an almost friendly familiarity. Countless events of equal but virtually forgotten ferocity transpired.

One such incident occurred in 1918 near Stafford, Arizona. In an atmosphere of intense social antagonism spawned by World War I, Sheriff Robert F. McBride and two deputies set out on a February day to locate three "slackers" resisting military service. At an isolated camp the lawmen came upon the suspects and so initiated what must surely have been one of the West's bloodiest but least reported gunfights. The exact events have never been fully determined. It will, perhaps, suffice to note that all three lawmen and an old man apparently with the party discovered at the campsite lost their lives.[34]

Scores of cases and reports illustrate similar events in western law enforcement. Some sheriffs, constables, and deputies died bravely in performance of duty. Among the killers of county peace officers, however, one name must be specifically mentioned —Gregorio Cortez. A strange mixture of Robin Hood imagery still surrounds the young man from South Texas who killed sheriffs of both Karnes and Gonzales counties and then received a pardon from the governor. Cortez even went on to become a lawman himself in Mexico's famed *rurales*.[35]

Examples of county officers falling in battle with badmen and desperadoes, however dramatic, are relatively rare. Several hundred such deaths occurred, or about 0.5 per cent of those serving in such law enforcement capacities. Most sheriffs and deputies rarely encountered violence and many found it quite unnecessary to carry firearms—a condition rather rare in the modern United States! Along the real frontier, difficult as it may be to imagine, most local lawmen primarily contended with boys playing pranks and an occasional noisy drunk.

Colorado demonstrates the limited danger of western law enforcement. Some 1,200 sheriffs held office in that state prior to 1964. Only seven were killed in line of duty, most of them in the twentieth century. Twenty-three sheriffs died naturally while in office, four were involved in fatal accidents, and three committed suicide. Twenty-five resigned, with one, Henry Robertson of Teller County, doing so upon threat of imminent lynching by enraged mine owners in 1904. Two sheriffs quit their posts to become federal marshals, one simply absconded, and two others found themselves reluctantly removed upon felony conviction.[36]

Western counties experienced a constant problem of replacing personnel. The sheriff's department at Denver in 1904 and 1905 experienced a consistent turnover of better than 100 per cent annually. With a total force of about twenty-five, half being assigned to jail work, a normal month included at least two dismissals.[37] The condition was chronic throughout the West, for employees seldom possessed any real qualification or interest in the job. Frequent misconduct or open disobedience prompted removals at a truly appalling pace, with little or no overall improvement in standards or service.

Routine duty varied considerably in the different agencies. Custom often determined specific functions. In some counties the sheriff personally concentrated on major criminal cases, while the chief deputy or undersheriff handled such ordinary civil matters as sales of property, collecting taxes, service of writs, and routine licensing. Along the early frontier, officers sometimes worked so closely with pioneer circuit judges as to accompany them on their rounds, dealing with incidents at the immediate scene. In the normal pattern, however, sheriffs devoted much of their time to petty crimes within the limited jurisdiction of county or justice of the peace courts. In addition the local officer handled all sorts of unexpected personal and local problems. The latter might include direction of rescue operations in time of crisis or lending assistance in removal of strayed or trespassing livestock.

To perform the functions of criminal investigation frontier sheriffs relied upon the same basic techniques employed by modern agencies. While the science of criminalistics had not appeared, some enterprising officers devised means of identification by comparison of boot and hoof prints. They relied upon contacts with the local criminal element to provide intelligence and utilized operatives and informers, and in the absence of radio communication the western lawmen used telegraph and later telephone networks with considerable success. Only the superficial means underwent significant modification with technological advances; fundamental procedures, on a practical level, have changed little during the past century.

A key element to interpreting county law enforcement in the West, and one which cannot be underestimated, constitutes a continuing plague to proper police work—politics. Despite misleading appearances, peace officers seldom embody true social power; instead, they normally represent the interests of community wealth and authority. Under the American system of local election, ultimate strength came to rely not so much upon actual constituents, but those with money and organizations which could consistently produce results at the polls. Sheriffs and constables possess positions of significant patronage control through discretion in appointing and removing deputies, jailers, and office personnel. The situation in the West merely reflected a pattern still prevalent throughout the nation.

Politicians, businessmen, civic leaders, and others of practical influence dominated choices of those nominated to almost all key law enforcement positions on the county level. In return for support elected officials could reasonably expect demands to serve appropriate interest groups. At its best this scheme produced a police agency subject to local control; at its worst, extreme subjectivity, discretionary enforcement, and outright collusion might result. In certain districts the criminal element itself elected those chosen to repress it; more often officials simply followed predetermined policy without serious interference from political sources. Many western sheriffs consequently allied themselves with particular classes, ethnic minorities, companies, economic blocs, or even vigilante movements.

Because of the usual alignment of wealth and social power the lawmen most often demonstrated a strongly conservative bias. Money produced votes, votes elected the sheriff, and the sheriff selected his deputies. In certain circumstances the cheapest way to maintain influence within an area came through support of a winning candidate. For some prosperous concerns reliable support of county lawmen could be obtained more cheaply than hired guns. While such a situation did not occur with great frequency it could hardly be described as rare.

The influence of inner politics is seldom easy to discover. At times, however, disputes between opposing groups swept beyond the voting booth and erupted into overt and violent conflict. New Mexico's famous Lincoln County War, including the ambush killing of Sheriff James Brady and subsequent involvement of Governor Samuel Axtell, is one example of such a situation in the American West. The Woodpecker-Jaybird battles of East Texas, leading to intervention by state Rangers upon the murder of a sheriff, also stemmed from intense political controversy.

While competition seldom extended to actual killing, the role of powerful economic elements, apart from usual party structure, often dominated. Before the discovery of gold in California John A. Sutter controlled the appointment of sheriffs for the enormous Sacramento district extending from Los Angeles to Oregon.[38] A generation later the vast cattle ranches of the Southwest selected their own men to win and retain various elected law enforcement offices.

In most counties nominees sought office by ordinary and quite traditional means, while settled areas had an established political system with peace officers fitting into the patterned party structure. In Kansas during the aftermath of the Civil War, where newspapers had to report crime news from Chicago and New York in the absence of nearby violations, local law enforcement became a matter of routine campaigning. As one article noted:

N. P. Pease of Mt. Pleasant Township, received the nomination of the Convention for sheriff. He is a young man of excellent character, great energy, and undoubted capacity. He has resided in the County about five years . . . as a school teacher; and lately in farming. He served, during the war, as a soldier in the First Minnesota Cavalry, and two brothers also served in the Union army. He will make as good a Sheriff as we ever had. He is not only competent in every way, but deserving and honest. He is an earnest Republican, and has always labored for . . . Republican principles.[39]

Even the more fearsome fighting lawmen, such as Bill Tilghman of Oklahoma, had to rely on publicity when seeking office. Broadsides spread the good word in 1907:

I desire to call the attention of the voters to the good work done by Wm. Tilghman during his term of office as sheriff of Lincoln County. During the first thirty days of Mr. Tilghmans' [sic] administration he received warrants for nine persons charged with horse stealing. He caught eight of the thieves, recovered the horse in the ninth case and afterwards caught the thief and sent him to the penitentiary, a record for thirty days never made by any sheriff before or since that time. During the ten years prior to his election there had been convicted and sentenced to the penitentiary thirty-nine persons charged with various crimes. During his terms of office eighty-four persons were convicted and sentenced to the penitentiary, being many more than has ever been sent to the penitentiary before or since his terms as sheriff. A large proportion of these were the hardest criminals Lincoln county ever had to contend with, a good many of them being horse thieves, bank robbers and murderers.

This record was accomplished by hard work. No sheriff in Lincoln county ever worked harder or more faithful than Wm. Tilghman did. When a crime was committed the night was never too stormy or too dark for him to go after the criminals. He went and he kept going until he captured them and landed them in jail and kept them until they were indicted and convicted. He then transported them to the penitentiary and delivered them to the warden of that institution.

Mr. Tilghman inaugurated a system of collecting personal taxes that saved to the farmers of Lincoln county hundreds of dollars. Lincoln county never elected an officer that worked harder or more faithful than did Bill Tilghman during his terms in office. Do you want Lincoln county over-run with horse thieves? Do you want to guard your pastures to protect your stock at night? Do you want Lincoln county to continue to be the banner county in Oklahoma for bank robbers? Do you want Lincoln county murderers to escape and go unpunished? Do you want your homes burglarized? If not vote for Wm. Tilghman on June 8th.

Yours very truly,
R. P. Martin[40]

The office of sheriff could be financially quite rewarding. It carried great power of disbursing jobs, provided a contact to investment and mercantile circles, permitted the collection of lucrative fees, and might even include free housing at the jail or office. The unscrupulous could, of course, add to the regular salary through bribes and graft, and more honest officers used their commissions to seek extra jobs within the community.

In the more populated regions a successful campaign meant an enormous expenditure of funds. "It was stated that Sheriff [S. F.] Scannell paid the democratic central committee [at San Francisco] $100,000, regarded as equivalent to election, for his nomination to an office with a salary of $12,000 a year for four years; and yet as times were, there was money in it. . . ."[41]

In 1864 San Francisco's sheriff received officially $8,000 a year while his two general deputies earned but $150 per month.[42] Such variation in salary endured throughout the West, as indicated by the formal monthly payroll for the sheriff's office at Denver in December, 1904:[43]

Sheriff	$383.33
Undersheriff	208.33
Chief Deputy	125.00
Chief Clerk	150.00
Assistant Clerk	100.00
Deputy (9)	100.00
Jail Warden	125.00
Matron	75.00

Jail Clerk	75.00
Guard (8)	75.00
Chief Engineer	100.00
Engineer (2)	75.00

Official salaries, however, could be quite misleading. Sheriffs ordinarily retained their fees of office and this might easily produce tens of thousands of dollars a year even in sparsely populated regions. In Cochise County, Arizona, John Behan garnered a reported annual income of about $40,000 a year; John Slaughter collected over $4,600 in one month.[44]

Obviously men had good reason to seek the office despite some danger, constant stress, and continuing work. Occasionally, however, the role of sheriff became a sudden nightmare when the society itself erupted in bloody upheaval. There have been many instances in the West when conditions combined to ignite an explosive cultural climate, usually with racial and/or economic overtones. Minority groups including Chinese, Irish, Germans, Mexicans, and others fell victim to injustice and violence. For the peace officer such situations posed an impossible problem; any action or inaction could be interpreted as bias or interference with serious results possible at the next election.

Beyond a certain stage, of course, the sheriff had to intervene; a few openly took sides in the early phases of social conflict. Jefferson Farr of Huerfano County, Colorado, apparently acted in behalf of mine owners during the prelude to the disastrous "Ludlow Massacre" of 1914.[45] Other prominent instances of intervention in Rocky Mountain labor disputes occurred at Crested Butte in 1891 and near Steamboat Springs in 1924. The actual purpose, whether merely to preserve order or to influence the outcome directly, usually disappeared in subsequent political debate and intense personal feeling.

The strangest involvement of a western sheriff in overt social struggle took place in 1917 in Arizona. Against a background of American preparation for World War I, direct conflict between the I.W.W. "Wobblies" and an alliance of the Phelps-Dodge Corporation with the Calumet and Arizona Copper Company broke out at the little border town of Bisbee. A strike developed, but workers split along ethnic lines, with Cornish "Cousin Jacks" willing to cross the lines of Central European "Bohunks." The principal issues concerned retention of injurious dry drilling operations and indirect support of the Allied cause. This obviously complex situation got completely out of hand by July.

Henry C. Wheeler held the crucial post of sheriff in Cochise County, and few men seemed better qualified to deal with the worsening problems at Bisbee. Born in Florida, he had served with the cavalry and become a captain in the renowned Arizona Rangers. By legend one of the finest gunmen in the West, but with a reputation for fair treatment, Henry Wheeler stood out among the colorful lawmen of the region. A sheriff of distinction since 1912, he apparently first attempted to quiet seething conditions in the copper fields. There has never been a satisfactory explanation for what then unexpectedly transpired. Theories have ranged from simple bribery to discovery of a secret plot to blow up the entire community. Whatever the actual cause, events underwent a rapid change by July 12.

Sheriff Wheeler deputized and armed hundreds of able-bodied citizens sympathetic to the mine operators and then directed what is still referred to in the Southwest as the "Bisbee Deportation." With little apparent discretion some 1,160 individuals, ranging from union organizers to innocent Mexican nationals, were herded to the railroad station and, amid agonized screams of women and children, loaded into waiting cattle cars. The Bisbee miners, given bread and water, finally escaped their rolling prisons some one hundred miles to the east, near Columbus, New Mexico. U.S. Army patrols finally gathered up the deportees and provided them with food and shelter. By September most had drifted away, but the story did not come to such a simple end.

Henry Wheeler resigned his office shortly after the deportation and quickly left for France with an army unit. Public outcry eventually forced an inquiry and indictment of the former sheriff, his deputies, and several mine officials. The acts at Bisbee were justified peculiarly as an emergency war measure with no convictions obtained. For the one-time hero of the Arizona Rangers the nightmare would not end. A changed man, he finished his days as a truck driver, dying in 1925 at the age of 50.[46] The memory of July, 1917, left a lasting impression on the western labor movement. Perhaps the most graphic recollection appeared by 1919 as the anonymous poem "Bisbee:"

> *We are waiting, brother, waiting*
> *Tho the night be dark and long*
> *And we know 'tis in the making*
> *Wondrous day of vanished wrongs.*
>
> *They have herded us like cattle*
> *Torn us from our homes and wives.*
> *Yes, we've heard their rifles rattle*
> *And have feared for our lives.*
>
> *We have seen the workers, thousands,*
> *Marched like bandits, down the street*
> *Corporation gunmen round them.*
> *Yes, we've heard their tramping feet.*
>
> *It was in the morning early*
> *Of that fatal July 12th*
> *And the year nineteen seventeen*
> *This took place of which I tell.*
>
> *Servants of the damned bourgeois*
> *With white bands upon their arms*
> *Drove and dragged us out with curses*
> *Threats, to kill on every hand.*
>
> *Question, protest all were useless*
> *To those hounds of hell let loose.*
> *Nothing but an armed resistance*
> *Would avail with these brutes.*
>
> *There they held us, long lines weary waiting*
> *Neath the blazing desert sun.*
> *Some with eyes bloodshot and bleary*
> *Wished for water, but had none.*

Yes, some brave wives brought us water
Loving hearts and hands were theirs.
But the gunmen, cursing often,
Poured it out upon the sands.

Down the streets in squads of fifty
We were marched, and some were chained,
Down to where the shining rails
Stretched across the sandy plains.

Then in haste with kicks and curses
We were herded into cars
And it seemed our lungs were bursting
With the odor of the Yards.

Floors were inches deep in refuse
Left there from the Western herds.
Good enough for miners. Damn them.
May they soon be food for birds.

No farewells were then allowed us
Wives and babes were left behind,
Tho I saw their arms around us
As I closed my eyes and wept.

After what seemed weeks of torture
We were at our journey's end.
Left to starve upon the border
Almost on Carranza's land.

Then they rant of law and order,
Love of God, and fellow man,
Rave of freedom o'er the border
Being sent from promised lands.

Comes the day, ah! we'll remember
Sure as death relentless, too,
Grim-lipped toilers, their accusers,
Let them call on God, not on you.[47]

Economic struggle clearly served as the basic cause of trouble at Bisbee and in a similar confrontation of 1916 at Everett, Washington, but local officers sometimes contended with other kinds of social unrest. In Texas during the World War I era, for example, sheriffs in several counties had to deal with actual plots of political revolution extending on both sides of the Rio Grande. Kidnapping, murder, and treasonous conspiracy created an atmosphere of great and continuing tension with the constant possibility of international involvement.

Social conflicts involving county lawmen did not exclude strife among the peace officers themselves. Individual differences led to assaults by one official upon another. At times this extended to armed disputes with police agencies in rivalry over jurisdiction and possible financial rewards.[48]

In the main, however, sheriffs worked fairly closely together and maintained generally good relations with other forces, success in office often depending upon mutual co-operation. County lawmen naturally had to co-ordinate their activities with those representing individual communities and neighboring jurisdictions. Transfers of prisoners, hunts for fugitives, and need for general information prompted regular communication. Sheriffs also remained in contact with state and federal officers. Occasional requirements for assistance found both the regular army and the state militia lending co-operation and aid where good relations had been established.

Routine association with other agencies eventually led to formal organizations dedicated to united county law enforcement. Texas pioneered such a group by 1879. With forty-two members, the Sheriffs' Association of Texas began holding annual meetings and urging greater legislative concern with general police needs.[49] Other states emulated the design and developed both regional and welfare organizations for peace officers.

Virtually no significant changes have occurred in the American system of county law enforcement during the past century. Most sheriffs and constables operate under the same basic laws and customs as existed at the creation of their posts. County officers continue to exist from the simple combination of precedent and political pressure. The fee system, while frequently limited by statute, endures in most jurisdictions as a primary source of income. Minimum standards for peace officers may eventually raise general conditions, but no rapid improvement can be anticipated. Everywhere the pressure of organized politics pervades the enforcement of law on the county level.

During the past fifty years the sheriff and constable stubbornly resisted two expanding forces—the state and the city. In a handful of counties along the West Coast energetic efforts transformed antiquated local agencies into modern and fairly efficient law enforcement units providing service to suburbs and unincorporated areas. In the main, however, elected police throughout the West have sharply declined in significance. Trapped by a changing ecological setting and incredibly outdated statutes, the American sheriff will probably never reassert the powerful position occupied on the frontier. With no functioning standards, virtually anyone can seek and win election as the county's chief law enforcement officer. The present system results in establishment of lucrative and virtually independent governmental monopolies under political domination and openly subject to corruption.

The situation of constables has been hopeless for two generations. Still chosen by precinct or township, serving routine process for justices of the peace, they exist as an unjustifiable link in the antiquated chain of American law enforcement. With no duties or responsibilities which could not be efficiently performed by other agencies of justice, the office, though officially recognized, no longer functions in some districts. With little or no compensation some posts remain vacant and so relinquish their legal powers.

Several western states do not provide for the office of constable. Nevada never established such positions on a general basis, the work being performed by sheriff's deputies or state patrolmen; Colorado in 1964 repealed provisions permitting constables on either an elected or appointed basis.[50] Such legislative steps point the way to additional progress in administrative reform. Other new laws permit temporary assignment of police across the traditionally rigid lines of geographic jurisdiction, while "home rule" in a few instances has led to virtual abandonment of the traditional law enforcement function for constables and sheriffs.

County lawmen have long dealt with a perplexing problem—how and where to house prisoners? The early frontier could not afford elaborate jail facilities. In the absence of even temporary lockups some regions saw persons chained to stumps or buildings; other areas resorted to immediate punishment by exile, whipping, or execution. Westerners recognized the evils imposed by these limited measures and in most cases quickly utilized existing structures or erected new buildings to serve as county jails.

State legislatures routinely enacted provisions designed to solve the difficulties of housing prisoners. In 1861 Nevada decreed:

Sec. 1. There shall be built, or provided, kept, and maintained in good repair, in each county, one common jail, at the expense of the county.

Sec. 2. The County Commissioners shall have the care of building, inspecting, and repairing such jail, and shall, once every three months, inquire into the state thereof, as respects the security thereof, treatment and condition of prisoners, and shall take all necessary precautions against escape, sickness, and infection.[51]

Those incarcerated, however, were placed under direct control of the chief local lawman. As stated in Texas, "Every sheriff is the keeper of the jail of his county. He shall safely keep therein all prisoners committed thereto . . . and shall be responsible for the safe keeping of such prisoners."[52]

As population increased, hundreds of places designed for extended confinement appeared. By 1890 no less than 3,523 of the nation's 19,861 momentary county prisoners resided in western jails. Throughout the entire United States women composed 9.1 per cent of the total jail population; females accounted for about 5.3 per cent on the closing frontier.[53] Since inmates normally stayed for a little more than one month, the total numbers held during a year were, of course, much higher. Those awaiting trial on all types of charges usually faced temporary confinement in county facilities; proven misdemeanants served their sentences in the same building while felons normally went on to larger prisons if such were available in the territory. As a result an incredible array of accused and convicted persons passed through the jails. The large majority of inmates had committed only the usual offenses of public drunkenness, prostitution, vagrancy, and petty theft. Murderers, rapists, runaway children, lunatics, and military deserters were others quite routinely confined together with only rudimentary attempts at classification and segregation.

Jails tended to expand in slightly more than parallel proportion to population increases. A few jurisdictions could afford the luxury of several different structures for confinement. By 1894 San Francisco had separate buildings for women and those already serving time.[54] But most counties fought a constant battle to enlarge facilities for steadily growing numbers of the incarcerated. As Sheriff Henry L. Davis stated with candor in 1864:

The County Jail [at San Francisco] in its present condition is totally inadequate for the accommodation of the prisoners now confined there, although great care and attention is bestowed by the keepers to the end, that the prisoners shall not suffer from personal uncleanliness, yet the sanitary interests of this Institution and common humanity require that some action be taken. . . .[55]

Poor physical conditions contributed to frequent escapes; in 1869 the 158 counties of Texas had eighty-two jails, but only twenty-four of these could be termed "secure."[56] Prisoners managed to saw off their shackles with eating implements, bribe jailers, overpower guards, or simply run when attention might be distracted. Some sheriffs took a most phlegmatic attitude toward such eventualities. When one accused murderer escaped the Denver jail in 1886, Fred Cramer refused to send a deputy in pursuit and predicted a voluntary return within the month.[57] Reactions of this nature prompted a few early legislatures to pass strong preventive measures; Washington's read:

If any jailor or other officer shall voluntarily suffer any prisoner in his custody, charged with or convicted of any criminal offence, to escape, he shall suffer . . . the like punishment and penalties as the prisoner so suffered to escape was sentenced to, or would be liable to suffer . . . and if the prisoner was charged with or convicted of a capital offence, he shall be imprisoned in the penitentiary not more than twenty years, nor less than five years.[58]

By any accepted standards conditions within the jails could be termed deplorable. For certain inmates the situation became so intolerable as to induce suicide. When one prisoner offended Deputy Sheriff E. L. Bracken at Garza, Texas, the enraged officer merely shot between the cell bars and killed him.[59] Some jailers brutally enforced lucrative "taxes" upon those confined; other lawmen permitted and even encouraged vicious "kangaroo courts" within the lockups they guarded. Sadism, personal gain, and simple indifference turned the jails into incredible human jungles of depravity.

Sheriffs enjoyed the privilege of profiting from both the imposition and relief of inmate suffering. Collecting fees for care of prisoners from various governmental units, they could then provide food and other items for prisoner use at unconscionable prices. By hiring guards, maintaining buildings, and supplying meals at the lowest possible actual cost, profits could be maximized. With such conditions condoned by those in responsible positions it is not surprising that many prisoners died through lack of supervision, mistreatment, or crude forms of outright physical and emotional torture.

The various western legislatures attempted through usually ignored laws to remedy the tragic conditions within the county jails. New Mexico required that prisoners be supplied with wholesome food, but only in quantities *"para el mantenimiento de la vida."*[60] Utah, along with other states, attempted to separate various and obvious classes of inmates as follows:

> Persons committed on criminal process and detailed for trial, persons convicted and under sentence, and persons committed upon civil process, must not be kept or put in the same room, nor shall male and female prisoners, except husband and wife, be kept or put in the same room. Females shall be under the supervision of a suitable matron. . . .[61]

In several states county sheriffs are still technically required, by statute, to visit the jail every month, inspecting individual prisoner welfare, and to cause the cells to be literally whitewashed three times a year.[62] It is tragic to state that adequate enforcement of such seemingly outdated laws could improve some present local lockups.

Jail occupants, usually under very close confinement, frequently fell victim to pestilence and disease. Whether temporary frame structures or ancient *calabozos* of Spanish design, housing for prisoners often constituted a grave fire hazard. With incarcerated persons, a routine blaze could quickly become a mass funeral pyre. California, in the era of the Gold Rush, had to outline the proper steps in case of conflagration: "When a County Jail or a building contiguous to it is on fire, and there is reason to believe that the prisoners may be injured or endangered, the Sheriff or Jailor shall remove them to a safe and convenient place. . . ."[63]

Many regions attempted to deal with overcrowded, dangerous, and nonproductive conditions by putting the prisoners to work, particularly on public projects such as roads, sewers, and parks. Some jurisdictions even permitted a financially rewarding contract system to be utilized.

Every Sheriff may hire out, or put to labor, any person or persons in his custody who shall be convicted of the following crimes: Petit larceny, grand larceny, burglary, assault and battery with intent to commit murder, bribery, perjury, and fraud, taking all necessary means to secure their safe keeping, and shall charge to earnings of said prisoners to himself, for the sustenance of said prisoners.[64]

If the inmates refused to labor or became disobedient, the guards "may inflict punishment upon them by confining them in dark and solitary cells"; but an officer supervising work by a prisoner also "shall protect him from insult and annoyance and communication with others."[65] Road gangs and other forms of public labor, however, did not fit well into the western scene. A combination of competition with private business, concern for inmate welfare, and an excess of cost over productivity forced general abandonment of such schemes by the early twentieth century.

It would be pleasant to report that the conditions described above have been eliminated or at least greatly alleviated. But one cannot say that deplorable jails are simply a bygone feature of the last century, a quaint memory of the old frontier. Actually, the situation remains fundamentally unchanged. Juveniles are still mixed with older felons and sexual deviates. Suicides, assaults, brutality, and murder remain paramount elements in appalling settings. While sheriffs no longer routinely reap great profits from inmate maintenance and cruelty by guards has been curtailed, county jails continue throughout the entire nation as detours to despair. They are the weakest link in the incredibly slack chain of American criminal justice.

"A Private Person May Arrest Another"

V

An unwritten but basic tenet of democracy places enforcement of the law within the domain of ordinary citizens. In early England, when no formal police forces functioned, the task of upholding order fell to the over-all community. Later generations found sophisticated agencies performing particular enforcement functions, but under principles of common law any man still possesses wide authority to protect himself, his family, and to some degree the general peace of the land. Policemen operate only under specific statutes and are given power only to demand adherence to particular regulations. While the concept is today increasingly ignored, every citizen is a policeman. The line delineating peace officers can best be viewed both by judicial interpretation and by custom as somewhat vague and relative. At perhaps no other place and time was this distinction less clear than during the western American frontier experience.

Voluntary associations of citizens working to assist in the capture and prosecution of felons and thieves constituted an influential element in the English system of criminal justice until well into the nineteenth century.[1] This practice extended to America and reached its culmination in the West. No one questioned the right of a wronged citizen to attempt redress of wrongs when no convenient police agency existed. In Texas, Colorado, Arizona, and other sections volunteer groups carried out functions now thought of as entirely encompassed by officially qualified units. In most instances these efforts comprised the only practicable law enforcement services available to the community. They did not challenge existing authority and they sprang from well-established precedent.

The very movement westward contained strong elements of community law enforcement. Wagon trains sometimes carefully prescribed such authority for certain leaders or committees. No group surpassed the sophistication of the Mormons in this regard. With such mobile police chiefs as Hosea Stout and the mysterious "avenger" Porter Rockwell their early camps existed under tight central control.[2] Later the Mormon leadership developed an extensive and powerful force for internal discipline. "The secret police of France was never more efficient than Brigham Young's; and, considering the much vaster territory that lies under his organized espionage, I might be justified in saying that in efficiency none ever equaled his."[3]

Citizens frequently acted as peace officers with both formal and unofficial blessing of operating law enforcement agencies. Under statutes routinely permitting inhabitants to act in prevention of many crimes the unique power of the police tends to blur. According to the law of Idaho:

A private person may arrest another: (1) For a public offense committed or attempted in his presence. (2) When the person arrested has committed a felony, although not in his presence. (3) When a felony has been in fact committed, and he has reasonable cause for believing the person arrested to have committed it.[4]

Apart from a slightly broader interpretation of "reasonable cause," a peace officer possesses no greater designated power and, like regular lawmen, citizens in most states can be authorized to serve formal warrants.

Private parties entered close alliance with the police in a number of fashions. The most popular, without doubt, came through the special commission. Issued by various agency chiefs, such designation usually brought with it the privilege of carrying concealed firearms, but no financial reward other than through facilitated private employment. The custom of issuing special commissions began when communities were desperately short of officers, but has continued with undiminished vigor in many sections. San Francisco utilized irregular policemen in the generation following the Gold Rush to such an extent that assignments came to be viewed as property rights.[5] From January to May of 1894 the sheriff in Arapahoe County, Colorado, appointed special deputies at the rate of more than ninety a month, many upon the simple recommendation of "self."[6]

Since commissions for ordinary citizens normally involved no pay, they provided officials with a free form of campaigning; in some counties virtually any voter can still obtain one with a minimum of trouble. Several hundred thousand such positions presently exist throughout the nation. In certain cases, however, the work of private persons on the frontier deserved monetary recognition. One territorial governor urged Congress in 1885 to reimburse citizens defending the peace against rustlers, and a recently enacted California statute permits indemnification for anyone injured while trying to prevent a crime.[7]

No discussion of the relationships between private persons and law enforcement can avoid mention of the vigilante. Popularly associated with the West, organized extralegal efforts at social control actually sprang from a European heritage and moved forward in America with the advancing frontier. One cannot in practice easily distinguish those frequently termed vigilantes from actual peace officers. The frontier did not afford technical delineation permitted by more sophisticated times. Community lawmen frequently functioned under authority incapable of withstanding close judicial scrutiny; they nonetheless constituted an operating police. Instead of representing violent cultural disharmony, the vigilante often fitted into a developing pattern of social control.

It is dangerous to generalize about over-all extralegal attempts to maintain community order. To characterize collectively the vigilante movements at Plattsmouth, Nebraska, in 1854, at Fort Griffin, Texas, in 1876, at Bakersfield, California, in 1897, and at Centralia, Washington, in 1919, would display gross ignorance. Every section of the West witnessed some organized opposition to rustlers, claim jumpers, labor organizers, corrupt officials, or other varieties of socially disapproved persons. Some vigilantes clearly acted at the instigation of particular interest groups, others just as certainly represented a great need for the preservation of local tranquillity.

Many efforts by Westerners to exercise privately and collectively quasi-judicial power operated within a basic legal framework. This conclusion does not require resort to semantic illusion. A few of the earliest vigilante groups operated beyond the geographic reach of formal law, but the overwhelming majority occurred after courts had become well institutionalized. While several movements demonstrated strong antipathy to existing judges and juries, direct opposition to police agencies was comparatively rare. This may, of course, be related to the obvious and immediate threat of violence associated with enforcers as distinguished from administrators; it may also spring from closer community ties maintained by local officers.

Vigilante justice tended to be informal, rapid, and harsh. It usually failed to provide the accused with his full rights under current constitutional interpretation, but many modern and formal trials are similarly derelict. A distinguished historian correctly stated that, "The existence of a vigilance organization is *a priori* proof of the absence of good government."[8] Popular extralegal activity frequently and unjustly filled a void where no practical equity from the courts could be obtained. The resulting situation along the frontier had many flaws as well as certain virtues.

Barbarous and uncivilized as this rough kind of justice is . . . I doubt whether it is not better than the systematic evasion of justice which is so commonly practiced throughout the Western country where the formalities of law are gone through, either by local magistrates or the officers of military establishments, but where criminals of all kinds usually escape with little or no punishment. I speak from actual knowledge when I say that my horse is safer in a coralle [sic] at Trinidad, than in an officer's stable in Fort Union.[9]

The odd partnership between law and vigilantism can be illustrated in many ways. Movements in Kansas, Texas, Arizona, Montana, and elsewhere often involved a community's fundamentally conservative element, the same strata of society which usually supports formal methods of enforcement. When police had not yet begun to function effectively these sound and productive groups formed regulatory forces of their own. The mining camps of California routinely created independent systems of justice with elected sheriffs and magistrates to provide enduring social control. A few years later the pattern reappeared in Colorado with actual codification of vigilantism. "It shall be the duty of the [District] President to appoint a Vigilance Committee, consisting of four persons, to examine into and report all criminal violations of the laws of this District, who shall serve for the period of three months. . . ."[10]

Early vigilante efforts sometimes clearly served as the forerunners of formal agencies. The first municipal police forces in both Los Angeles and San Francisco were composed of volunteers acting without formal authority. In other regions vigilantes obviously functioned in a well-structured manner lacking official recognition. Arizona had "Outlaw Exterminators" before its territorial police could be formed. Texas simply transformed its illegal "Partizan Rangers" into a cavalry regiment at the outbreak of the Civil War.[11]

Vigilantes often operated with co-operation and even encouragement from regular law enforcement agencies. Extralegal groups were utilized by Confederate authorities in hunting deserters and maintaining order. California sheriffs relied upon San Francisco's famous vigilantes to collect debts, seize property, and receive transferred prisoners. In other regions central authorities quietly asserted administrative control after citizen forces had already established general peace and relative tranquillity. Only in rare instances did vigilante movements meet direct conflict from functioning police agencies.

Extralegal efforts to enforce customary laws may be distinguished from simple lynch mobs or riotous assemblages. The true vigilante movement indicated conformance with established procedures and patterns of structured leadership. This does not, however, remove them from the commission of heinous mass offenses and disregard of individual rights. Vigilantes of the West exiled, hanged, maimed, branded, whipped, and otherwise misused their victims without regard to fundamental safeguards and formalities, but one should recall that the punishments and practices of formal courts were often little better.

Leaders of vigilantism often came from the educated and wealthy segments of the community. John X. Beidler, a key figure in the popular Montana movement against Sheriff Henry Plummer, served as a deputy federal marshal and customs collector; William T. Coleman, one primary personality in San Francisco's committees of 1851 and 1856, became a noted trader and mine operator.[12] Under the guidance of such men vigilante justice came to include its own rough procedural protections. Judges, juries, administrative councils, and fully structured police units characterized at least some of the western extralegal systems of enforcement.

Conceptualized as a crude system of justicial administration, the vigilantes possessed an authority beyond that of mere force. So viewed, they cannot be distinguished from the ordinary police by virtue of power, but rather through lack of control by governmental formality and detail. The vigilantes served as a peripheral form of social control through law enforcement. Such community responses constituted extremely informal police action far removed from usual agency functions.

A wide collection of quasi-public and private organizations developed in the gap separating forces with official sponsorship and popular movements. These practical law enforcement agencies, often operating under special statutory recognition, occupied a vacuum formed by weak or simply nonexistent police structures.

When citizens became sufficiently aroused, they obtained legal authority and merely proceeded to protect desired interests. One outstanding example in western history is the famous group of deputies known as the "Dodge City Peace Commission" of 1883. With Wyatt Earp as chairman, Luke Short, "Bat" Masterson, and others functioned for more than a week against the town's leading elected officials.

Another form of citizen service started in San Francisco about 1917. The Law Enforcement League of California concerned itself primarily with vice control. With several thousand members the group employed regular investigators, successfully agitated for recall of judges, furnished intelligence to military forces in World War I, and briefly took over the gathering of information on prohibition violations when federal officers had no available funds.[13]

Some private forces received direct support from commercial interests. Beginning soon after World War I and enduring for more than a generation, branches of the American Bankers' Association backed special protective units in several hundred primarily rural counties of the American Midwest. Ordinarily deputized by the local sheriffs and paid by the banks, these auxiliary forces acted in the absence of the regular police units with specialized functions and wide jurisdiction.[14]

Business sponsorship of law enforcement started with the earliest days of the frontier. Agents of fur-trading companies carried out such duties at their most isolated outposts, often with active co-operation from the Indian tribes. With the development of other types of mercantile activity came additional needs for private policemen. Railroads, ranchers, mining concerns, oil field operators—all established their own investigating and law enforcement agencies. In larger communities businessmen banded together to form special forces frequently known as the Merchants' Police.

The officers supported directly by business usually received legal recognition through easily obtained special commissions.

States were most dilatory in establishing viable control over this practice and left matters almost entirely in the hands of local sheriffs and chiefs of police.[15] A multitude of representatives from all kinds of commercial undertakings consequently became duly commissioned peace officers. During the period from 1892 to 1894, for example, the sheriff of Arapahoe County, Colorado, appointed special deputies for "Elitche's Garden," "Depot," "Furniture Dealer," "Union Brewery," "Electric Light Co.," "Windsor Hotel," "Jeweler," "Athletic Park," "Durang Land Co.," "Arcade," "Tramway Co.," and countless others.[16]

A logical step occurred with the development of large and privately owned protective systems offering services for diverse business enterprises. Special detective forces, with eventual licensing from the state, appeared upon the scene in great numbers. They utilized a gamut of methods from routine and discreet investigations to open terrorism and extortion. It would be too great a simplification to deal collectively with representatives of Furlong's, Burn's, Curtin's, Vennatta's, and numerous other agencies.

At their worst such organizations constituted a combination of the protection racket and violence for hire. Jim Courtwright's Commercial Detective Association at Fort Worth, Texas, is an outstanding case in point. "Long-Haired" Jim, once a rather well-known Southwestern desperado, operated his extortion schemes and suppressed labor unrest until Luke Short killed him in 1887. J. W. Cottrell ran quite a different kind of private agency in Austin. His Protective and Detective Association of America offered membership to anyone willing to subscribe $3 a year. In return Cottrell promised fortunes in rewards, a certificate for framing, subscription to a newsletter, and "a star made of solid silver, handsomely engraved."[17]

At its best, a private detective force could provide real services with integrity and discretion. No agency probably enjoyed a better reputation than that of Harry N. Morse, with central offices in San Francisco. The former sheriff of Alameda County, California, refused divorce cases and rewards of all types. Morse em-

133

phasized persistence and efficiency, maintained agents as far away as Japan, and built his detective and patrol systems into a sustaining enterprise of great size and scope.[18]

Most widely known of the private forces was that founded in Chicago in 1850 by the son of a Glasgow, Scotland, policeman. Allan Pinkerton gained his early experience on the Midwestern railroads, and his major clients came from among these vast transportation networks. The "Pinkertons" involved themselves in protective work across the nation. They guarded Buffalo Bill's Wild West Show, tracked down John Wesley Hardin in Florida, conducted the investigation leading to the conviction of Albert "Harry Orchard" Horsely for the murder of Idaho's Governor Frank Steunenberg, and maintained a central index of wanted criminals long before the involvement of federal agencies. But the agency's men also became subject to marked public antipathy. Under the direction of William "Big Eye" Pinkerton, Allan's son, the agency became closely associated in the West with conservative industrial and transportation interests. Rumors persisted that detectives secretly worked on both sides of the same case, kidnapped witnesses, bribed juries, commonly used violence to break strikes and coerce confessions, and then stole from their clients.[19]

The Pinkertons were accused of providing assassins for a sufficient remuneration. Tom Horn, former deputy in Arizona and Colorado, reportedly killed seventeen men on assignment from the agency. Such charges could never be proved in court and Horn personally denied any duty of the sort, but the Pinkerton men nevertheless became a widely distrusted force among working-class Westerners by the end of the nineteenth century.[20]

Opposition to major private agencies culminated in a number of highly significant state provisions. Any constitutional mention of police authority is rare, but several western jurisdictions became so concerned with growing utilization of foreign forces as to forbid their employment. Among the earliest of such enactments was that adopted in Wyoming. "No armed police force, or detective agency, or armed body, or unarmed body of men, shall ever be brought into this state, for the suppression of domestic violence, except upon the application of the legislature, or executive, when the legislature cannot be convened."[21] North Dakota, Montana, and Idaho included similar constitutional protections immediately upon their admission to the Union.[22]

Other states followed such examples by attempting to prevent misuse of police power. Utah and Arizona directed their provisions specifically against corporations while Nebraska attached a large fine to companies importing personnel for the suppression of disorder.[23] At least two jurisdictions outside the West, Kentucky and South Carolina, also passed constitutional sections to insure that armed persons would not be brought into the state by private interests.[24]

The widespread fear of external police authority did not extend to relations between ordinary law enforcement agencies, even when the connections existed on a private and semisecret basis. During the last few decades of the nineteenth century western lawmen enjoyed the services of a unique and extremely influential organization which clearly defies all efforts at simple classification. The Rocky Mountain Detective Association was neither public nor private, official or extralegal. It existed as a loose and voluntary confederation of officers serving in an era before complex communications systems and agencies of wide jurisdiction to capture hundreds of wanted persons.

Under the careful direction of David J. Cook, former chief of police, sheriff, deputy federal marshal, and general of the Colorado National Guard, the Rocky Mountain Detective Association expanded from its formation at Denver about 1866 to include "correspondents" throughout the West. Although the membership maintained relatively independent field districts it also provided a flexible means by which rapid and dependable assistance could be expected from a distance of hundreds of miles. Only a pledge of co-operation bound the officers to giving aid; there were no dues or regular staff and any rewards went to lawmen directly responsible for the arrest or recovery.

With such outstanding members as Thomas Jefferson Carr,

Frank A. Hyatt, Nathaniel K. Boswell, and W. Frank Smith to call upon, the Rocky Mountain Detective Association grew to become one of the strongest but least-known law enforcement organizations in the history of the United States. From his office in Denver General Cook impartially but firmly supervised overall operations. In later years he permitted limited publicity and commercial utilization of the informal structure. Shortly before his death in 1907, however, Cook determined that the need for the Rocky Mountain Detective Association had largely disappeared and allowed his creation to dissolve slowly.[25] Changing social and technological conditions brought the organization to a peaceful and natural conclusion.

The closing of the American frontier directly involved a transportation revolution. Within a generation the West witnessed a transition from covered wagons to army airplanes. Each of the major phases brought into play specialized agencies of private law enforcement. Beyond the Mississippi two forms of transport became closely connected both in truth and the popular mind with the frontier legend. One of these has been transformed, largely by motion picture, into a symbolic representation of the Old West—the stagecoach. In reality it may usually have been a crowded and uncomfortable wagon pulled slowly by mules, but in the popularized and now more significant form it endures as a thundering microcosm drawn by six galloping horses endlessly chased by renegades.

Outlaws did attack early stagecoaches and freight wagons. Western express companies responded to these robberies by organization of private protective forces. Different conditions required unusual means of commercial response. When the army failed to protect the Butterfield line in Texas, the company hired as drivers such personalities as William A. "Big Foot" Wallace and sometimes assigned several armed outriders as escorts. The Overland Express obtained the services of the notorious Joseph A. "Jack" Slade as supervisor of its vast district extending from Missouri to Utah. With no special legal authority he exercised great power under both Alexander Majors and Ben Holladay. Slade maintained a kind of order along the line from 1859 to 1863, ending his career as the victim of a lynching party.[26]

No company achieved a greater reputation through its law enforcement operations than Wells Fargo. Its representatives in Panama imported several Texas gunmen in the Gold Rush years to conduct a sanguinary campaign against desperadoes on the Isthmus. In California the company soon provided shotgun messengers and developed ironclad coaches for troubled routes.

Wells Fargo eventually created an investigative division under Chief Detective James B. Hume. His unique force not only captured the famous Charles E. "Black Bart" Bolton, it later recruited him as an operative! Hume succeeded in controlling the number of fruitful robberies through rewards, special officers, and persistent prosecution of highwaymen. Between 1870 and 1884 approximately three hundred Wells Fargo stages were held up and over $400,000 in treasure stolen. But the company spent more than $500,000 in the same period to keep losses at a minimum.[27]

The agents of Wells Fargo protected many shipments by train and, consequently, worked closely with the private forces of the West's second transportation symbol—the railroad. California commissioned special detectives for express, steamboat, and rail systems alike in the decade following the Civil War. Some officers worked jointly for several such concerns, such as those simultaneously employed in the Southwest by Wells Fargo and the Southern Pacific. Such alliances demonstrated the co-operation and mutual aid extended by many of the commercial protective units on the frontier.

Railroad police exemplify the foremost development of quasiofficial law enforcement. Supported entirely by private interests they normally operate under special statutory authority. The history of these forces is lengthy and has a unique tie with the West. Before the Civil War the railroads contracted with private detective companies such as that of Allan Pinkerton to obtain protective services. Within less than a decade, however, many lines had begun to employ their own special agents on a large scale. The western roads led in the establishment of internal police units.

Sparsely populated expanses between the Mississippi and the Pacific left transport facilities at the mercy of thieves and robbers. Companies such as the Union Pacific, Chicago and North Western, Denver and Rio Grande, Santa Fe, and Southern Pacific found that private security personnel contributed greatly to operational efficiency and reduced losses.

The next step taken by the railroads led to formation of separate detective departments, usually at a high administrative level. Two roads, the St. Louis and San Francisco and the Union Pacific, had such independent structures established no later than 1891. In 1896 officers formed the Railway Association of Special Agents and Police and by World War I most of the major lines maintained centralized forces of considerable size. Agents formed a well-integrated system cutting across company lines and uniting the rail networks of the country. They had to co-operate with one another for a single officer might be assigned an entire district with thousands of miles of track to protect.

Railroad and steamboat police, unlike most private agents, operated under clear statutory authority. Although Canadian lines had appointed constables with the power of peace officers since 1860, the first specific recognition in the United States occurred in Pennsylvania about 1865.[28] Under subsequent legislation in other jurisdictions railroad representatives gained a wide variation of authority. Western enactments tended to be both broad and early. Wyoming extended limited power of arrest to conductors, while North Dakota at first permitted only special company policemen and then declared all trainmen to be peace officers.[29] Oklahoma granted the right of appointment in a rather generous fashion. "Railway companies . . . are hereby authorized and empowered at their own expense to appoint and employ policemen at such stations or other places on the lines of their railroads within this State, as said companies may deem necessary for the protection of their property, and the preservation of order on the premises. . . ."[30]

Most states in the West provide for formal commissioning of railroad officers through either the governor or county sheriffs upon company application and bonding. Terms range from one year to indefinite and geographic jurisdiction may be quite restricted or statewide. Most statutes concerning the railroad police have gone unchanged for many decades and, as a result, now create certain technical difficulties. It is not unusual for a special agent to carry several separate commissions to insure proper legal authority in conducting investigations or making arrests.[31]

Railroad police performed an assortment of tasks. Chasing train robbers, even in the early West, rarely occupied a significant amount of time. Special agents guarded supplies against petty thieves, caught embezzlers, and kept the lines clear of obstruction. Their overzealous protection of company facilities and prevention of surreptitious free travel by transients, however, could create unpleasant situations and resultant bad publicity. Railroads recruited detectives according to local need. The Santa Fe lured James B. Gillett from the ranks of the Texas Rangers with an offer of $150 a month in 1881, three times his state sergeant's pay.[32] When the same line became involved in Colorado's famous Royal Gorge dispute, it imported noted gunman Ben Thompson to guard the roundhouse at Pueblo. The Santa Fe spent its money in vain—Thompson quickly surrendered when offered $20,000 by the opposition.[33]

Railroad detectives frequently represented company interests in the bitter labor disputes which spread along the tracks of the West. Thomas Furlong, chief agent for the Missouri Pacific, directed one such violent campaign in the great railroad strike of 1886.[34] The active participation of special agents in economic and social conflict led certain jurisdictions to restrict the authority of commissioned lawmen in private employment: ". . . peace officers so appointed [by the governor upon railroad application] shall not have authority to act or perform any service or be used as peace officers with reference to strikes or labor troubles."[35]

The common realities of law enforcement on the western tracks often fell short of dramatic holdups of trains in the night. When J. A. Presley wished to accompany his livestock across Texas, for example, he was permitted to ride in the caboose. But he, perhaps in an intoxicated condition, somehow managed to secrete himself within a freight car. When trainmen demanded his egress Presley produced a pistol and said, "That was his ticket . . . and further stated in effect that he would fill with holes the first man who came into the car."[36] Such were the incidents to enliven the work of the western railroad agent on a routine basis.

While duties varied in different times and regions some insight into development is possible from the history of one line's special force. No company's police have a more distinguished past than the Union Pacific's. Single guards and detectives certainly served the railroad when its first tracks reached out from Nebraska to Utah; Pinkerton men were regularly employed as police into the 1870s. By 1880 divisions along the line maintained undercover operatives and investigators such as M. F. Leech, N. K. Boswell, and James Smith. In the sparsely populated Rockies these agents sometimes trailed suspects and developed extensive intelligence networks without assistance of public officers. Times were dangerous, stakes high, and the railroad policemen often worked alone.

Centralization of detective services came for the Union Pacific in 1891 with appointment of Chief Special Agent William T. Canada. As an indication of the great stability of railroad protective organizations it is interesting to note that only three other men held this position during the next seventy years.[37] Canada forged a unified and tough organization of professional law enforcers. He promoted close relations with officers from other railroads as well as representatives from local and federal agencies.

Chief Special Agent Canada also supervised formation of the Union Pacific's unique "ranger" company to fight train robbers at the turn of the century. Following several major bandit attacks in Wyoming the railroad assigned more armed express guards and organized a well-equipped posse composed of the best trailers and riders in the region. A special train designed to quickly transport the agents with their fast horses to the location of any robbery usually waited, loaded and ready, at Cheyenne. The Union Pacific's elite force operated for a number of years and succeeded in driving the foremost bandit gangs, such as Butch Cassidy's, into other areas and endeavors.

America's railroads experienced their worst siege of robbery not in the frontier West but across the entire nation immediately after World War I, following two years of direct federal control. In 1921 the Protective Section of the American Railway Association met for the first time to inaugurate even closer ties between the lines of Canada and the United States. Changing conditions within the past fifty years have modified but not required major alteration in the role of the railroad police. Today several thousand commissioned officers guard some 400,000 miles of track belonging to hundreds of independent lines. The detective forces have greatly increased in sophistication and skill, but social movements continue to provide new problems. Special agents of the present deal far more frequently with juveniles and safety than did their predecessors of the last century, but the primary task remains one of lonely patrol along the tracks and in the giant freight yards of the West.

The railroad police demonstrate commercial response to various forms of lawlessness directed toward a broad enterprise. When similar victims were more numerous and only loosely connected over great areas, a different reaction could be expected. Stockmen on the western frontier did not possess the organization or broad economic power of the railroads, but they found themselves beset by rustlers and thieves. Private attempts at law enforcement varied in different regions and required a number of years to achieve clear form. Stock raisers quickly discovered that public police agencies, however sincere, could not prevent the disappearance of horses, cattle, and sheep. These herds and their ranges comprised the primary bases of wealth in much of the West, and owners soon accepted the problem as personal and vitally important.

Larger ranches could afford the luxury of maintaining special forces to combat rustlers and others encroaching upon land. The great cattle raisers of West Texas personified this response, and organizations like the XIT and LS led the way. By 1885 both of

141

these enormous ranches had established private police forces. The LS imported no less a personage than Pat Garrett, former New Mexico sheriff and killer of Billy the Kid, to organize a unique company known as the "Home Rangers." With blessing from the state government these private lawmen conducted a campaign against outlaw bands and certain small ranches in the Texas Panhandle. The LS force's most dramatic encounter left four men dead on the streets of Tascosa. Unfortunately a dance hall girl rather than cattle thieves served as the cause of violence!

On the expanse of the XIT former Texas Rangers Ira Aten and John Armstrong directed operations. Although never publicized, the "Syndicate" maintained armed patrols along its boundaries for approximately thirty years. Both Aten and Armstrong (the latter was killed in 1908) carried the title of foreman, but their real duty demanded protection of XIT lands and herds. Only with dissolution of the Syndicate in 1912 did the need for such means of private guards along the Texas–New Mexico border come to an end.[38]

Although the effort did not achieve notable success several detective companies attempted to provide protective services, for a fee, to stockmen throughout the West. Pinkerton's, Turtle's, Thiel's (as illustrated by Appendix C), and other agencies entered the field in the 1880s. These private detective organizations stressed the value of skilled and experienced men under central supervision. Most western ranchers, however, turned to other means of law enforcement. Smaller stock operations could not afford individual police units. When public officials proved unable to cope with bandits and rustlers they had to seek additional remedies. Despite the representations of fiction this response rarely took the form of open and bloody vigilantism. Most Westerners wished to assist rather than displace the regular system of justice. In a large area this could be accomplished through a unique fraternal order known as the Anti-Horse Thief Association.

Shortly before the Civil War a Missourian named David McKee founded an organization of private citizens dedicated to support of public order and protection of property. His Anti-

Horse Thief Association spread slowly westward across the Great Plains. By 1912 some 1,100 chapters enrolled members in Missouri, Illinois, Iowa, Nebraska, Kansas, Wyoming, Colorado, Oklahoma, Arkansas, Texas, and New Mexico.[39] During the decades around the turn of the century this fraternity experienced phenomenal growth, dropped its quasi-secret character, and to some degree replaced the Rocky Mountain Detective Association as a bulwark of unofficial law enforcement.

The constitutional preamble of an original branch illustrates the general purpose of Anti-Horse Thief involvement:

> We, the citizens . . . being a part of, and acting with the National Order of the A.H.T.A., for better protection of ourselves against the depredations of thieves, robbers, counterfeiters, incendiaries, tramps, and all criminals, do hereby pledge ourselves to cooperate with and assist the civil authorities in the capture and prosecution of all such offenders, and to aid each other in the recovery of stolen property. . . .[40]

Lodges of the organization took especially deep root in Oklahoma. With admission to the Union and loss of direct federal police service early settlers substituted formal semiofficial agencies. By 1913, for example, the Anti-Horse Thief Association's Oklahoma Division reported 262 functioning chapters and recovery of better than 80 per cent of stolen property. The legislature even enacted a provision specifically permitting authorized members of lodges to carry firearms while in pursuit of suspects.[41] To this day Oklahoma statutes grant that ". . . the sheriff may appoint one lodge deputy sheriff for each organized A.H.T.A. lodge in his county, when the applicant is endorsed by the president and secretary of the lodge, with the seal of the lodge attached."[42]

Support for the Anti-Horse Thief movement came largely from middle-class farmers and ranchers. The association reached its maximum growth shortly before World War I and declined in strength through the next several decades. By 1932 membership had fallen to about eight thousand and "Horse" disappeared from lodge titles.[43] Citizen involvement continued in other fashions, but fraternal structure withered away.

Concern with stock depredations also embarked on a slightly different course following the Civil War. Powerful associations of ranchers appeared throughout the West to combat range criminals. The concept of such private organizations for law enforcement apparently had independent origin in at least two geographic locations. By 1873 the often victimized stockmen of both Texas and Wyoming organized to provide mutual aid against rustlers and bandit gangs; early associations involved neither dues nor formalities.

Laramie County, Wyoming, and Young County, Texas, served as birthplaces for much larger and more powerful organizations. Leaders in both locations supported the hiring of detectives to safeguard the ranges. By 1875 the Laramie County Stock Growers' Association employed five agents; within six years the Southwestern Cattle Raisers' Association also levied dues upon its membership to retain full-time inspectors. In 1883 the Wyoming Stock Growers' Association, an expansion of the Laramie County organization, called a special meeting to form a unified detective bureau. Nathaniel K. Boswell, former sheriff of Albany County, served as director of this private force until resignation because of ill health in 1887.[44] The stock detectives had been established as part of the western scene.

Examples set in Texas and Wyoming prompted emulation by different groups in other regions. Montana ranchers sponsored inspectors after 1884 to create an atmosphere of close co-operation which regularly transcended political boundaries. Some agents carried commissions from more than one state or territorial authority to facilitate investigation and pursuit. Associations even joined together to employ personnel jointly and share expenses. Not all western range organizations existed to protect large ranchers against rustlers. The Stockmen's Association of Wyoming's Shoshone Valley fought encroaching sheep interests and the Homesteaders' Protective Association of Sherman county, Kansas, represented the grangers battling cattlemen.

Various types of recognized private organizations employed range detectives. While not drawing public salaries, they still possessed limited power as peace officers. Montana statutes provided,

sec. 38 . . . stock commissioners are hereby authorized, and it is made their duty, to appoint such stock inspectors and detectives as they may deem necessary for the better protection of the live stock interests of the [Montana] territory, and such inspectors and detectives shall have the power to summon a posse. . . .

. . .

sec. 40 Said stock inspectors and detectives are hereby empowered, and it shall be their duty, to arrest all persons who shall violate the stock laws of this territory. . . .[45]

The power of range associations, in close alliance with regular law enforcement, to reach across the West cannot be underestimated. Detectives from Wyoming could, for example, also hold Montana commissions and even obtain appointment as special deputies in Minnesota to facilitate the hunt for fugitives.

Forces of range inspectors became fairly expensive propositions for the major cattle and sheep organizations. The Wyoming Stock Growers' Association levied a small charge upon its members for each head of livestock, but also demanded payment in advance for special services. A typical range detective received a monthly salary of from $100 to $150 with additional funds for expenses and travel. During the period from 1885 to 1888 the detective bureau for Wyoming stockmen spent approximately $15,000 a year with almost half the costs resulting from prosecution rather than investigation.[46]

Associations of beef or wool raisers hired inspectors on a rather informal basis; men worked without written contract on either county or state bases. Most agencies attempted to recruit from the ranks of experienced peace officers, but also resorted to former cowboys with reputations for courage and initiative. Since salaries and working conditions tended to be quite competitive with opportunities in public organizations the stock associations generally attracted capable and efficient personnel.

No man better serves to exemplify the range detective than the mysterious and somewhat sinister Frank M. Canton. He drifted north to Wyoming from Texas shortly after the Civil War, but his real name was Joe Horner and he originally came from Virginia. Canton, as he chose to be called, became sheriff of Johnson County and a field operative for local range organizations. In 1887 he replaced N. K. Boswell as chief of detectives for the Wyoming Stock Growers' Association and continued the extermination efforts begun by his predecessor. Canton was a taciturn and calculating man with an unfortunate tendency to become vicious when drinking. He thoroughly understood the ranges of the West and a near compulsion drove him on a continuous search for suspects. Canton wandered on to Alaska at the close of the nineteenth century to be commissioned as a deputy federal marshal. Later he went to Oklahoma and served for nearly a decade as the state's adjutant general. The former officer died peacefully in 1927, leaving behind a multitude of legends and unanswered questions.[47]

Another personality that cannot be clearly separated from the range protection movement is that of Tom Horn. Born in Missouri about 1860, he first became noted as a guide in the Arizona Territory. With a reputation as an expert tracker and outstanding frontiersman Horn readily found employment as a deputy sheriff in Colorado's Gunnison County. While subsequently serving as a Pinkerton agent he obtained a commission as deputy federal marshal and opportunities of a still disputed nature on the cattle ranges of southern Wyoming.

Canton, Horn, and other stock detectives serve as one reasonable basis for legends surrounding the hired gunmen of western fame. From them also probably sprang the myth of the bounty hunter. In truth no one could support himself on the frontier by earning rewards offered for the capture or killing of wanted men. The foremost peace officers had great difficulty in collecting such sums; a private citizen would have starved to death seeking to pursue fugitives as a vocation. But men of wide repute, like Horn, could work for private interests demanding a very wide variety of protection. This might constitute an agency of respectability and honor; it could also lead in rare extremes to murder for profit.

Tom Horn came to Wyoming as a detective for the Swan Land and Cattle Company in 1894. With the brief interruption of service with the army during the Spanish-American War he continued to perform duties for leading ranching interests into the twentieth century. What Horn's actual duties comprised and specifically for whom he acted has never been disclosed. Although events remain subject to conjecture, the evidence indicates that the frontiersman either became a hired assassin or regarded himself as a dedicated exterminator of criminals, depending largely upon point of view. The courts of Wyoming convicted Horn for the 1901 murder from ambush of fourteen-year-old William Nickell largely upon the basis of a confession apparently obtained through duplicity. He reportedly admitted, "Killing men is my speciality. I look at it as a business proposition, and I think I have a corner on the market."[48] The tragic life of Tom Horn came to end by legal execution in 1903; many Westerners believe the full story will never be told.

Some ranchers undoubtedly resorted to extralegal means of range protection. In a few instances stock associations sponsored major attacks on suspected cattle and land thieves. Montana experienced one such excursion in the great vigilante movement of 1884. With apparent federal support, ranchers and stock detectives lynched at least fifteen persons.[49] The most notorious of range disputes, often termed the Johnson County War, came in 1892. Major ranching interests, working through the Wyoming Stock Growers' Association, determined in 1891 to bring an end to rustling attributed to homesteaders. An invasion was launched, spearheaded by imported gunmen from the Southwest under a deputy federal marshal from Texas named Tom C. Smith. He received $2,500 for recruiting G. R. Tucker, Buck Garrett, and about twenty additional fighters at the rate of $1,000 each. The troop gathered at Denver and moved by special train to Cheyenne where Frank M. Canton, the stockmen's chief detective, waited with a force of similar size composed largely of range detectives and dependable ranch foremen. The Johnson County War erupted at Buffalo, Wyoming, with unexpected results.

Homesteaders fought the carefully selected gunmen with such success that only timely intervention by the army saved the invaders from probable disaster. Taken into protective custody the raiders spent short periods in confinement but could never be convicted. The leaders of the imported faction soon returned to formal law enforcement. Tom C. Smith died in the Indian Territory, once more with a federal commission as a deputy marshal, before the Wyoming trials came to an end. Tucker and Garrett, his principal lieutenants in the Johnson County War, both later became peace officers at Ardmore, Oklahoma.[50]

Stock detectives normally operated within legal limits. Most worked on assignment according to local needs; only a county committee might be informed of an agent's secret identity, for infiltration into organized gangs constituted a popular technique. Detectives and inspectors (the two titles could be used interchangeably) used an assortment of methods and procedures. Stationed throughout the territory they could be quickly alerted by telegraph or telephone to watch for wanted persons. Major stock associations also maintained closely guarded "blacklists" of suspects and cattlemen deemed untrustworthy. Range detectives sometimes "cut trail" alone or in small groups and frequently appeared at roundups and rail stations both to provide protection and maintain general order. A good inspector memorized countless cattle markings used in the West, could spot all but the finest modifications at a distance of several yards, and could read up to ten thousand brands in a day.

In unusual circumstances the range interests would join together and send operatives considerable distances to help combat rustlers. When William Bonney's gang posed a major threat in the Southwest, several Texas ranches and the Panhandle Cattlemen's Association sent a team of agents to aid Pat Garrett in New Mexico. John W. Poe, one of this group, led the sheriff to his final encounter with Billy the Kid in 1881.

Unscrupulous stock detectives apparently resorted to highly suspect means of enforcement at times. Some associations paid set rewards for captured thieves and agents could profit from the art of entrapment. By suggesting or encouraging criminal activity and subsequently making arrests, an aggressive inspector could gain considerable extra remuneration. The practice naturally created an unfavorable impression and met most unpleasant legal receptions throughout the West.

In most regions, however, the stock inspector earned acceptance and high regard. One unfamiliar with current conditions might assume that the need for range detectives ended long ago. Such is not the case. The modern West still contains many agents in the employ of various stock associations but carrying governmental authority occasionally reaching, in Texas, to the coveted commission of Special Ranger. Detectives continue to fight constantly changing styles in rustling and thievery. While appearance has been greatly altered in the last century, basic problems endure.

Railroad and stock police are but two outstanding examples of private officers of the present. Today the primary emphasis is upon security forces of retail establishments and major industrial operations. Some guards and detectives not in public employ possess special, reserve, auxiliary, or honorary commissions while others do not. In sophistication they reach from the lone watchman at a store to an officer of a large and well-equipped agency at a leading defense or space program contractor. There are probably sixty thousand such varied individuals throughout the current West who clearly demonstrate that the private policeman remains an essential element in protective service.

"There Shall Be a Corps
of Rangers"

VI

The frontier can be best identified by an absence of people. In the American West vast areas of very low population density still exist. Thousands of square miles with less than two persons resident upon each may yet be found in Arizona, Nevada, Idaho, Wyoming, and other western states. Today these regions may lie close to cities of considerable size and be laced with highways, telephone lines, and fences. But this great land has only been touched by such modern innovations within the last few decades. Little more than a century ago most of the West comprised a high expanse almost entirely devoid of people. The Indians could, when they wished, fade into the wilderness. A few tiny outposts of traders and Spanish settlers existed in virtual isolation from one another. Aside from certain large pueblos maintained in the Southwest, the country awaited its fated and irreparable contact with civilization in lonely majesty.

As colonists spread across the West after the Civil War they brought customs, values, and social roles developed in Europe and east of the Mississippi. The undeveloped territories posed new problems and also proved more resilient to immigration. Distances remained great in the West while climate and soil defeated many efforts at settlement. These conditions forced certain changes within institutionalized forms of government. For law enforcement such modifications could hardly be termed sweeping. Existing patterns of community and county police found acceptance and even increased emphasis. Ordinary citizens discovered a heightened necessity for self reliance and economic interests resorted to marked utilization of special officers. Some industries, such as railroads and livestock, turned to formation of new types of private police forces. But the enormity of jurisdictional limits and the difficulty of cultural problems demanded still another innovation. The spatial scope of law enforcement demanded expansion with the land. A possible solution came from Texas.

English-speaking settlers moving into the region opened by Stephen F. Austin discovered a need for protection. Mexican authorities offered no real assistance regarding the Indian threat in East Texas and left the colonists to their own defensive resources. During the period from 1823 to 1826 the isolated communities raised several small militia companies. A few mounted units ventured into the plains to scout and patrol the frontier; the settlers called them "Rangers."

When Texas embarked on revolution and independence it retained the unique force which had proven so valuable in the previous decade. "There shall be a corps of Rangers under the command of a major, to consist of one hundred and fifty men, to be divided into three or more detachments, and which shall compose a battalion, under the Commander-in-chief when in the field."[1]

Throughout the Republic of Texas the Rangers appeared at intervals to guard the frontier against Indians and Mexicans. They did not achieve permanent status until about 1840 under Captain John C. Hays. With the beginning of the Mexican War the Rangers developed into an informal mobile striking force armed with special new Colt revolvers. When General Zachary Taylor advanced across the Rio Grande the Texans' mounted frontier guards went along as scouts; later a unit accompanied the invasion force moving inland from Vera Cruz to Mexico City. The Rangers proved to be distinguished fighters but almost hopeless soldiers. Lack of discipline, disreputable appearance, and a reputation for bloodthirsty conduct helped form the basis for a legend already in the making.

Shortly before the Civil War, following a decade of intermittent service in times of danger, the Rangers began to demonstrate a new function. They remained an informal quasi-military force but became increasingly involved in the complexities of internal disorder. The original standing company under Hays had been used in 1841 to protect traders from bandits along the Rio Grande; by 1857 conditions along the road between San Antonio and Port Lavaca prompted additional assignments of similar nature. Frequently positioned as a buffer between Texan and Mexican communities, the Rangers also served as unofficial border guards. They not only captured *peones* fleeing northward from Nuevo Leon, but chased slaves escaping from the southern United States. Interestingly, the Negro fugitives faced return to their masters while the Mexicans were frequently hired by the state's quartermaster or permitted to find other employment in Texas.[2]

Ranger units of the era operated in a highly informal manner. Almost anyone desiring to do so could, with cause, obtain permission to raise a special company. No uniform qualifications for recruitment existed and some sections supported detachments which used German rather than English as a language. During the 1850s:

The men furnished their own horses (American or large mustangs), saddles, pistols, and knives—the state providing only rifles. The pay was $25 per month. . . . Rations of hard bread and pork, or, sometimes, fresh beef, flour, rice, sugar, and coffee, were served out once in four days, with a bushel of corn and hay for the horse. If sent on a separate scout, where rations could not be taken, they were drawn and sold on their return, the party subsisting on game.

They carried no tents, and seldom employed baggage-wagons. Where they were to make a long camp, they usually built log huts, otherwise, lay, rolled in their blankets, wherever they pleased, within the lines of their sentinels. . . .

Men and officers were on terms of perfect equality, calling each other by their Christian or nicknames. Their time, when not in actual service, was spent in hunting, riding, and playing cards. The only duty was for four (out of seventy) to stand guard. Men were often absent, without leave, three or four days, without being reprimanded. They fought, when engaged, quite independently, the only order from the commander being—"All ready, boys? Go ahead."[3]

By the outbreak of the Civil War the thrust of Ranger duty clearly involved additional police activity. In 1859 John S. "Rest in Peace" Ford chased raiders into Mexico and two years later he suppressed a related insurrection against the Confederate government in Zapata County. But the Ranger leader also continued to insist that his men constituted a military rather than a civil force. Ford once refused to arrest white men accused of killing Indians by claiming a lack of authority in ordinary criminal matters. His reluctance probably originated not with legal technicalities but a somewhat biased attitude amid already tense conditions.[4]

Ranger operations decreased during the conflict between North and South and came to a temporary end with Reconstruction. The provisional government of Texas discontinued the force and created a substitute.

Gov. [Andrew J.] Hamilton issued a proclamation [in 1865] . . . in which it was recited that lawlessness and disorderly persons were causing much trouble in many portions of the State. The Governor empowered the chief-justice of the several counties, where outrages had been perpetrated and in which there were good grounds to anticipate acts of violence and disorder; and where the civil authorities were inadequate to correct lawlessness, to select a prudent and discreet citizen, having the confidence of the community, to act as chief, or captain, of police; and, with the advice and consent of the chief-justice, raise and organize at the expense of the county, a company to consist of not less than ten nor more than fifty men, who shall be sworn to support the constitution and laws of the United States and the State of Texas, the company to act as a police and assist the civil authorities in preserving law and order, and all times be subject to the officers of the law. Members of this special police force were enjoined to offer no violence to any one, advised that they were simply to be conservators of the peace and informed in advance that policeman [sic] guilty of violence or outrage upon any persons, was to be arrested and held for trial.[5]

Reconstruction efforts to provide internal security for Texas culminated in 1870 with formation of a new State Police. Few agencies of law enforcement in the West provoked so unpopular a public response. Regardless of actual purpose the overwhelming majority of Texans clearly regarded the unit as an arm of tyranny and oppression. To some degree the State Police certainly earned their unpleasant reputation. One of the captains, Jack Helms, had to be dismissed quickly for misconduct. Adjutant General James Davidson, director of the agency, embezzled over $30,000 and fled to Europe, only to be promptly replaced by the governor's brother-in-law.[6]

Although authorized strength totaled 257, the State Police never attained its full complement of men. Negroes held nearly half of the positions, and most of the whites who served were apparently regarded by the general public as renegades. Several counties found themselves under martial law enforced by the State Police, but the agency actually seemed to concern itself most frequently with arrests for such routine crimes as gambling, assault, and theft. Most Texans felt the officers were in truth political spies permitted to search without warrant, disrupt peaceful meetings, and even murder those opposed to Reconstruction domination. In 1873 the newly elected legislature abolished the State Police and within a year enactments permitted re-establishment of the unit associated with prior independence. The Texas Ranger once more rode the plains.

Within forty years a legend in state law enforcement became thoroughly entrenched. One should not assume that Rangers were necessarily full-time professional peace officers. A great number held special and temporary commissions. These sometimes composed minute companies, served in unusual circumstances, or represented strictly private interests. The great bulk of writing on the Ranger service has largely ignored such members; instead it has concentrated unreasonably on the more spectacular and better reported activities of the regular detachments.

Texas' unique mounted force met three major problems in the generation after the Civil War: law enforcement on a developing frontier, continued threats from Indians, and a simmering international border. The Ranger role evolved gradually from the second to the first while hostility along the Rio Grande proved an enduring difficulty. Duties included collecting taxes, protecting courts and prisoners, chasing Mexican cattle thieves, maintaining order at elections, escorting strike breakers, assisting local posses, and arresting a wide variety of suspects. The Rangers might be called out to quell riotous conditions such as those at El Paso in 1877 and Brownsville in 1906. They might also be ordered on more unusual assignments, including prevention of illegal prizefights, medical assistance in smallpox epidemics, or rescue of dogs from Indian raiders.

Tales of Ranger fearlessness require no further retelling. They are endemic throughout the Southwest and most are based upon fact. Appointments generally went to young men demonstrating both interest, ability, and desire for excitement. As one pioneer recalled,

I will give you a description of the Texas rangers, as they were at that time. In the first place he wants a good horse, strong saddle, double girted, a good carbine, pistol, and plenty of ammunition. He generally wears rough clothing, either buckskin or strong, durable cloth, and generally a broad-brimmed hat, on the Mexican style, thick overshirt, top boots and spurs, and a jacket or short coat, so that he can use himself with ease in the saddle.

A genuine Texas ranger will endure cold, hunger and fatigue, almost without a murmur, and will stand by a friend and comrade in the hour of danger, and divide anything he has got, from a blanket to his last crumb of tobacco . . . he is not so bad after all. He generally settles down into a quiet, sober citizen.[7]

During the late nineteenth century the Rangers normally worked in relatively small units assigned on a semipermanent basis to particular geographic sections. Operating from fixed camps they scouted in teams, frequently with operatives and guides supplied by local citizenry. Upon discovery of enemy personnel the force would stage a rapid, quiet displacement and raid, identifying their men at night with pieces of white cloth.[8]

The state officers maintained a somewhat sanguinary reputation. They occasionally adopted the Mexican *ley de fuga* by killing "escaping" prisoners and seemingly enjoyed comparative immunity in such matters from the courts.[9] At times the Rangers' extreme techniques received very bad publicity. A notable instance of such occurred during fence-cutting disputes between cattle interests. The governor finally intervened to prevent the employment of dynamite bombs connected by officers to vulnerable stretches of barbed wire. A less spectacular and more successful measure consisted of a printed booklet issued to each Ranger camp. Compiled from information supplied by various law enforcement agencies it listed and described wanted men and constituted a frequently consulted reference device.

In general those with state commissions enjoyed good relations with other peace officers and the overall population. Citizens sometimes presented awards to Rangers who ordinarily worked in fairly close association with local sheriffs and marshals. There were instances, however, of jealousy between law enforcement agencies which even exploded into armed conflict and killing.

The Rangers exercised general power as lawmen throughout all of Texas, yet overstepped even these bounds. On several occasions detachments entered Mexico illegally on a variety of missions. They also were known to torture and lynch captives. Such activities along with other indictments of misconduct resulted in several trials throughout the state. The greatest legal blow to the force came in 1900 when the attorney general ruled that only Rangers with ranks higher than sergeant had authority as peace officers. The legislature quickly decided otherwise.[10]

Many of those in state service served for very short terms. Volunteers for special companies usually remained with the command only until the emergency ended. Even the regular officers could ordinarily resign on short notice. Many men worked for only a few weeks or months but returned when needs arose. The Ranger force had a surplus of applicants and could choose recruits with care. Compensation amounted to about $40 a month and rations, but the service carried remarkable distinction, adventure, and pride. Those accepted into a company in the late nineteenth century continued to furnish their own horse and saddle together with blankets and revolver. The state provided inferior carbines, ammunition, and $100 for a horse lost in service. Enterprising officers could usually obtain a suitable mount for considerably less money and keep the rest as profit.[11]

Much of Ranger activity necessarily centered around base camps throughout the state. These were often established conveniently near a community and frequently became small villages with wooden cabins replacing tents. A few leaders brought their wives and established temporary homes within the camp. Ranger life rarely resembled that pictured in today's mass media. A steady flow of visitors and guests, including girls from nearby towns, prevented monotony from becoming a problem. The Rangers also amused themselves in a number of ways. Ordinary gambling constituted a breach of discipline and could only be practiced without official notice, but horse racing and shooting contests caused no difficulty. Officers could also hunt, keep an assortment of pet animals, and perform extraordinary practical jokes upon one another. Some Rangers were quite well educated, many played musical instruments. They could enjoy a game of croquet or give a benefit minstrel performance and still remain the most feared law enforcement agency on the American frontier. Quarrels between members occurred occasionally, but a persistent troublemaker soon found himself isolated and discharged.

Real work usually fell to those detailed as scouts. Operating far from camp in small groups the Rangers demonstrated personal initiative and resourcefulness. The picture changed little over a period of several decades.

The rations are placed in sacks. . . . Each man carries a tin cup on his saddle and a hunting-knife in his belt. On the trail each Ranger is allowed 22 ounces of flour, 20 ounces of bacon, 3 ounces of sugar, and 3 ounces of coffee per day. The coffee is issued green and is parched as needed, the ground berries being macerated for use in a tin cup, the handle of a six-shooter being used for a pestle. Each man carries 60 rounds of ammunition for his carbine and 30 rounds for his revolver. He places one pair of blankets and his overcoat on the pack mule.[12]

Rangers rarely experienced difficulties with citizens. When the legislature failed to appropriate funds in 1877, townsmen collected enough money to provide temporary support. Close personal ties often led to resignation. In many instances a departing company would leave behind a number of former Rangers married to local belles. It proved a popular method of bringing law and order to the wild frontier.[13]

Regardless of the accomplishments performed by the state force during the final decades of the nineteenth century, the Rangers are frequently accorded a significance unfair to other peace officers. The great bulk of law enforcement in Texas remained the duty of county and community agencies. The Ranger image developed from wide authority and easily obtained unit records rather than actual social effect. All sections demanded the continued services of local deputies, marshals, and policemen. Some districts in Texas neither required nor desired Ranger service.

The twentieth century imposed new conditions on law enforcement. Open ranges, unorganized counties, and isolated communities dwindled away. The Rangers no longer met the same needs, but recognition of these modifications required a full generation. Public support for the state force declined with a closing frontier and increasing urbanization. The title lost much of its former distinction. World War I found some one thousand "emergency" Rangers commissioned for service largely near the Rio Grande.[14] Several governors contributed to wholesale introduction of the spoils system into state law enforcement. Miriam A. "Ma" Ferguson not only discharged the entire force, she issued over 2,300 "special" Ranger commissions, including some to former convicts.[15]

Between 1915 and 1935 the force's reputation fell to a dismal low. An entire company was dismissed after indiscriminate arrests through the Big Bend region in 1917. Charges of murder, torture, drunkenness, and political involvement eventually led to an unsuccessful reorganization and restrictions on assignment. Prohibition laws brought even further decline in public respect. Officers faced charges of theft, embezzlement, homicide, gaming, and other types of misconduct.[16]

The Rangers also moved into several booming oil communities to control public disorder amid political intrigue. In Borger, state lawmen demanded the resignations of all local peace officers, closed down gambling and drinking houses, and then found the jail to be in such terrible condition that prisoners had to be removed to Amarillo. But the townspeople soon tired of centralized authority and petitioned for recall of state control. Complaints culminated in a bitter suit to enjoin the Rangers from acting as political spies and informers, thus hindering operations of local government.[17]

In 1935 a reform administration restructured state law enforcement under a central Department of Public Safety. After some dispute the legislature retained the Rangers as a separate division to assist rural areas and work on special assignments. A maximum of three hundred Special Rangers might be appointed, but no more than ten could be in the employ of single interests except in emergencies.[18] Since 1935 the service has expanded very slowly and remained under fairly close Department of Public Safety supervision. Rangers have endured as an entity separate from other state law enforcement agencies because of provincial tradition and political pressure. The modern force has consistently withstood charges of ethnic bias and coercive measures to become well entrenched as a living symbol of the frontier West.

The Texas Rangers formed the oldest state police agency in America and clearly influenced developments throughout the country. This should not be taken to indicate that early territories had no means of central law enforcement. The usual recourse in times of severe disturbance was to involvement of the militia and later the National Guard. Range wars, labor disputes, political controversies, and other causes led governors in Texas, Colorado, Idaho, California, and elsewhere to declare martial law for the suppression of disorder. State police systems, distinct from the militia, did not leap suddenly upon the scene. The process of emergence proved gradual and involved. Texas' contribution of a mobile force of centralized responsibility failed to strike an immediately responsive note. In the midst of the Gold Rush, California briefly experimented with its own Rangers. Terror attributed to Joaquin Murieta led to legislative approval in 1853 of a small company of twenty men under Harry Love. In less than three months the California Rangers destroyed Murieta's gang and were themselves disbanded.[19]

Between Reconstruction and World War I several American jurisdictions experimented with various forms of state police. Massachusetts recognized "Constables of the Commonwealth" in 1865 to demand observance of vice laws; the force eventually became a small detective force under central control.[20] Connecticut formed a similar unit in 1903 as an outgrowth of a semiofficial "Law and Order League." These New England organizations possessed limited authority and had minimal effect. The East's first real state police appeared in 1905 under direct supervision of Pennsylvania's governor.

It is difficult to estimate the influence British Commonwealth law enforcement may have had upon developments in the United States. Organizations similar to a state police had existed for several decades in Australia, Canada, and South Africa. The Philippine Constabulary organized shortly after American occupation also may have been a significant model.

In the West, however, the Texas Rangers clearly served as the primary basis for emulation. Within the first decade of the twentieth century at least three jurisdictions created central police systems—Arizona, New Mexico, and Nevada. These experiments along the fading frontier marked not only the continuing battle of order against lawlessness, but served to express politically the social and economic struggles then underway. State police appeared in the West because of a thinly scattered population and geographic limitations traditionally imposed on local lawmen. They proved to be a firm springboard for the unique image of the western peace officer.

Territorial governors of Arizona recognized the need for a police company under central control during the restless 1880s. John J. Gosper recommended strong measures to control raiders and outlaws operating along the Mexican border and apparently extended broad powers to selected deputy marshals.[21] F. A. Tritle supported vigilante movements in the area and painted a graphic portrait of conditions in 1883:

In view of the comparative security which isolated and unsettled portions of the territory afford to criminal fugitives from other territories and States, and the southern boundary bordering upon a foreign nation, the territory of which immediately adjacent possesses the same peculiarities, it is a very difficult thing for the civil authorities to prevent crime. Cattle-stealing in these localities is carried on to such an extent along the border as to render protection to the citizens a proper subject for the attention of the general government. I would suggest that Congress provide for the establishment of a mounted patrol or police along the border of Arizona and New Mexico.[22]

Tritle renewed his recommendation, without success, the following year.

The presence of a well organized and vigilant mounted border patrol or police with authority to arrest criminals in addition to preventing smuggling . . . would discourage the banding together of men who . . . develop into criminals of the most abandoned character. Through its agency the organized stealing of cattle . . . would in time be entirely broken up, and criminals guilty of such and even more atrocious crimes who now find refuge in the sparsely populated portions of Arizona and Sonora, could be soon apprehended and brought to justice.[23]

In 1901 the Arizona legislature quietly approved a bill allowing the governor to organize a company of fourteen men "for the pursuit and arrest of criminals in the mountain fastnesses and frontier regions."[24] Burton C. Mossman, a ranch superintendent, served for several months as captain of the semisecret Arizona Rangers. Following a dispute involving professional gamblers at Bisbee and the daring removal of a fugitive from Mexico, he resigned. Mossman's successor, Thomas H. Rynning, reorganized the Rangers and in 1903 the legislature allowed an expansion to the legendary "twenty-six men."[25] The records of the unit during the next several years reflected considerable and steady activity:[26]

Fiscal Year	Total Arrests	Murder Arrests	Felony Arrests
1903–4	453	5	155
1904–5	1052	9	264
1905–6	704	5	187
1906–7	614	11	191

Much Ranger work dealt with the ordinary offenses of drunkenness, disorderly conduct, and simple assault. Livestock theft constituted a major problem for the lawmen.[27] Arizona Rangers, usually operating in small teams, maintained the peace during roundups and detected rustlers by such devices as coins implanted beneath the skin of cattle for subsequent identification.

Although the territorial police cost more than $30,000 annually, they provided a highly mobile and versatile company which could disregard county boundaries and provide support in cases of local need. Rynning reported that in an average month the few Rangers rode an astonishing total of 10,140 miles.[28] As officially described in 1904,

They are used as peace officers, preserving law and order wherever they may be in the Territory. The force is composed of fearless men, trained in riding, roping, trailing, and shooting. The very best men to be found are enlisted, and they come for the most part from the interior parts of the Territory, where they can be detailed for important work with assurances of success owing to their knowledge of the country.[29]

Arizona's Rangers enjoyed much better relations along the international border than did their Texas counterparts. Higher Mexican officials co-operated with the lawmen to a remarkable degree and permitted manhunts and extradition of United States citizens in a most informal manner. When, in 1906, a mob threatened the isolated mining community of La Cananea, Sonora, Rynning led the Rangers and several hundred other Arizonans across the border to be sworn into emergency service by Mexican officers and dispatched by train to the strife-torn community.

In 1907, amid growing opposition to the force, Henry C. Wheeler succeeded Rynning to become the last captain of the Arizona Rangers. During the next two years charges against the unit slowly multiplied. Since their organization the Rangers had been used in labor disputes at Globe, Clifton, Morenci, and elsewhere in the Territory. They antagonized many local lawmen and prosecutors throughout Arizona. Some groups felt the force attracted unfavorable publicity, consisted largely of hardened gunmen, and interfered in community affairs without cause. In 1908 Jeff Kidder, the leading *pistolero* of the Rangers, became involved in a battle with Mexican policemen and died without medical treatment in the Naco jail. According to unverified reports officers then slipped across the line for revenge on those deemed responsible.[30] Events culminated the following year in a bitter political battle which led to abolition of the Rangers. After a mixed history of less than a decade the unit closed its files and faded into the legends of the West with only one officer, Carlos Tafolla, killed in line of duty.

The Arizona Rangers enjoyed the height of their prestige about 1905 and led to creation of a similar body in bordering New Mexico. Appendix D contains the act of organization for this special contingent of peace officers. Arizona's governor properly commented that, "One of the strong arguments advanced for the creation of a force of 'mounted police' in New Mexico was found in the fact that many dangerous criminals were known to be hiding in that Territory having been frightened out of Arizona by the activity of the rangers."[31]

Within a few weeks of approval command of the New Mexico Mounted Police passed to the durable and energetic Captain Fred M. Fornoff. During the remaining nine months of 1905 he enlisted thirteen men:[32]

Name	Age	Occupation	Born
Octavio Perea	36	Deputy Sheriff	New Mexico
Herbert McGrath	30	Deputy Sheriff	Illinois
Cipriano Baca	45	Deputy U.S. Marshal	New Mexico
William E. Dudley	36	Teacher	California
Robert W. Lewis	39	Deputy Sheriff	California
George Elkins	27	Cowman	Texas
Julius Meyers	39	Deputy Sheriff	Alabama
John J. Brophy	42	Cowman	Missouri
Charles R. Huber	49	Deputy Sheriff	Texas
L. F. Avent	48	Stock Business	Wisconsin
Robert G. Putnam	36	Stock Business	Minnesota
Rafael Gomez	39	Laborer	Texas
E. R. Stewart	32	Stockman	Kansas

Throughout the next sixteen years the New Mexico Mounted Police remained a small and carefully selected force of dependable and versatile officers. Many individuals volunteered themselves for commissioning. William Jackson wrote as follows:

I understand through a friend that you are thinking of putting a man at this place [San Rafael] if so I would be pleased if you would consider my application for same. The different factions are fighting one another and the place is in a turmoil all of the time with people shooting up the town and fighting all of the time. I am deputy sheriff at Grants but Eliseo Barela is deputy at this place.[33]

Another applicant from Silver City stated frankly, "I have cut out drinking so dont see many rows and fights now, havent taken whiskey for two months."[34]

With an ordinary force of no more than ten or twelve regular officers Fornoff could directly supervise most operations from his central post at Santa Fe. The limited size and purpose of New Mexico's Mounted Police may be indicated by the meager list of office assets recorded by the captain in 1906:

> 1 box rubber bands
> 1 carpet
> 4 maps
> 1 set brand books
> 1 stove
> 3 pair chain handcuffs

9 boxes 30/40's [rifle ammunition]
3 boxes 45's [revolver ammunition][35]

As with other law enforcement agencies, membership in the Mounted Police sometimes went to special officers. Sheriffs, stock detectives, Texas Rangers, and representatives of the state Cattle-Sanitary Board received such commissions. Personnel of this type did not always conduct themselves in an exemplary fashion as indicated in a telegram dispatched from Carrizozo by Governor George Curry to Captain Fornoff: "Special mount Policeman Recently appointed here shot a man tonight in depot Come or send responsible man . . . at once."[36]

The small band of regular state officers performed a wide variety of functions. They kept the governor informed of local conditions and attitudes, enforced federal liquor laws relative to the Indians, co-ordinated activities of other agencies, maintained records of stolen horses, and performed numerous investigations involving officials or otherwise notable figures.

Correspondence files of the New Mexico Mounted Police abound in examples of the peculiar assignments given officers. A sheriff wrote from Aztec, New Mexico, in 1909:

I am convinced that this county [San Juan] is infested with an organized gang who are bent on doing a deal of mischief.

I am able to do all that any man known in this vicinity can do but this case demands the services of a first class man and he must be an absolute stranger. You will oblige both myself and law and order if you can dispatch an absolute strainger [sic] to my aid at once. It is *imparative* [sic] that you cause him to leave his present location *secretly*.[37]

An interested and concerned citizen, justly alarmed over rustling on the Salado Range, expressed his alarm while also requesting aid in clear, somewhat confused, but original English: ". . . it is going to Be Pretty bad here this winter about steeling meat and by all means thay ought to be a mounted Polse around here clost for the winter for a mounted Polse is better then 14 county sherefs to my ider."[38] Calls for assistance poured into Captain Fornoff's office from all sections of New Mexico. With only a handful of officers in service he did his best to keep the scattered force informed of local conditions. A note to Mounted Police Lieutenant John Collier is typical.

Dear John:

I have been advised that gambling is being carried on and a saloon is being run on Sunday at Encino. This saloon is known as Brown's saloon and I want you to take a sneak over there some Saturday evening, and put a stop to it if possible.[39]

For the fiscal year 1906–1907 the eleven-member unit reported 152 arrests, with those for livestock theft and carrying illegal weapons being the most prominent. The force cost $12,126.16 in salaries with an additional $1,524.43 going for contingencies.[40] New Mexico Mounted Policemen encountered a wide variety of violations. Their office records reveal cases of till tapping, saloon loitering [?], goat theft, murder, arson, "taking rock," practicing medicine without a license, indecent exposure, stealing pickets, train robbery, wife whipping, shooting up a tavern, forgery, killing a wild turkey, and abduction of a girl under the age of consent. In the latter incident the officer duly reported that he obtained the parents' consent and subsequently gave instructions that a marriage license be promptly sought. With many ordinary arrests for disturbing the peace, drunkenness, and assault, life in the Mounted Police could hardly be termed dull.

Although members of the centralized force possessed broad authority and normally supported local law enforcement there were occasional instances of great friction. In 1910 two territorial officers arrived in Mogollon to investigate a series of stage robberies and murders. A bitter dispute led to the saloon killing of Deputy Sheriff Charles Clark by Mounted Policeman John A. Beal. Local citizens clearly resented interjacence in community affairs and demanded an immediate indictment and trial for murder. Beal, bonded by mining interests, was eventually cleared and returned to duty.[41]

The New Mexico Mounted Police functioned from 1905 to 1921, withstanding the transition to statehood in 1912. During World War I the force functioned administratively under a Council of Defense, but social changes quickly produced different conditions and political pressures which finally led to abolition of the colorful Mounted Police. Remaining central law enforcement functions passed quietly to the state attorney general's office.

Nevada also developed a state police system in the first decade of the twentieth century. The region experienced very rapid population growth shortly after 1900 and possessed no militia organization to support local officers in time of major social unrest. In 1908 the legislature created the unique Nevada State Police when faced with a major labor dispute:

Sec. 2.   The said "Nevada State Police" shall consist of a Superintendent of Police, to be appointed by the Governor, one Inspector, four Sergeants, twenty-five subordinate police officers, and two hundred and fifty reserves.

Sec. 3.   The Superintendent of Police shall, subject to the approval of the Governor, appoint all officers and members of the said "Nevada State Police," and may remove any such officer or member without notice.[42]

The officers received full authority to make arrests, suppress riots, serve criminal warrants, and investigate offenses. They could not execute civil process of any type, but possessed special power in public disorders:

Sec. 8.   Whenever the Governor shall declare martial law within any county or counties in this State, or when he shall declare any county or counties in this State to be in a state of insurrection, after the date of such declaration, and until the same shall have been revoked, the said "Nevada State Police" shall have full and absolute power to take any and all steps necessary for the preservation of life and property and the restoration of peace and order.[43]

The legislative act of creation provided members of the force annual salaries ranging from the handsome sum of $3,600 for the superintendent to $1,200 for a regular policeman. Reservists received either $20 per month or $5 a day if in active service.[44]

Actual expenses never approached the amounts originally envisioned. By 1916 monthly costs, including salaries, totaled less than $900. One of the most active units in the Nevada State Police at this time was the Criminal Identification Bureau. Every month the central office processed hundreds of Bertillon descriptions and, after 1915, fingerprint records. They also issued an illustrated bulletin and transmitted information from other jurisdictions.[45]

State Police functions expanded greatly during World War I. During this period the director of the state prison at Carson City also served as police superintendent. He directed a regular force of about twenty-five with approximately one hundred actual reservists. In addition, Nevada issued some State Detective commissions directly through the governor's office. The loyalty issue and suspected danger from radical elements prompted widespread use of special officers during World War I. The large copper companies employed considerable numbers of Nevada State Policemen as watchmen and paid them salaries accordingly. Conditions and attitudes are illustrated by one letter from Reno favorably received by Governor E. D. Boyle in 1918:

Again the need for some one in authority at our [Riverside] Mill was presented only two days ago, when an I.W.W. presented himself at the Mill wishing to purchase flour without substitutes and really acted disagreeable. Such need a rebuke and a reminder that they are wrong and endeavor to show them the proper attitude to take during these crucial hours of war.

In accordance with our recent conversation, please have me appointed as a member of State Police without salary. If there is a badge or anything for identification, please forward same. If any expense the writer will remit to you.[46]

During the generation following World War I the Nevada State Police underwent a transition unique in western law enforcement. While reduced in size, by 1923 the force began assigning men to traffic patrol on highways and such duty slowly grew in significance with passing years. The state officers, however, continued to serve diverse police functions. They inspected pharmacies for drug violations, checked hunting licenses, maintained order during strikes, investigated explosions and reports of cattle theft, tracked train robbers, and assisted local lawmen upon request.

A primary concern remained that of major social disorder. Alert officials recognized the potential problems posed by large numbers of special commissions among private interest groups and attempted to curtail widespread issuance. In 1922 the Nevada State Police also obtained several hundred dollars worth of arms and military equipment on loan from the army. Superintendent Thomas J. Salter explained the general functions of his unit to a high-school student in the following year:

> The duties of the force are to aid and assist the sheriff and other officers in the various counties of the state in the enforcement of law and order and their services are very valuable in districts where strikes occur and where property is apt to be destroyed by irresponsible persons.
> The Nevada constabulary is specially advantageous in Nevada in view of the fact that we have no national guard in this state. I know of no disadvantage in the system. In states where highly trained men, such as we have, can be called at a moment's notice there results in greater efficiency than by the use of the national guards. The national guard system is a cumbersome method for this kind of work.[47]

Between 1925 and 1935 State Police expenditures jumped from about $500 to more than $4,300 per month. The major cause of expansion came through increased enforcement of traffic laws. By 1925 Nevada stationed individual officers on main roads, primarily for the collection of fees and fines. Within a few years a highway patrol system developed within the structure of the State Police. After World War II this unit came to dominate its parent organization. In 1949 Nevada separated the Highway Patrol and permitted it slowly to assume all central law enforcement functions. For nearly twenty years officers carried joint commissions in both forces, but obvious duplication led the legislature in 1967 to end the history of the Nevada State Police as a formal entity.

As noted previously, World War I brought marked changes to western law enforcement. Social conditions and public alarm in certain sections brought about greatly increased interest in state agencies. Both the Texas Rangers and the Nevada State Police expanded operations considerably during this period and at least two additional western jurisdictions formed short-lived and politically oriented units. Colorado and Oregon established significant state police forces along obvious paramilitary lines in 1918.

The Central Rockies suffered from serious labor strife throughout the early twentieth century. The "Ludlow Massacre" of 1914 and other conflicts left especially bitter memories in Colorado. For the supposed protection of essential war industries the legislature in 1918 permitted organization of two companies of Rangers, each composed of approximately fifty men. After 1919 unit strength declined by about one half under supervision of the state adjutant general. The Colorado Rangers were quite active in the coal mining areas' labor disputes of 1921 and 1922. They earned a reputation for efficiency, antagonism with local officers, and political misuse. After prolonged controversy among representatives and administrators Governor William E. Sweet simply vetoed the Ranger appropriation in 1923 and permitted the force to pass out of existence.[48]

The Oregon Military Police functioned under the State Council of Defense with Major Richard Deich as commanding officer. Organized "to guard against obstructions to the laws of the State, breaches of the peace, and to prevent destruction of property,"[49] the force primarily guarded shipyards on the Pacific Coast and certain timber operations. The Oregon Military Police consisted of approximately 230 men in four companies. While announced plans dealt with prevention of sabotage a primary function continued to be the application of force in labor disorders.

A variety of small, centralized state law enforcement agencies appeared in the decades after World War I. California created a Bureau of Criminal Identification in 1905 to maintain records on wanted persons and those in confinement. The successful experiment prompted emulation in Nevada and other western states. Utah formed its identification service in a basement hallway of the state capitol in 1927. Beginning with only about 10,000 prison fingerprint records, the bureau had by 1941 compiled information on 230,000 individuals.[50]

Several jurisdictions on the Great Plains modified the pattern by establishing central agencies with general investigatory power. In 1935 South Dakota assigned broad duties involving communications, statistics, and secret fact-gathering to such a special unit within the attorney general's office. Four years later Kansas followed with its Bureau of Investigation, or K.B.I., accorded national recognition in the 1960s by Truman Capote's *In Cold Blood*.[51] These small forces usually possess broad technical authority but normally operate under direct orders from high executive officials or when requested by local agencies. They do not perform ordinary police functions.

In the decade after World War I several Rocky Mountain states created administrative departments of law enforcement. Wyoming's unit dealt primarily with new problems created by automobiles and prohibition. The Colorado agency expanded briefly from about six men to a force of seventy-five during labor struggles in 1927. After a vicious battle involving state officers at the Columbine coal mine, the governor summoned troops and the police unit declined to its original size.[52]

Other jurisdictions in the Northern Plains utilized the position of state sheriff. Nebraska still retains the office as one directly responsible to the governor and charged with the duty of investigating felonies and maintaining public safety.[53] The state sheriff for South Dakota in 1930 had an annual budget of $34,450 and a considerable staff of special agents. They made numerous arrests for violation of liquor and vehicle laws in addition to the usual offenses of assault, gambling, and prostitution. Representatives of the state sheriff also issued permits and licenses to physicians, druggists, and peddlers.[54]

South Dakota took a promising step toward emergency control over diversified law enforcement agencies in World War II. A 1943 act created an extensive state constabulary under the attorney general. Membership not only extends to all sheriffs, deputies, policemen, and constables, it permits the granting of peace officer authority to game wardens and others in critical times.[55]

Such a force, under suitable regulation, could be of great assistance toward promoting general standardization and in cases of domestic emergency.

A quite different, and potentially dangerous, method endures in the Texas statutes. Under 1920 legislation the governor possesses the power, without declaring martial law, to supersede completely existing local law enforcement authority and assume "full and complete police jurisdiction" wherever commerce may be interdicted. The governor also is given authority to employ "any number of men to be designated as special Rangers" and to remove all prior rights of arrest.[56] Texas has a long tradition of central police activity exemplified by the oldest state law enforcement agency in the nation. This heritage appeared in 1934 with the special team of officers created by executive order to find and destroy the notorious gang of Clyde Barrow and Bonnie Parker. Within four months the small force of investigators under former Texas Ranger Frank Hamer located the desperadoes, crossed the line into Louisiana, and successfully ambushed them.

Between 1931 and 1937 most of the western states created new agencies to deal with problems directly relating to increased highway traffic. The trend generally began on the Pacific Coast and swept eastward to the Central Plains. By World War II every state in the West maintained some type of motor-patrol system. The enormous increase in automobile traffic after introduction of the Model T Ford in 1909 led to a need for mobile officers of wide geographic jurisdiction and centralized control. Many of the highway law enforcement organizations did not spring suddenly upon the scene following a particular legislative act. Several units evolved from rudimentary motor-patrol systems operating under a variety of governmental offices. Many states had a highway police several years before such found specific statutory recognition. Texas and Oregon presented representative patterns in the development of automobile oriented agencies.

The Texas unit rapidly passed through several distinct phases. The state had maintained a few license and weight inspectors for about three years prior to establishment of a highway patrol in

1930. This force of fifty men, selected from 1,600 applicants, showed a profit of more than $18,000 during the first few months and led to legislative approval of a regular unit with a strength of 120 by 1931. The Texas Highway Patrol made a conscious and successful effort to earn public respect and popularity throughout the state. Officers conducted thousands of free and voluntary auto-safety inspections. The motto of "Courtesy, Service, and Protection" had to precede rigid enforcement of traffic regulations. In 1935 the patrolmen became the major element in a new Department of Public Safety and received the technical authority previously reserved for the Ranger force.[57]

Oregon created its state system in 1931 through combining functions previously divided among five administrative law enforcement agencies. After much debate and opposition Marine General Smedley D. Butler from Philadelphia began the task of organizing a unit along distinctly military lines. Most of the initial force of ninety-five men were assigned to the new highway patrol. While an upsurge of robberies led to approval of the State Police, a primary contribution came through increased safety. During the first year of patrol, traffic fatalities in Oregon decreased by better than 33 per cent, falling from 309 in 1930–31 to 205 in 1931–32. The force issued some 140,000 warning tickets in one year and soon settled down to making approximately 10,000 annual arrests with road offenses comprising approximately 50 per cent and violations of the game and fish laws another 25 per cent.[58]

State highway patrols of the early 1930s confronted three distinct problems: winning public acceptance, enforcing traffic regulations, and resisting political domination. Efforts to accomplish such goals proved largely successful; each may be recognized within the ten general orders of the Arizona Highway Patrol for 1933:

1. To familiarize myself with the Highway Laws of the State of Arizona and to enforce those laws to the best of my ability and in an entirely impartial manner.
2. To remember at all times the motto of this organization; COURTESY

AND SERVICE: courtesy alike to all, and to the point of human endurance when the person addressed does not exhibit courtesy; service to the traveling public when seeking information or in dire trouble.

3. To refrain from the use of intoxicating liquors or narcotics, in any degree or at any time or place.

4. To refrain from smoking while in direct contact with anyone, in my official capacity.

5. To keep myself in good physical condition, body clean, my uniform neatly pressed and in order, fully buttoned and otherwise as ordered by regulations.

6. To keep my car and other State equipment entrusted to me in good repair, cleaned and polished and fully accounted for.

7. To vote my convictions as a citizen on all public questions and political races but to take no other part in any public question or campaign; to make no statements for publication nor give interviews for the same purpose.

8. To remember that my employers expect me to conduct my business in a quiet voiced manner; to warn but never to threaten; to be firm but courteous; to remember that arguments are seldom effective but explanations in a courteous manner are.

9. To follow and obey orders and instructions and to be familiar with them at all times; to take up matters affecting me or my position only with my immediate superior or through proper channels and to remember that my superintendent will always be glad to receive through proper channels any suggestions for the betterment of the service.

10. To at all times both on and off duty, conduct myself, in such a gentlemanly manner that I may merit the voluntary commendation of all law abiding citizens and visitors with whom I come in contact, both those with whom I meet in carrying out my duties and those I shall live among as a citizen; in order that credit may be reflected on the State Highway Department.[59]

Most state units made sincere efforts to create an initially favorable public image. They ordinarily selected mature, married men and created training schools for recruits. The first months of operation normally saw very few actual arrests; officers had no desire to begin work under conditions of pronounced public antipathy. Patrol on highways of the 1930s did not directly resemble that of the present. Many states maintained border posts to collect fees from travelers, issue permits, and check truck weights. As two-way radios did not appear on a large scale until about 1940, officers had to resort to "flag stations" for telephone communications. It was not unusual for a single patrolman to be assigned a district of 20,000 square miles with virtually no practical supervision or assistance. Yet the state officers soon earned a reputation for efficiency and impartiality.

Political involvement always posed major difficulties. Oklahoma's unit emerged from a small and ineffective patrol force of "spoils system" appointees. A primary legislative battle occurred over various commission-fee schemes that permitted officers to retain a percentage of collected fines. Not until 1937 did an attempt to have state representatives directly select highway officers meet defeat.[60] Some jurisdictions required that, "As nearly as may be, the patrolmen shall be appointed equally from the several counties."[61] Within a few years, however, the western state police units generally operated under forms of civil service with relative immunity from overt political pressure.

Powers extended to highway patrolmen clearly reflect the heritage of particular regions. California, which created the first large traffic unit in the West in 1929 and later supplied instructors to several other jurisdictions, still possesses no state agency with general police authority.

All members of the California Highway Patrol have the powers of a peace officer; provided, that the primary duty of the department shall be the enforcement of the provisions of this [vehicle] code or of any other laws relating to the use or operation of vehicles upon the highways, and patrol members shall not act as peace officers in enforcing any other law except:

(a) When in pursuit of any offender or suspected offender.

(b) To make arrests for crimes committed in their presence or upon any highway.[62]

Nebraska and North Dakota also restrict their state patrolmen primarily to traffic functions and direct co-operation with local sheriffs and police; Kansas statutes contain similar limitations which have even been subject to an unusual interpretation technically depriving highway patrolmen of the "peace officer" designation.[63]

175

No state imposes tighter legislative regulations than Colorado. A long and bitter heritage of central involvement in local and labor disputes left the "Courtesy Patrol" with very restricted police authority except at the annual Pueblo fair.[64] The state officers possess only the power of arrest for traffic violations except, as noted in Colorado's statutes,

. . . in an emergency, and with the approval of the governor, they are authorized and empowered to assist and aid any sheriff or other peace officer in the performance of his duties. . . . Furthermore, they shall not be deputized as deputy sheriffs or as other peace officers by any local or state authority, nor shall they be required to serve or act on strike duty, riots, lockouts, or other labor disputes, nor shall they perform any of the functions commonly performed by the national guard.[65]

Prohibitions upon assignment in connection with strikes may be found in the laws of Arizona and other western states. For thirty years Montana patrolmen could not act in labor disputes or even to congregate or act as a unit to suppress riots or preserve the peace. Since restrictions were, however, removed in 1965, officers may now also perform most ordinary police duties in rural areas and small towns upon official request.[66]

Other western states extend wide authority to state patrolmen. A few, including Utah and Wyoming, include restrictions on service of civil process but otherwise grant the general power of peace officers.[67] Many jurisdictions charge state policemen with the duty of enforcing all penal and regulatory provisions, although primary attention is often directed to traffic offenses. Idaho specifically demands liberal construction of enactments on its State Police to aid the efficient enforcement of criminal laws.[68]

Extension of power as a centrally commissioned peace officer is not restricted to full-time employees. Two states in the Southwest, Arizona and New Mexico, permit large systems of state police reserves.

The superintendent of the Arizona highway patrol may provide for the organization of an auxiliary volunteer organization to be known as the Arizona highway patrol reserve, which organization shall consist of male citizens, residents of the state of Arizona, over age twenty-one years, who shall render auxiliary support, without compensation, to the patrol under such rules and regulations as the superintendent may prescribe.[69]

New Mexico statutes recognize two separate reserve law enforcement units at the state level. One exists as a paid arm of the regular State Police while the other, termed the "Mounted Patrol," is located directly under the governor as an honorary force which can be used to assist other officers.[70]

Current western agencies vary greatly in size and responsibility; state law enforcement agencies on the Pacific Coast and in the Southwest tend to have numerically strong forces while those on the Northern Plains remain relatively small. Most of the present western patrols are composed of carefully selected, thoroughly trained, and well-equipped officers. They benefit from specialized assignment and relative freedom from political influence. State police organizations generally demonstrate an active efficiency comparing favorably with other law enforcement agencies. The New Mexico system is representative of these aspects. During 1967 the force of about 240 officers and ninety civilian employees maintained ten patrol districts and twelve radio stations. In one year the New Mexico State Police made 62,709 arrests, with 37,881 falling in the category of moving traffic violations. During the same period officers reported on 6,895 highway accidents, recovered 773 stolen automobiles, and were responsible for the collection of $1,228,820.10 in fines, costs, fees, and other charges. In addition the Special Investigation and Intelligence Section handled cases of murder, narcotics, armored car robbery, and the major social disorders at Tierra Amarilla.[71]

Western state police forces maintain a generally high professional esprit and distinctly favorable public image. Many communities actively seek to have a post located in their immediate vicinity. It is not uncommon for small towns to present petitions, offer free housing, and even purchase communication equipment to obtain the presence of a patrolman. The state police of the modern West still permit a considerable degree of independent action; single-man posts may still be found where an officer operates under only occasional supervision. Such autonomy is, however, slowly disappearing with increased population and more rapid means of transportation.

The particularly colorful history of the state police gives little indication of possible future trends. With a blurring of clear jurisdictional lines caused by ever-expanding urban regions and the deepening complexity of road networks, centralized systems are likely to increase in significance. In many western areas they now stand as a positive model and perform a cohesive service for local agencies. The state police normally provide a center of information, means of distant communication, technical and scientific assistance, and educational opportunities for local lawmen. Any distant strides forward in domestic administration will undoubtedly require consolidation. General state systems, the most logical basis for such efforts, are generations overdue. There is, unfortunately, no guarantee that any centripetal flow of law enforcement authority will not become subject to bureaucratic domination or political misuse.

Ex Parte Crow Dog

VII

Settlers of European ancestry did not bring the first police to the American West. Every organized society probably demands some form of law enforcement, though this might include little more than the simple authority of a leader to require adherence to ordinary standards. Extended groups logically delegate power to enforce institutionalized behavior patterns, while sophisticated cultures naturally require specialized agencies with duties of police. Each of these varieties of law enforcement probably existed among Indians in the West, even before arrival of Spanish colonists.

Existence of a police agency does not require a complex and technically advanced civilization. Anyone with recognized authority to demand observance of social rules, whether customary or written, actually serves in a law enforcement capacity. Despite the emphasis of recent times, such power need not emanate from governmental institutions. Religious, economic, and other cultural structures can develop their own forms of a police.

Very early agencies of the American West occupied no rigorously defined role and functioned through wide societal variation and the lack of formal codification. Nevertheless, many of the indigenous cultures possessed police systems with accepted powers and duties. The laws and regulations may have been expressed at times by tradition or force, but various Indian tribes maintained some means of enforcement long before being influenced by immigrants moving westward.

The primitive societies, despite general adherence to customary rules, dealt with occasional transgressors. Invasion of personal and property rights is by no means original with European cultures. The western Indians enforced rules governing disposition of food, ownership of animals, procedures for changing campsites, and peace within the community. Maintenance of such apparently simple standards sometimes became the special duty of individuals occupying a status directly parallel to the modern concept of a police.

No tribe more clearly demonstrated activities of formal law enforcement agencies than the Cheyenne. This nomadic people of the Plains had six separate military societies to perform a police function. The Fox Soldiers, Dog Men, Elk Soldiers, Northern Crazy Dogs, Shield Soldiers, and Bowstring Soldiers could be entered by any worthy warrior. Popularly referred to in collective terms as the "Cheyenne Dog Soldiers," they gained a later reputation for discipline and bravery in wars against white invaders. Prior to the onslaught of the frontier, however, these units functioned as key elements in the preservation of internal tranquility. They restrained undesirable raids, maintained order during buffalo hunts and ceremonies, kept marches moving smoothly, inflicted punishment determined for offenders, investigated reports of serious crime, supervised public works, and otherwise performed duties directly comparable to any real police force.[1]

Military societies of Plains Indians, of course, had diverse roles beyond law enforcement. Kiowa, Sioux, and Cheyenne cultures contained organizations to perform a variety of functions relating to social control. In some tribes police duties only appeared during mass gatherings and might subside after a few weeks or season of the year. Some societies, including that of the Comanches, maintained no recognizable separate unit for law enforcement purposes.

The most fully developed form of Indian police moved into the West from an original home in the South. The Five Civilized Tribes created a complex institutionalized system of agencies to demand adherence to formal regulations. In 1808 the Cherokees appointed "regulators" to suppress horse theft and robbery; by about 1820 the Choctaw Nation started a structured and significant force of mounted policemen termed the "light-horse."[2]

Driven into the Indian Territory by 1840 from the South, the Chickasaws, Cherokees, Seminoles, Choctaws, and Creeks brought along their advanced systems of tribal law enforcement. Each society developed and modified its police agencies; the major elements appeared dramatically among the Choctaws. During the 1840s the United States government indirectly supported the light-horse with gifts of pistols; Indian officers then concentrated their efforts toward control of the liquor trade, keeping children in school, and generally preserving the peace. The tribe also maintained sheriffs during this period to perform all of the usual duties associated with local law enforcement.

In 1860 the Choctaw Nation reformulated their written statutes on policemen. Each county received authority to elect both a "ranger" and a sheriff for two-year terms. The latter, upon commissioning by the principal chief, could appoint deputies and take charge of those confined to jail. The light-horse continued as an arm of the central tribal government. A corps of six national officers remained directly under the principal chief to serve as messengers, suppress riots, preserve the peace, and enforce all criminal laws. From one to three additional light-horsemen, with annual salaries of $150, were assigned to the different districts. They were specifically directed to search for intoxicants, keep order at elections, and aid the Indian agents when so directed.[3] In 1867 the salaries of Choctaw sheriffs amounted to $1,200 while expenses of deputies came to $5,760. During the same period the national light-horse cost $950; district detachments of the force received $2,400.[4] It is quite obvious that this culture independently evolved a complex police structure comparable to others found at the time within the United States.

During the 1870s many tribes created formal systems of law enforcement. The high sheriff of the Cherokee nation, with the assistance of an organized posse of officers, operated a regular prison at Tahlequah. Navajo depredations led to formation of a small internal disciplinary force under the war chief Manuelito in 1872. Supplied with Army uniforms, pistols, and carbines, this "Mounted Cavalry" grew to about 130 men. Lack of sufficient pay proved to be a great problem with the agency-sponsored Navajo police. Although it was officially disbanded in 1873, it actually continued to function on a sharply reduced scale.

In 1874 Indian Agent John P. Clum created a small police unit among the San Carlos Apaches. The force increased quickly in size and proved so successful that all troops were withdrawn from the reservation by the following year. Clum's Apache lawmen received $15 a month but proved loyal to their sponsor and later directly aided in the capture of the feared Geronimo.[5]

In 1878 the United States Congress finally appropriated funds for a system of Indian police. Within less than two years a majority of the approximately sixty agencies formed or increased the size of already existing law enforcement contingents. The first official uniforms came from guards at the Centennial Exposition, while revolvers soon replaced the originally issued rifles.[6] These officers performed a vast assortment of duties. Congress intended them to demonstrate the virtues of formal regulation to the Indians.

. . . let us give them law, let it be executed with justice and humanity, let them feel its protecting power over the weakest as well as the strongest, against whites as well as Indians, and they will learn to love it, to trust it, and to shelter under it.[7]

In practice the Indian policemen represented official decrees of the local agents. The officers chased encroaching ranchers and lumbermen off reservations, tracked rustlers and bootleggers, and returned far-ranging hostiles to camp. They gave advice on civil matters, served as messengers, and took the census. At most agencies Indian lawmen also served as general handymen who dug ditches, cleaned wells, and repaired bridges. Their most controversial duty probably consisted of demanding attendance, often by force, at schools.

Representing a dominant but alien culture, the Indian police met much resistance. As with most law enforcers they were not generally well liked and strong internal opposition continued for many years. Conflict over the imposition of such undesired authority culminated with a dramatic sequence of events described legally in Ex parte Crow Dog. The Sioux police for the Rosebud Agency in Dakota encountered particularly bitter opposition from the tribal council. Captain Crow Dog, a successful leader of the agency force, became involved in a bitter personal struggle with Chief Spotted Tail over position and stature in the tribe. Although the discontented officer resigned from the police shortly before the actual incident, he engaged the chief in a dramatic confrontation in 1881 and killed him. Crow Dog was taken into custody by federal officers, tried for murder, convicted, and sentenced to death. In 1883 a writ of *habeas corpus* brought the case before the United States Supreme Court. The decision freed Crow Dog and established indirectly the essential role to be played by the reservation police and later judicial systems. Crimes committed by one Indian against another on agency lands could not be taken under federal jurisdiction. Neither statute nor treaty created any direct criminal authority over the tribes.[8] Within a few months Congress established certain major offenses as falling within the federal system, and by 1888 Indian policemen clearly acted as representatives of the United States government.[9] The peculiar legal status and relative independence of the tribes nevertheless endured and demanded existence of separate systems of law enforcement.

In the final decades of the nineteenth century Indian police assumed varied forms among the different tribes. Sioux agencies tended to maintain powerful paramilitary units trained in basic cavalry or infantry maneuvers. These officers were directly involved in the Ghost Dance episode leading to the death of Sitting Bull in 1890. At the other extreme many of the Indian nations in Oklahoma operated community and district police agencies, with marshals and sheriffs similar to those common throughout the United States.

The Five Civilized Tribes continued to possess strong systems of central control. Within the Indian Territory, now eastern Oklahoma, the light-horse served as the primary police agency. They guarded the region against whisky traders, drove out straying cattle, and maintained the peace. Many routine problems arose from excess drinking, and the tribal officers devised simple but adequate measures for dealing with such offenders. Contraband bottles could be shattered on the spot; and, "When an Indian got drunk [at a community picnic or dance] the Indian police would take him and handcuff him to a tree and leave him there until he sobered up and then turn him loose."[10]

Light-horsemen also conducted many of the official sentences pronounced in the region. Since the Choctaws, Creeks, and other nations maintained courts of sovereign authority over Indian offenses, their police applied an assortment of corrective measures. Seminole justice typically involved the administration of corporal punishment for lesser offenses. The police used seasoned hickory sticks approximately four feet in length. The victim would be stripped to the waist and tied to a whipping post. Then, as one early settler described a memorable scene,

Big Peter [a leader of the light-horse] took a switch by the tip and called to one of his men. The man pointed out would remove his gauntlet, spit on his hand, and then take a careful grip on the butt of the switch. He was not allowed to change that grip in any manner after he took it. If the switch should break or fly out of his hand, the condemned man was saved that many of the remainder of 25 lashes. As soon as twenty-five were administered, the chief signaled for another man for the next twenty-five. It was administered in doses of 25, 50, 100, and 150 according to the sentence of the Council. There was absolutely no "throwing off" in the whippings. They were methodically administered with about all the muscle that could be put into it. Each lash either gashed the skin or left a fearful welt. I never saw an Indian manifest the slightest interest in it while he was being whipped. Not a muscle of the face would change. But they seemed to delight in the whipping of a "Freeman," a negro who held tribal citizenship because he or his parents were slaves of the tribe before the war.[11]

For serious crimes the tribes might give the death penalty. Again, the duty of actual imposition fell to the Indian police. At one final court session,

Two Seminole "Light Horsemen" shot the condemned with Winchesters, shooting at a small white mark pinned over the heart . . . if a man was shot and lived over it, he was free. In fact a light-horseman was pointed out to me who had been condemned. His friends bribed two officers detailed to shoot. One of them shot too high, hitting him through the shoulder. The other one only half cocked his gun and cut his finger to the bone trying to fire. They cussed him for negligence in half cocking his gun, but they knew blamed well the other one missed purposely so they chased him out of the country.[12]

As the nineteenth century drew to a close the Indian police comprised approximately 800 individuals scattered throughout most of the West. On many reservations they existed in a transitional status representative of the varying process of tribal acculturation. The primary problem of administration consisted of a lack of funds with which to attract and retain worthwhile personnel. Leo E. Bennett of the Union Agency, Indian Territory, reflected the general attitude in his formal report for 1892:

An Indian policeman, to perform his duty acceptably, must not only be a moral man and be courageous and faithful, but he must be a man of considerable discretion. This character of man is far from being a rarity among the Indians of this agency, yet it is not always possible to find in every locality one of this high character who is willing, or can afford to make the personal sacrifice of time and business interests necessary to the discharge of the duties of an Indian policeman at the pay allowed, $10 a month. Deputy United States marshals and all other peace officers are much better paid and their standard of morality and efficiency is not, as a rule, up to that of the Indian police. . . . Besides they should be properly armed with the best grade of Winchester rifles and Colts revolvers. The weapons with which they are supposed to be furnished (for none of them will carry the guns now on hand at this agency) are not only worthless, but a source of immediate danger to those who might use them . . . the Dalton gang of train robbers and murderers is operating within this agency, with improved weapons for offense and defense, and staying close together, it would be but suicide for the police force of this agency to seek their capture unless better armed than they are now.[13]

Deficiency of remuneration prompted many officers to urge various forms of additional pay. Captain Albert L. Myer, detached from army service to the San Carlos Agency in Arizona, relied upon his Apache protectors to perform all types of police and military duty. In 1895 they suffered greatly from lack of transport. The officer wrote, "I feel they are somewhat imposed upon, being compelled to furnish horses themselves without feed, or walk the long distances some of them are required to go. All of them should be allowed forage for a pony."[14]

Indian police organization continued to reflect a variety of administrative patterns and duty assignments. Most agencies decentralized their forces by 1900. As the military format slowly declined in significance, towns and farming activity caused the officers to be detached on rotation to outlying camps. Agent S. G. Reynolds reported in 1906 that,

Our police force [at the Crow Agency, Montana] was too small the past year to get the best results out of the individual Indian located at different places than it was when working in a community. This refers only to the lazy and indolent. The force was increased the first of the year and is now well organized for good work. Outside trespassers take much of their time.[15]

Duties continued to involve such diverse tasks as fighting forest fires, investigating occasional serious crimes, repairing roads, apprehending runaway school children, arresting drunks, and maintaining smallpox quarantines. The policemen also were supposed to provide a bridge of adjustment between the tribal and pervasive American civilization. One agent in 1892 wrote from North Dakota that, "Their influence is for the advancement and the abolishing of old Indian customs."[16] An effort to recruit only English-speaking officers helped this gradual process of acculturation.

While most police systems functioned with praise from their white supervisors, many problems existed. G. H. Newman reported on his law enforcers in the state of Washington as follows:

The police force at this agency is composed of 2 officers and 20 privates. Their service during the past year has not in the main been very satisfactory. But owing to the rough character of the country and the long distances they sometimes have to ride, I suppose better service cannot very well be expected.[17]

A major difficulty concerned the lack of jurisdiction over non-Indians on reservation lands. Although towns might appear on the agency, community marshals and patrolmen had no authority or legal control of white inhabitants. Related obstacles sometimes developed with increasing contact between the native subcultures and white settlement. The Indian law enforcement system thrived upon isolation but could not function without contacting other police organizations. As one interested supervisor commented,

While the local authorities have rendered small aid, they have not intentionally hindered. In fact the proposition has been one that most persons are willing to leave to Federal authority. One of the most gratifying results is the unmistakable evidence [at Fort Totten, North Dakota, in 1906] that the tribe itself rejoice over the stricter enforcement of the law as much or more than others.[18]

Tribal members ordinarily continued to look with open disfavor upon their police force. Officers felt a natural reluctance, intensified by social reaction, to enforcing regulations contradictory to custom. They usually demonstrated a marked sympathy with children fleeing schools and those wanted for offenses traditionally regarded as subject only to informal social sanction, such as many rules governing morality.

Indian policemen occasionally encountered danger and excitement fully comparable to those of other peace officers. A routine operation could easily provoke resistance leading to death. Such conditions had several consequences. Federal prosecutions resulting from the killing of a "squaw man" named William Fielder by a posse from the Cheyenne River Agency of South Dakota led the entire police force to threaten resignation in 1895.[19] About the same time Dew M. Wisdom, in charge of the Union Agency in the Indian Territory, felt his officers were delinquent in the hunt for renegade bands. He ordered the Cherokee light-horse into the field with orders to "shoot them on the spot" and then stated: "If you are afraid to carry out this order, send in your resignation and I will appoint better men in your places. This is no time for cravens and cowards to hold official positions and wear the badges of office."[20]

Most of the fights involving Indian police did not involve feared bandits and outlaws. A typical incident occurred at the Umatilla Agency, Oregon, in 1901:

> Quite an exciting affray took place recently near this agency, when an attempt was made by an Indian policeman to arrest two Indians, both notoriously bad men, who were under the influence and had liquor with them. One of the culprits, Black Horn, struck the policeman a blow on the head with his pistol, felling him, while the other bad man, Toc Nass Et, came at the policeman with a huge dagger, lunging at him with it repeatedly. The policeman snapped his pistol at the miscreants, but the weapon failed to explode. He then used it as a club and succeeded in knocking the knife out of the hand of the one man and bringing the other to the ground. At this time other policemen who were on their way to the scene of trouble were seen by Black Horn and Toc Nass Et, and they immediately jumped on their horses and put spurs, with the policemen in pursuit. Black Horn turned in his saddle and fired at his pursuers, missing them; he then fired again and failed to hit his mark. The policeman then opened fire. Black Horn was pierced by bullets in two parts of his anatomy, and Toc Nass Et was shot through the shoulder, but withal they escaped in the darkness. . . .
> Black Horn was found a day or so later at the home of his relatives . . . Toc Nass Et has not been seen since upon the reservation. . . . The policeman who attempted the arrest in the first place was put to rights by having a few stitches taken in his scalp. The dagger was captured and is a very dangerous looking weapon, being 1 foot in length.[21]

The twentieth century brought considerable change to the Indian police. Only a few years after pioneering achievements in India and England, fingerprints came into use as a means of identification. James McLaughlin of the Rosebud Agency in South Dakota popularized the method by 1905; other reservations in the West soon found the technique of significant value.[22]

Agencies slowly lost their independence, with lasting effects on law enforcement; the principal trend was toward centralized authority. Difficulties with the liquor traffic prompted the Office of Indian Affairs to appoint William E. Johnson as a special officer for the Indian Territory and Oklahoma by 1907. In one year his men seized some 12,000 gallons of contraband intoxicants. Liquor appeared hidden in otherwise legal shipments of such 2 per cent beers as "Uno," "Hiawatha," "Tin Top," and "Mistletoe."[23] Although much of the work consisted of searching railroad cars and wagons, it sometimes posed grave danger. The Commissioner of Indian Affairs knew the problem: "Two of Mr. Johnson's men and one posse man have been killed in skirmishes with boot-leggers, and 10 violators of the liquor laws have met a like fate. Mr. Johnson has had several narrow escapes himself, and during a good part of the time has worked in the face of a reward of $3,000 offered by the outlaws for his assassination."[24] Experimentation with operatives directly under central federal control proved quite successful. William E. Johnson became chief special officer for the suppression of the liquor traffic. From headquarters in Salt Lake City he directed efforts to curtail the use of intoxicants on western reservations which produced about one thousand convictions yearly.[25]

Table 5 of Appendix A shows the number of Indian policemen on duty in 1912. Total strength had remained relatively stable at approximately 800 for a generation. Over 90 per cent of the officers could be found in the West, where the greatest concentrations existed in the Far Northern Plains and Arizona. The figures given do include approximately twenty authorized special officers then working under central direction to fight the liquor traffic.

In some areas the Indian police slowly lost their powerful position in social control. By 1911 the Five Civilized Tribes, with a combined enrolled population of 101,221 citizens, maintained less than forty officers. The fabled light-horse of the Choctaws and Seminoles had been replaced by local policemen and deputies. Changed conditions required different duties:

Thirty-six members of the Indian police force are scattered throughout almost all of the 40 counties of the Five Civilized Tribes, the larger number of them being detailed to the district agencies where their services are utilized in various ways, largely as interpreters. Practically no policemen are now employed who can not fluently speak English and the language of the Indian tribe to which they belong, and in this manner practically no expense is incurred in the employment of interpreters. The police force is also used in placing allottees in possession, as required by the different acts of Congress, in assisting in the protection of tribal property, the collection of rentals therefrom, and the suppression of the liquor traffic on tribal and other lands still within the control of the Government.[26]

Alcohol continued to pose a major problem among the Indian population. The primary technique utilized to curtail the importation and sale of forbidden intoxicants required employment of decoys, or operatives unlikely to attract suspicion. Growing numbers of investigators dispatched by the Office of Indian Affairs came to rely almost entirely upon this often disputed method of catching bootleggers. Commissioner Robert G. Valentine reported on the problem in 1912:

Decoys are in many instances as essential in our work to suppress the sale of liquor to Indians as a special officer. It requires the services of the officer to procure the evidence and the services of the decoy to produce the evidence. There are innumerable instances where the officer has every reason to believe that certain individuals are trafficking in liquors with the Indians, and yet it is next to impossible to procure evidence of that fact sufficient to warrant prosecution. In such instances the decoy, who ... should be a person about whose race there is no question, is an essential element and renders valuable service.

I have taken steps to eliminate to a certain extent one of the objectionable features of this work, and which has been the subject of criticism. Heretofore many deputy special officers were employed on a fee basis, namely, they were paid a certain fee for a certain service performed. While this method still continues, it has been reduced and the chief special officer authorized in its stead to employ deputy special officers on a monthly basis at varying salaries, at not to exceed $75 a month.[27]

Within a year the number of fee deputies fell from 184 to 67 scattered through Oklahoma, California, Idaho, New Mexico, and Wyoming, but intoxicants continued to form the greatest percentage of agency arrests throughout the West, paralleling conditions found in white settlements.[28] Drunkenness could be easily attained either through cheap locally made alcohol or by purchase of powerful patent medicines available in most stores.

Indian policemen continued to spearhead the often tragic effort to eradicate tribal customs. Subcultural traditions withered under steady pressure to promote general standards of acceptable behavior. Clothing, leadership patterns, marriage, religious beliefs, festivals, and countless other aspects of society fell under well meaning but often misguided forms of repression. Most tribal entities eventually dissolved or underwent pronounced modification. The destruction of familiar values also left many Indians without the stable foundations essential to any adaptation to a complex civilization. Enduring difficulties with drunkenness, gambling, and other means of personal escapism resulted. By 1911 the danger signs of yet another threat to Indian integrity had spread from the Southwest:

A relatively new intoxicant of a peculiarly insidious form has come into favor with Indians in many parts of the country. From a cactus growing wild in the arid regions of old Mexico just South of the Rio Grande the crown is cut off and dried, becoming the peyote bean of commerce. Among the tribes it is commonly known as mescal. As these beans sell for $3 or $4 a thousand, and three or four beans suffice to give the full effects of the intoxicating drug in peyote, indulgence is within the reach of all.[29]

During the second and third decades of the twentieth century Indian police declined in significance along with the importance of tribal organizations. Under the administration of Franklin D. Roosevelt, however, conditions began to change. Failure to orient successfully large numbers of Indians to the basic American culture finally forced adoption of a rejuvenated policy of support for native groups. As was reported in 1941:

The destruction of Indian social organization and the breakdown of Indian leadership made it extremely difficult for the Indian tribes to administer law and order. For many years the Department maintained a rough and ready sort of justice. . . . Since the passage of the Indian Reorganization Act [1934], however, tribes are once again assuming responsibility for the maintenance of law and order. Tribal courts have been created, law and order codes adopted, native Indian police employed. . . .

Indian administration of law and order has been especially successful on closed reservations (those in which lands have been allotted but remain in tribal status). In allotted areas where Indian and whites are interspersed the problem is much more acute. Indian courts in some of these areas have not functioned for years. Often the county enforcement officers have undertaken the task of maintaining law and order.[30]

During the most recent generation tribal justice has steadily expanded in significance. Today there are approximately as many Indian policemen as have ever existed at any one time. Currently they fall into three major categories. Most are employed directly as tribal officers; a smaller number work under contract with the government; still others hold positions within the Bureau of Indian Affairs itself. The Department of the Interior also maintains special investigators for certain offenses, and the Federal Bureau of Investigation has agents available to handle crimes within their statutory authority. Patterns change, frustrations remain.

Many larger reservations presently possess forces affording considerable specialization. Some have positions for jailers, matrons, game wardens, juvenile or probation officers, rangers, radio operators, and various ranks beyond that of patrolman. No tribe has an internal system of law enforcement as complex as that of the Navajos. In 1968 that tribe maintained a police strength of approximately 200 men with an annual budget of $1,800,000. Administration of the Navajo force, far more independent than those of most communities, involved five districts and many substations. Operations included a complex radio network, jails, and formal relations with other police agencies, not altogether unlike those between friendly countries.[31]

The legal status of Indian reservations is unique in the United States and creates a need for special answers to the law enforcement problem. In effect, the federal government has never exercised jurisdiction over any but the most serious of crimes committed by Indians upon their own tribal lands. Congress has granted authority over reservations, with qualifications, to a number of states. Kansas, California, Nebraska, and Oregon are among the western jurisdictions granted such power. Nevada and Washington have also asserted state criminal control over Indian lands, without objection. In much of the West, however, minor reservation offenses remain under the practical control of only the tribal officers. State policemen cannot, for example, arrest an Indian for a traffic violation on a federal highway where title to the land formally remains with the independent and quasi-sovereign Navajos.[32] In many areas, of course, the problem is simplified by tribes commissioning local or state lawmen as special officers.

The Indian policeman is still a very important part of the western scene. He has become a separate variety of peace officer with new pride and capability. Through attendance at state training schools such lawmen have acquired many of the sophisticated skills demanded by modern law enforcement. In 1969 opportunities for professionalization were further increased through organization of an Indian Police Academy at Roswell, New Mexico.[33] Instead of vanishing, the officers appear to be entering another and enduring authority reminiscent of their unique heritage.

As the Indians required their own versions of police, they also indirectly led to another type of law enforcement agency on the frontier. The overt danger of hostility, or actual conflict, between European settlers and native societies required the presence of martial power in the form of regular army detachments and later through militia units. These forces frequently became involved in the maintenance of internal order in many communities of the

American West and they often provided an ultimate variety of police protection in times of social upheaval.

Spanish colonists in the early Southwest depended upon soldiers to guard against Indian marauders and preserve the general peace. In New Mexico, Texas, and California a basic pattern existed, for the only practical means of control in most of the region occupied by Spain remained in the presence of armed troops. Some areas eventually developed functioning civil and religious systems, but the military continued as the primary form of police in sparsely populated regions.

As settlers from the United States crossed the Mississippi the army moved westward to patrol the changing borders of the nation. Along the frontier troops carried on lengthy warfare against hostile Indians and enemies from Mexico. Such service constituted overt and armed conflict between opposing nations rather than international law enforcement. Yet, apart from these activities, the army engaged in many duties ordinarily associated with the civil police.

Major functions of the military naturally revolved around the Indian nations. The army usually served as a buffer between the cultures of the frontier. Aside from preventing excursions on settlers by hostiles, troops had to guard the Indians against white encroachment or molestation. Since tribal law only applied to members of the native societies the army often enforced federal statutes violated by those of European ancestry. The military also protected all government property in the territories, kept opposing Indian groups apart, and attempted to prevent the flow of contraband guns, ammunition, and alcohol.

Army units performed various peace-keeping functions among white settlers. In time of social unrest only the military could maintain order in many isolated regions. Troops appeared to clear Wyoming ranges in fence-cutting wars, prevent battles between opposing ethnic groups at El Paso, and stop riots against the Chinese in Colorado. Soldiers additionally acted in many capacities as protectors of internal law. They guarded such western trails as the Santa Fe, Oregon, and Chisholm, and wagon trains of newcomers had occasional recourse to military posts in matters of criminal justice.[34]

Stage and rail systems relied upon the army for protection against outlaw bands and road agents. Detachments often accompanied travelers in dangerous regions, but their efforts did not always engender high respect.

> Troops stationed at the respective forts throughout that bleak interior were . . . lazy, careless, indifferent, and stupid; laborious days and sleepless nights were less attractive than comfortable quarters and regular potations. There was little glory in catching. . . . If sheriffs cannot catch rogues, assuredly soldiers cannot. In mechanical slaughterings soldiers do very well; if well trained, they have not the intelligence and will sufficient to flee danger when they see it. This is all as it should be for posts, to shoot and be shot at; but as detectives they are of little value.[35]

If the military failed to rid the West of criminals the regular peace officers did little better. As always, the army moved at a ponderous rate and faced countless regulations not applicable to civilian agencies. In chasing suspects, "The cavalrymen had to be careful not to ride their horses to death . . . a sufficient reason for the ease with which the desperadoes eluded them."[36]

Federal legislation of 1878 kept local military commanders from assisting civil authorities in time of disturbance. This restriction, sometimes circumvented, plagued leaders in the thinly populated West. John J. Gosper, acting governor of Arizona in 1881, felt that only the military could bring order in the territory. He commented as follows:

> On account of the greatly disturbed condition of the public peace along the border of the United States and Mexico, and the seriously apprehended disturbance of the present peaceful conditions between the two governments as a consequence thereof, and the utter inability of the local civil authorities at all times to keep the peace and bring to justice the large numbers of reckless and abandoned men in the counties forming a part of this border, I would very respectfully urge upon Congress the wisdom of so far amending the law now prohibiting the Army from actively participating in aggressive efforts to keep the peace, and protect the lives and property of the citizens of the country, so far as the same relates to this Territory.[37]

Gosper's plea did not go unheeded. In his first annual message, President Chester A. Arthur called attention to the problems relating to limitations on the direct use of military force in the West.

> The Acting Attorney-General also calls attention to the disturbance of the public tranquility during the past year in the Territory of Arizona. A band of armed desperadoes known as "Cowboys," probably numbering from fifty to one-hundred men, have been engaged for months in committing acts of lawlessness and brutality which the local authorities have been unable to repress. The depredations of these "Cowboys" have also extended into Mexico, which the marauders reach from the Arizona frontier. With every disposition to meet the exigencies of the case, I am embarrassed by lack of authority to deal with them effectually. . . .
> I will add that in the event of a request from the Territorial government for protection by the United States against "domestic violence" this government would be powerless to render assistance. . . .
> It seems to me, too, that whatever views may prevail as to the policy of recent legislation by which the Army has ceased to be a part of the *posse comitatus*, an exception might well be made for permitting the military to assist the civil Territorial authorities in enforcing the laws of the United States. This use of the Army would not be within the alleged evil against which that legislation was aimed. From sparseness of population and other circumstances it is often quite impracticable to summon a civil posse in places where officers of justice require assistance and where a military force is within easy reach.[38]

Restrictions on military assistance were eventually eased as troops served in instances of serious social conflicts. Perhaps the most dramatic example occurred over activities of the Western Federation of Miners. On several occasions during the 1890s federal troops went to Idaho upon gubernatorial request. Strikes at Coeur d'Alene and Silver City led to extreme violence with lasting animosities in the Northwest. The army's commonly disputed interventions in Texas, Nevada, Colorado, Montana, and other areas are still open to question but undoubtedly provided a stabilizing influence in the midst of severe economic unrest.

Soldiers also served a very different police function in the West. For instance, from the initial creation of the Yellowstone pres-

First police force in Vancouver, British Columbia, 1886. Courtesy Provincial Archives, Victoria, British Columbia.

Headquarters of U.S. Marshal Robert Galbreth, Oklahoma Territory, 1890. Courtesy Oklahoma Historical Society.

North West Mounted Police at Fort Saskatchewan, Alberta, 1894.
Courtesy Royal Canadian Mounted Police, Gendarmerie Royale du
Canada, Ottawa, Ontario.

Bill Tilghman, serving as chief of police in Oklahoma City, 1912. Courtesy Western History Collections, University of Oklahoma Library.

Marshal Heck Thomas. Courtesy Western History Collections, University of Oklahoma Library.

Denver police in 1896. Courtesy Library, State Historical Society of Colorado.

Denver police detectives, 1894. Sam Howe is seated, far left. Courtesy Library, State Historical Society of Colorado.

Denver police "Motor Bandit-chaser," 1921. Courtesy Library, State
Historical Society of Colorado.

Arizona Rangers at Morenci, 1903. Twenty-five of the legendary "twenty-six men." Courtesy Arizona Pioneers' Historical Society Library

Manhunt with hounds and bicycles in Salem, Oregon, 1902. Courtesy Oregon State Library.

Police dispersing Wobblies with fire hoses, San Diego, 1912. Courtesy
University of Washington Library.

Bisbee deportation. Courtesy Arizona Pioneers' Historical Society Library.

June, 1913 (3) Falconer Henry (5) Wade Dick (6) Parr My J.E. (8) McLaughlin Dave (10) Taylor Bill (11) James Jesse (18) McCauly Billy (14) Whitson (15) De Flore, Felix (17) Anderson Frank (19) Parry, Jess (22) H
(7) Davis, Frank Cuningham Ed (9) Malone, John (12) Hector Lyda (13) Hockett, Bert Cal (16) Earth, Henry (18) Crumbeck, Jesse (20) Rogers, B.M. (23) M

Reunion of U.S. Marshals at Fort Smith, Arkansas, 1908. Left to right: Bob Fortune, Henry Falconer, Ace Wade, Maj. J. T. Farr, Frank Bolen, Price McLaughlin, Ed Armor, Bill Taylor, John Malone, Jesse Jones, Lyde Rector, Billy McCauly, Ben Hackett, Cal Whitson, Felix De Flore, Henry Bernier, Jess Perry, Frank Anderson, B. B. Rogers, Joe Gramlich, H. L. Rogers, Lige Fannin, William Ross, Joe Peters, John F. Priest, unidentified, C. B. Rhodes, S. O. Harris, Attorney Osborne, J. K. Pemberton, Frank Parks, Dave Lee, Tobe Pinson, Jim Cole, Jim Patty, Dr. Woodrow Hammond, Sam Minor, Sid Johnson. Courtesy Oklahoma Historical Society.

Wyatt Earp in 1926. Courtesy Western History Collections, University of Oklahoma Library.

U. S. Marshal E. D. Nix, Al Jennings, and Deputy U.S. Marshal Chris
Madsen at the 1937 National Frontiersmen Association meeting in
Houston. Courtesy Western History Collections, University of Okla-
homa Library.

Sacramento traffic officer, 1922. Courtesy California State Library.

ervation area until World War I, they guarded the national parks. As enacted in 1883,

The Secretary of the Army . . . is authorized and detailed to make the necessary details of troops to prevent trespassers or intruders from entering the park for the purpose of destroying the game or objects of curiosity therein, or for any other purpose prohibited by law, and to remove such persons from the park if found therein.[39]

For many years detachments of regular troops policed reserved regions in Wyoming, California, and elsewhere. Major H. C. Benson, assigned from the 14th Cavalry Regiment to act as superintendent at Yosemite, reported in 1907:

Twelve patrols, varying in size from 2 to 5 men each, were stationed at various points throughout the park at distances varying from 20 to 75 miles from the main camp, for the purpose of preventing trespassing. These patrols were visited and inspected by an officer as soon as practicable, and they were invariably found to be performing their duties in an efficient and satisfactory manner. No sheep whatever crossed the border and only an inconsiderable number of cattle have been found within the park limits. . . .[40]

Service in the national parks did not, however, always attain great success. Enlisted men received assignments with little regard for either interest or ability. Undeveloped regions demanded a specialized police of packers and woodsmen, while the army had to maintain a basic emphasis on ability in time of war.

The role of the military in law enforcement has continued into the twentieth century. During World War I soldiers acted in several parts of the West to suppress sabotage and crush strikes. In the same period the army dispatched Colonel Brice Disque to the Northwest for the purpose of forming the Loyal League of Loggers and Lumbermen, or "4 L's," in an effort to combat activities of the powerful Industrial Workers of the World.[41] In the 1920s Marines guarded mail shipments and navy oil reserves, while the army intervened in rail strikes. World War II found military police devoting themselves to troop discipline and protection of government property. These functions continued on a large scale in recent decades, as the tens of thousands of such personnel now on duty clearly demonstrate. Each of the armed services has grown to constitute a new American subculture. Every large military unit and base maintains an internal police force as part of several gigantic and diversified law enforcement systems now international in scope.

In the United States the armed forces only indirectly serve to maintain internal peace and order. The situations in other countries, including those sharing the American West, possess quite different heritages. Mexico and Canada experienced problems in frontier law enforcement quite similar to those of the United States. Their basic solutions to common difficulties, and the role of the military therein, illustrate remarkable comparisons in national culture.

The Canadian frontier carried with it traditions shared by the United States. By the middle of the nineteenth century, however, the British Commonwealth already recognized the general benefits of central police authority with high standards and relative isolation from political pressure. Canadians continued the appointment of regular and special constables by local magistrates. Law enforcement agencies along city and provincial lines developed by the 1860s. Indian peace officers served to enforce requirements long before such official recognition in the United States.

British Columbia met the needs for police through a force of about fifteen efficient constables established under Chief Inspector Chartres Brew. Between 1858 and 1865 this very small and underpaid unit managed to keep order and prevent widespread crime on a booming mining frontier. Low salaries prompted appointment of men with outside income; in emergencies a reserve of special constables might be called to duty.[42] The unit subsequently became the British Columbia Police, which endured as a separate provincial force until 1950.

The general withdrawal of British troops in 1871 created many problems for Canadian law enforcement. In the interior regions of the early West they had performed many police functions in a fashion similar to that of the army in the United States. A means of maintaining order, particularly among the Indians, became of paramount importance. Canada had permitted a small "Mounted Police Force" to be raised in districts and counties since 1845.[43] This early authority to appoint militiamen-constables served as precedent for creation of a standing unit with wide authority.

In 1873 the Canadian Parliament passed "An Act respecting the Administration of Justice, and for the establishment of a Police Force in the North West Territories." This significant legislation allowed initial formation of perhaps the most famous law enforcement agency in the world—the Mounties.

10. The Governor in Council may constitute a Police Force in and for the North West Territories, and the Governor may from time to time, as may be found necessary, appoint by commission, a Commissioner of Police, and one or more Superintendents of Police, together with a Paymaster, Surgeon and Veterinary Surgeon, each of whom shall hold office during pleasure. . . .

13. No person shall be appointed to the Police Force unless he be of a sound constitution, able to ride, active and ablebodied, of good character, and between eighteen and forty years; nor unless he be able to read and write either the English or French language. . . .

15. The Commissioner and every Superintendent of Police shall be *ex-officio* a Justice of the Peace; and every constable and sub-constable shall be a constable in and for the whole of the North West Territories: and may execute the office in any part thereof, and in Manitoba. . . .[44]

Other sections of the act created a minimum enlistment of three years, allowed land grants of 160 acres to those completing satisfactory service, and established pay scales ranging from a maximum of $2,600 yearly for the commissioner to $0.75 a day for subconstables. Assigned duties included the preservation of peace, prevention of crime, attendance upon the courts, and conveyance of prisoners.[45]

A cadre of experienced lawmen was imported from the Royal Irish Constabulary to become a nucleus for the 300-member North West Mounted Police. Initial recruits included former clerks, farmers, telegraphers, bakers, professors, sailors, gardeners, students, and a bartender. Uniforms emulated those worn by British dragoons in the Crimean War; equipment followed military standards and came directly from England. Within a short time the frontier forced several modifications. White helmets and gauntlets proved hopelessly impractical in the West and were discarded. The standard British "Universal" cavalry saddle found a replacement in the heavier California stockman's version. But the scarlet tunics and guidon-lances became enduring parts of a great image. Armed with carbines and revolvers, supported by a small artillery unit containing light field guns and brass mortars, the North West Mounted Police set out to tame the Canadian frontier.[46] It largely succeeded.

Under the leadership of Superintendent James M. Walsh the force controlled some 100,000 Indians on the plains and forest reaches of Canada. By 1887 the nearly one thousand Mounties maintained order over a vast region. With completion of the Canadian Pacific railway white settlers moved into the interior in sharply increasing numbers. The North West Mounted Police served all with quiet courage and friendly efficiency rather than raw power.

Within twenty years the Mounties earned and received support of courts and public unmatched by lawmen in the United States. Better law enforcement even contributed to immigration northward to Canada. Settlers preferred the dependable and equitable protection of a central force to local constables or vigilance committees. Indians, outlaws, and ordinary citizens alike came to respect the North West Mounted Police as upholders of the law.

In 1920 Parliament reorganized the force as a Royal Canadian Mounted Police for the entire country. Currently the Mounties operate on all levels of law enforcement. Their responsibilities extend from traffic control to national security. Many towns and most provinces in Canada do not maintain an independent law enforcement system; they contract for protection with the Mounted Police and consequently obtain the benefits of a well-trained and highly regarded force of lawmen at a minimum cost.

On the other border of the United States a far different pattern of police service emerged. Mexico, which enjoyed no tradition of democracy or slowly developed concepts of individual freedom, also faced an enduring frontier. The country experienced various foreign and internal dictatorships during the nineteenth century and possessed no real heritage of a citizen police. Dependence on the military for internal control left Mexico with frequent banditry and Indian depredations. According to legend, President Benito Juárez first determined to use former outlaws as policemen. With the offer of salaries higher than might be expected from robbery, the famous buckskin-clad *rurales* came into existence. Under Porfirio Díaz the unit achieved a reputation for ruthless enforcement of federal policy. The *rurales* constituted the only practical police force on Mexico's northwestern frontier. They battled Indians and bandit gangs, but additionally repressed resistance by *peones* in many parts of the nation.

Generally, Mexican authorities co-operated with peace officers from the United States as long as citizens of Mexico were not involved. Many extraditions could be accomplished in an informal manner; *rurales* and other troops sometimes joined in international hunts for noted desperadoes or renegade Indians. Similar procedures also existed with Canadian officials for the expeditious handling of potentially involved legal matters.

No discussion of Mexican frontier law enforcement is possible without mention of a unique personality—Colonel Emilio Kosterlitzky. Born in Russia about 1853, he apparently emigrated to serve briefly with the United States Army. By 1873 Kosterlitzky appeared in northwestern Mexico and joined the cavalry as a private. He quickly rose through the ranks to become commander of the feared *la cordada,* an elite mounted unit that ranged in strength along the frontier. Kosterlitzky retained many close friendships with various peace officers in Arizona and New Mexico and his assistance led directly to the capture of many outlaws and renegades.

Rurales under Kosterlitzky's command comprised one of the

most colorful forces operating in North America. They ordinarily wore uniforms of dark gray whipcord with black braid but when desiring to make an impression would change to the traditional *charro* costume with giant hats and decorations of gleaming silver. The appearance of *la cordada* in a town constituted a dramatic scene. Kosterlitzky would leave his coach on the trail and mount a white charger to lead a thundering cavalcade of well-disciplined and heavily armed riders.

After the 1911 departure of Díaz and outbreak of the massive Mexican social revolution, the *rurales* lost governmental support. Kosterlitzky managed to continue operations for several months but finally crossed the border at Nogales to surrender himself to the protection of United States forces. His friendships, experience, and fluency in several languages proved of significant worth in later years. The former commander of *la cordada* worked for the Department of Justice in Los Angeles prior to his death in 1928.[47]

The revolution completely changed Mexican law enforcement. Amid enduring social turmoil entirely new police systems replaced prior means of control. Nevertheless, strong federal and particularly military influence continued. While states and cities in modern Mexico have operationally independent police agencies, they retain centralized tendencies. Higher-ranking officials are ordinarily commissioned members of the armed forces. While law enforcement appears highly fragmented, it nonetheless can function with considerable efficiency. There is, for example, a special and well-qualified federal agency responsible for protection of banks. Governmental involvement and structural eminence serves as a cohesive element among the Mexican police. The *rurales*, disbanded during the revolution, now operate as a type of militia and arm of the dominant political party. Their influence is less obvious and exists at a different level from that of the past.

Experiences of various cultures demonstrate markedly divergent approaches to law enforcement. The North American frontier represented different problems and demanded assorted solutions in each social setting. Indians, the military, Canadians, and

Mexicans established related but distinctive police systems. A comparative survey reveals that law enforcement is largely a product of its heritage and custom. Where peace officers succeed in maintaining order and protecting society against elements within itself, they also possess public respect and unit pride. This requires far more than physical force and legal power. The best police agencies of the West, regardless of nationality, upheld fundamental standards of their culture with a firm humanity based upon mutual confidence. Such principles, though frequently ignored, remain fully applicable today.

"¡Alto, Federales!"

VIII

The federal government has been directly involved in western law enforcement since the initial phases of the frontier. The army orginally performed many functions of a civil police but eventually relinquished such duties to other agencies. With actual settlement of the land came additional needs for specialized systems to maintain order and protect property. The large role occupied by the United States government in the development of the West left an enduring legacy of dependence upon central power. Only Texas and California entered the Union with any pronounced heritage of independence and self-rule. The other regions of the West experienced many years of federal supervision before leaving Territorial status. This extended reliance on national support and control, while not always locally desired, contributed to the appearance of several types of police service sponsored directly by the United States.

Constitutional dual sovereignty posed the need for a means of national law enforcement with formation of the country. Establishment of a federal judiciary in 1789 demanded officers to perform certain police duties. Congress apparently relied upon precedents of English admiralty courts in creating appointed positions of marshals to carry out such tasks. By the middle of the nineteenth century these lawmen had acquired the primary duty of enforcement within the territories. Formation of regional governments included recognition of the marshal's authority. As typically worded for Idaho in 1863, "There shall also be a marshal for the territory appointed, who shall hold his office for four years, and until his successor shall be appointed and qualified, unless sooner removed by the President of the United States, and who shall execute all processes issuing from the said courts. . . ."[1]

While statehood somewhat altered the duties of marshals it did not change their political nature. Appointments were hotly disputed and the source of endless connivance. Marshals rarely attained office on the basis of simple honesty, law enforcement experience, or personal courage. With the exception of a few peace officers of note, such as Christian "Chris" Madsen in Oklahoma and Thomas Jefferson Carr in Wyoming, appointments occurred with reference to past political performance. Those loyal to the party and on good terms with representatives and judges stood out as likely prospects in an ordinary surplus of applicants. The nature and importance of Presidential selection is indicated by quite typical reactions to an opening in New Mexico during 1882:

It is said . . . that the resignation of U.S. Marshal John Sherman was demanded. His resignation is very fortunate for the people of New Mexico and none the less so for the Republican party. He belonged to a certain clique of republicans, who wanted to reform the party by appointing democrats to office. Charges of embezzlement had been repeatedly made against him and damaging reports by grand juries against him were the order of the day.[2]

. . .

The President is still holding off in the matter of the appointment of U.S. Marshal for New Mexico, although Mr. Sherman's resignation was received three weeks ago at the department of justice. It is understood, there are fifty one applicants with sixty four bushels of petitions and seventy three barrels of recommendations on hand. The President however is evidently waiting to give some of the back counties a chance, as the returns are not all in yet.[3]

Early marshals battled to maintain close ties with administration officials. Some, like Ben McCulloch of Texas, spent much time in Washington and managed to obtain lucrative appointments for close relatives and friends.

An insight into the attractions of office may be gathered from a survey of the early Colorado succession. During the first century of operation (1861–1961) twenty men held the position. The first territorial marshal, Copeland Townsend, arrived in the company of Governor William Gilpin. The lawman fought groups suspected of sympathy to the Confederacy but was himself accused of embezzling federal funds. Within a year his replacement, Alexander Cameron Hunt, placed Townsend under arrest and removed him from office. The new marshal had been judge of the people's court in Denver and distinguished himself by chasing outlaws in Colorado. Hunt subsequently became territorial governor under President Grant, but was removed from the higher post in 1869.

The third marshal, Uriah B. Holloway, served from 1866 to 1868. He resigned facing charges of larceny and passing counterfeit money. Next came the popular Mark A. Shaffenburg. As fourth federal marshal he held office for some eight years, but was finally convicted of making fraudulent claims against the government and sentenced to two years at Leavenworth penitentiary. Appointment of Charles P. Tompkins, who resigned within a year, brought the bleak history of the position under Territorial rule to an end.

With statehood in 1876 Colorado's federal marshals apparently improved somewhat in general quality. Philip P. "Old Peak" Wilcox, in office from 1877 to 1882, had been a successful attorney and subsequently became superintendent of the San Carlos Indian reservation. Zephamiah Turner Hill, who served under President Cleveland, was once active in leading the militia against striking miners, but later became editor of *Cosmopolitan* magazine in New York. Those appointed in later years included a wholesale liquor dealer, local politician, merchant and miner, lawyer, state representative, real estate agent, county assessor and rancher, hardware merchant and bank appraiser, sheriff, and soft drink manufacturer.[4] Obviously the popular image of the western federal marshal as an incorruptible fighting man evidences some distortion. And the early Colorado experience is by no means unique.

Federal marshals could select and command their deputies, whose ranks sharply increased in time of domestic disorder. During the great rail strike of 1922, for example, over three thousand "specials" were sworn into service. Today such personnel are covered by civil service regulations within standards of the Department of Justice. Some confusion results from popular usage of the term "marshal." Many town officials carry the title and federal deputies are often still addressed by the same reference.

Authority to appoint deputies gave the marshals a sturdy lever of political patronage. They ordinarily selected men for designated office or field positions and could also issue temporary commissions in emergencies. Regular selections required a formal report of the individual's name, age, residence, occupation, and proposed assignment. Bureaucracy is not a recent innovation. Marshals received instructions to employ men with great care in 1898 and were warned that appointments "other than as the public interest may require will be canceled."[5]

The number of deputies varied greatly with the district. In certain parts of the East a marshal might have only two or three positions to fill. But in the West an entirely different situation existed. A single district might contain sixty or seventy authorized office and field deputies under such unusual situations as those within the Indian Territory at the end of the nineteenth century. Most western regions encompassed vast geographic expanses and required the marshal to scatter his force accordingly. In 1894, for example, W. K. Meade of the Arizona Territory concentrated men in Tucson and Phoenix, but also placed deputies at Florence, Winslow, Prescott, Williams, Solomonsville, Bisbee, Yuma, Globe, and Tombstone.[6] Upon such isolated officers the reputation of the federal marshals most clearly rests.

Deputies originally made their living from fees, routine expenses, and occasional rewards. The United States government refused to pay incidental costs commonly incurred in secret investigations. Most districts, nevertheless, operated at a consistent profit as fees tended to produce very large sources of revenue even after payment of clerical and administrative salaries. In 1882 Nebraska reported gross earnings of $9,829.15 and office expenses of $5,043.32 for a net of $4,785.83. In the same year Utah showed comparable figures of $6,801.78, $1,516.50, and $5,285.28. During this period the total costs for marshals' offices soared across the nation. Expenses leaped amazingly from $25,502.87 in 1878 to $610,731.21 in 1881, due in part to the upkeep of prisoners in Arizona and New Mexico.[7]

Rising costs prompted efforts toward the close of the nineteenth century to effect maximum economy. Deputies had to obtain vouchers for lunch, file reports of any fare reductions on railroads, and make statements concerning delays in transit. Although officers were required to list all expenses when traveling, they could charge their account only $2 a day. Special restrictions existed on expenses relating to persons in custody:

It is the duty of the marshal personally to see that guards are employed only when necessary. For short trips and daylight travel guards are usually unnecessary, unless of the number and known dangerous character of the prisoners. The action of any marshal in allowing his deputies to employ guards, except in plain cases of need, will not be favorably regarded by the Department. . . .

Prisoners in the custody of an officer must be subsisted in the most economical manner. Extravagant charges will not be allowed.[8]

A major problem in remuneration arose over the use of costs and fees. The marshals and their deputies originally received compensation largely determined through individual effort and initiative. The system could lead to misuse of power as indicated in a government report of 1881:

Instances have been brought to my attention where numerous prosecutions have been instituted for the most trivial violations of law, and the arrested parties taken long distances and subjected to great inconvenience and expense, not in the interest of the government, but apparently for no other reason than to make costs.[9]

By the 1890s critics recommended that marshals and their deputies be placed on fixed salaries with fees to go into the public treasury. Such proposals met strong opposition from those who felt that regular pay would merely promote inefficiency and inequity of compensation in the field. Reform finally won the day and the old fee system allowing deputies to retain portions of their earnings underwent thorough modification. "Under the act of May 28, 1896, United States Marshals receive annual salaries which are fixed by law and paid monthly by the Department of Justice, and are allowed in business, actual and necessary expenses for lodging and subsistence, not exceeding $4 per day, and actual necessary traveling expenses."[10] The new scheme meant that fees would not go directly to the individual officer concerned but field deputies continued to obtain a portion of charges for service of civil or criminal process. In fact, double fees were authorized for Oregon, Nevada, New Mexico, Arizona, Idaho, Wyoming, and North Dakota.[11]

In unorganized regions under United States control the federal deputy marshals sometimes served as ordinary peace officers. With the development of county governments and subsequent statehood their activities naturally fell into a far more restricted sphere as local lawmen appeared to fill immediate needs. Popular representations of marshals investigating ordinary crimes of violence and driving out local badmen are almost entirely incorrect. These were jobs for the normally uniformed community police even in the famous trail and mining towns. Federal deputies spent most of their working time issuing and serving subpoenas, returning trial venires, conducting sales of property, locating witnesses, empaneling juries, and executing innumerable writs and warrants. Most of this activity concerned civil rather than criminal matters.

At times the western marshal's work encompassed high adventure more closely resembling romanticized fiction. Deputies could be dispatched whenever federal law was either threatened or broken. Marshals frequently acted to safeguard the mails and railroad property; train robbers might be chased for hundreds of miles across several state or territorial borders. Unusual circumstances brought federal lawmen into action in many dramatic instances. Deputy United States marshals worked for twenty years to trace, arrest, and finally execute the leader of Utah's "Mountain Meadows Massacre." The investigation, which was often thwarted by Mormon citizens, spanned the Civil War and came to an end on the original site of the religious battle.

Another assignment of a deputy marshal in the West prompted a very significant Constitutional decision. A domestic relations matter led the colorful David S. Terry of California to threaten United States Supreme Court Justice Stephen Field with horsewhipping. The federal marshal of the region assigned a special deputy, David Neagle, to guard the justice and his wife. On the train from Los Angeles to San Francisco Justice Field and his protector encountered Terry in the dining car. When a fist fight developed, the deputy marshal tried to intervene. At this point Terry drew a knife but Neagle fired twice and killed the assailant. The sheriff of San Joaquin County then placed the lawman in custody on a charge of murder and the case rose to the Supreme Court of the United States, with Field taking no part because of personal involvement. In 1890 the highest bench ordered Neagle released; the federal executive had implied power to preserve the peace, the deputy acted in line of duty, and the state accordingly lacked jurisdiction.[12]

Many of the difficulties encountered by marshals in the West involved their prisoners. Most areas lacked suitable local or state facilities and no federal correctional system existed. The marshals therefore operated both jails and territorial prisons; inmates could also be leased for private employment and commercial profit. Terrible conditions within the federal institutions and among the prisoners on hire existed well into the twentieth century and may still be found in local jails commonly used to temporarily house prisoners of the national government.

Persons in custody frequently required transfer between courts and places of confinement, with such movements occasionally constituting periods of real danger. When United States Marshal

Hal L. Gosling of the Western District of Texas needed to transport two prisoners from Austin to San Antonio in 1885, he took the usual precautions. James Pitts and Charles Yeager, convicted stage robbers, were handcuffed together for the train trip. Marshal Gosling and his deputies permitted the wives, mothers, and sisters of the prisoners to accompany the group returning from trial. Apparently the women supplied weapons to Pitts and Yeager, for suddenly they commenced a fusillade in the smoking car. Gosling died at the scene and Deputy John Manning received serious wounds. A posse from New Braunfels soon gathered and took up the trail of the two escaped prisoners. Pitts's corpse was discovered only two hundred yards from the scene of the shooting; deputies captured the wounded Yeager about eight miles away.[13]

A few years later another dramatic incident occurred in the federal transport of prisoners. In 1889 the five Marlow brothers had been arrested on federal charges and held at Graham, Texas, after a shooting incident that left a sheriff dead. A mob attacked the jail but the rioters were apparently driven off by club-wielding prisoners. The federal marshal for the district dispatched Ed W. Johnson, a one-armed deputy, with orders to transport the Marlows to Weatherford. This officer, in turn, selected several unfit guards, chained the brothers together, and commenced the fifty-mile journey. His cavalcade, perhaps by design, rode directly into a night ambush. Johnson and the guards promptly surrendered their weapons, but the prisoners seized arms and resisted attack unaided by their official protectors. Alfred, Aaron, and Llewelyn Marlow were killed while George and Charles removed their shackles by hacking off the limbs of the dead and, although badly injured, managed to escape the ambush. Although convicted years later, the lynchers were never punished; the surviving Marlows eventually obtained their freedom and went on to a deserved fame in North Texas.[14]

Few of the West's more famous lawmen received appointments as full United States marshals, but many of them served as deputies. James Butler "Wild Bill" Hickok first turned to law enforcement after service in the Civil War. He worked sporadically as a deputy federal marshal in Kansas between 1866 and 1869. Hickok's primary duty then consisted of chasing army deserters and suspected horse thieves at Fort Riley. The military and marshals often co-operated closely along the frontier with the lawmen and soldiers, sharing problems and solutions. Hickok's experience as a scout and army escort rider well suited the role of a federal deputy, but the lure of politics and night life eventually drew him toward the trail towns of Kansas and employment as a local peace officer.

Many marshals selected their men from the ranks of those already experienced in law enforcement. Wyatt Earp had gained considerable notoriety in Kansas as a community policeman; he seemed a sensible choice as deputy federal marshal at Tombstone, Arizona, where he worked briefly for the sheriff. The United States lawman typically retained other interests; Earp remained an active partner and occasional dealer in a saloon. Simultaneously he worked as an agent of Wells Fargo to handle robbery investigations. The western express and railroad companies maintained extremely close and usually cordial relationships with federal officers. Earp's famous problems in Tombstone, however, resulted not from outside employment but from a continuing political controversy. His conflict with local elements, which festered over the selection of the county sheriff, reached a dramatic climax in the legendary 1881 gunfight at the O.K. Corral. Tombstone warfare continued for many months, but the Earp faction finally left the territory and barely managed to escape extradition from Colorado. The former deputy went on to considerable success as a gambler, sportsman, and developer of oil and mining properties. He died quietly in Los Angeles in 1929.

Although active throughout all the West, the federal marshals took their most notable role as the frontier closed in what is now Oklahoma. The expanse reserved for the Indian tribes existed for many years under the jurisdiction of the federal district for Western Arkansas; by 1889 conditions of lawlessness and a growing population led to division of the region into two enormous administrative areas. Thomas B. Needles received his appointment as first marshal of the Indian Territory; William S. Lurty obtained the comparable office for the Oklahoma Territory, immediately to the west. Needles held his post for four long and difficult years, when the equally durable James J. McAlester arrived to replace him.[15]

Oklahoma Territory proved to be perhaps the most challenging appointment in the nation for federal marshal. Lurty, from Vermont, quickly decided that the plains offered no personal future; he resigned in less than three months to be succeeded by his chief deputy, William L. "Bill" Grimes. The new marshal, a Republican political leader, experienced some difficulty finding men to work in the field and was removed from office in 1893. Evett D. Nix received the next appointment. He had been a wholesale grocer at Guthrie and determined to bring the orderly procedures of business into Oklahoma law enforcement. The 32-year-old marshal summoned a large force of deputies for a meeting and outlined policies to be followed. With his father as chief clerk and other relatives to assist him officially, Nix directed operations for three years. He maintained contact with most deputies through weekly reports and letters; his men, five of whom were to lose their lives, responded with some 60,000 arrests.[16]

After 1895 the succession of marshals in Oklahoma became increasingly complex. Expanding population and a heavy work load led to creation of additional federal districts. By 1903 the old Indian Territory encompassed no less than four separate offices:[17]

District	Deputies		Salaries	Gross Fees
	Office	Field		
Northern	12	15	$12,717.33	$17,748.80
Central	7	31	12,630.10	24,269.49
Southern	12	22	15,509.82	31,711.58
Western	10	21	13,317.95	22,104.55

Marshals in Oklahoma often had dozens of emergency deputies to reinforce regular office and field personnel. Some districts experienced periods when a majority of employees held special and temporary commissions. Deputies came with diverse qualifications and skills; many were recruited from the rougher elements of the territories. Several members of the famous Dalton gang worked as deputies before turning to bootlegging and bank robbery. One of the officers assigned to Cherokee lands promptly killed his immediate predecessor and served a long sentence at Leavenworth as a consequence. Troubles at Muldrow between white and Indian factions prompted Thomas B. Needles to dispatch a deputy described later by a resident as "a mean man and a very dishonorable fellow who drank, gambled and defied the activities of the church."[18] The lawman proved so corrupt that citizens petitioned for his eventual removal; a successor to the post soon died in a gunfight with settlers who were subsequently acquitted.

Deputies had many duties in reference to the Indian tribes and some agencies obtained commissions for tribal officers directly from the federal marshal. Thus, Reverend Dennis Roberts, a Choctaw convicted of stealing a pig, received thirty lashes and "That make good fellow out of him, so he 'point hisself a United States Marshal."[19] The presence of deputies on reservation lands proved expeditious and beneficial. Indian agents requested special commissions without pay for their dependable employees, reasoning they would serve as a deterrent to crime and disorder.

Appointments as deputy federal marshals went to all sorts of men. Charles B. Rhodes, a former schoolteacher in the territory, knew many fugitives as students rather than outlaws. The typical deputy, however, came with primary early experience in law enforcement. Many had relatives in federal employment and most lived in the region for several years before receiving their commissions as United States officers. A surprising number of the deputies were Negro. Apart from a few policemen in urban areas, however, the black peace officer was a rarity in the frontier West. In Oklahoma the presence of many former slaves, existence of Indian subcultures, and the continued dominance of federal authority led to commissioning many Negroes. These included Grant Johnson, Ike Rogers, Ed Robinson, Wiley Escoe, Robert Love, Edward Jefferson, and Bass Reeves. The Negro deputies performed all of the usual duties, often with outstanding valor and distinction. While many were themselves former slaves with virtually no educational background, they successfully carried on the functions of office and had relatively little attention paid to color.[20]

A trio of deputies made a particularly lasting imprint in territorial history. Bill Tilghman, Chris Madsen, and Heck Thomas constituted Oklahoma's "Three Guardsmen" as the nineteenth century drew to a close. Born respectively in Kansas, Denmark, and Georgia, they became fellow deputies by quite different routes. Tilghman first worked as a buffalo hunter and city marshal. Madsen immigrated to the United States about 1870 and joined the army. Thomas fought for the Confederacy and then drifted to Texas to become an express company messenger. The three men were federal deputies together, although rarely as a team, in the 1890s for the western Oklahoma Territory. They battled whisky smugglers, investigated family feuds and racial conflicts then raging in the region, carried out extraditions of fugitives from other jurisdictions, and chased gangs like that of Bill Doolin.

For many years Tilghman, Madsen, and Thomas remained active in law enforcement. While permitted to retain their federal commissions, they eventually obtained other related employment. Tilghman held several positions as city policeman and sheriff but was twice frustrated in efforts to be selected as a full United States marshal. Only Madsen received such a position through a temporary court appointment in 1910. Thomas became Lawton's chief of police but lost an election and returned to federal service. The life of each man came to an end in Oklahoma. Tilghman was killed by a United States prohibition agent at Cromwell in 1924. Madsen continued to work for the federal government for many years; he died peacefully at Guthrie in 1947. Thomas suffered a heart attack as a volunteer fireman and died at Lawton in 1912.

In the early days of the Indian and Oklahoma territories deputy marshals ventured far afield from their district federal courts. The officers usually moved in small groups and might travel for several weeks and cover hundreds of miles. A scarcity of jails necessitated special needs for transport of prisoners, as those suspected of serious crimes had to be taken to court for eventual hearings and trial. The deputies utilized wagons with special rings mounted in the sideboards. Lem F. Blevins, an early settler at Cherokee Town, recalled the scene:

> I have seen them come through there on their way to Fort Smith, Arkansas, with forty or fifty prisoners. Some of the prisoners would be wounded and they would haul them in wagons and drive the ones that were able to walk in front of the wagons like cattle.[21]

While on the trail the deputies kept outriders in front and behind the cavalcade to prevent escapes. At night the prisoners were chained together, secured to convenient trees or the wagon wheels, and provided with blankets in cold weather.

The obvious inconvenience of transport prompted the solution of taking justice into the frontier. Marshal Leo E. Bennett, once superintendent at the Union Agency, directed operations of the "brush court" active in the Indian Territory around the turn of the century. Deputies accompanied United States commissioners, who could hold primary judicial hearings, on regular circuits with tents or borrowed stores as courthouses. Prisoners could have original charges presented and bail set without the necessity of distant transport. Those needed for full trial would then be taken on to regular seats of justice.

By the beginning of the twentieth century Oklahoma had earned the reputation of a refuge for frontier outlaws. Fugitives from state law could achieve immunity in the Indian Territory, for they could be extradited only for federal offenses. Chris Madsen described the situation confronting the early marshals:

> The opening of the country to settlement and the closing of many of the large cattle pastures, left a number of cowboys out of employment. They had been used to the free and roaming life on the open prairie, and they could not content themselves to be confined to a farm half a mile square, so they soon took up other vocations, principally peddling whiskey to the Indians, rustling cattle, robbing trains and banks, as they advanced from one of those crafts to a higher class.

Hundreds, yes, thousands, of contests over the land which has been opened, soon flooded the land office and the Courts with cases, imposing additional work on the marshal's force, as in the majority of cases perjury would be charged, and indictments presented for the offense.[22]

Parts of the territory were infested with settlers highly suspicious of federal officers. The overwhelming majority of citizens demonstrated no truly criminal behavior, but many had personal reasons for mistrusting the law and developed a sympathy with fugitives. R. B. Holden remembered conditions on the Oklahoma frontier as follows:

> In those days all horses were barefooted. If we discovered a horse's track which showed that the horse was shod we knew a United States Marshal was in the neighborhood. The word was spread abroad that those for whom the marshal was looking could hide or run away. . . .
>
> . . .
>
> I went to the Choctaw Nation after a bunch of cattle and I noticed signs printed with black paint on boards nailed to trees along the M.K.& T. right-of-way on the west side of the railroad, which said, "Mr. United States Deputy Marshal, this is the dead line. When you cross this line you take your life in your own hands." These signs were placed by the outlaws and desperadoes to keep the United States Marshals from invading their territory, but the marshals paid no attention to these warnings.[20]

Federal deputies penetrated the farthest regions of their districts and sometimes operated for months in the field. They tried to remain on constant guard, for attacks might come from ambush. During meals at hotels or stations the deputies often kept watch and ate with weapons across their knees. In especially dangerous areas they traveled in teams using wagons with one officer facing to the rear. Frequently the deputies resorted to investigations involving decoys and disguise. George Louis Mann, who worked as an aide on some expeditions, has this to say:

> We would set a course, then follow the Indian trails as far as they went our way, then cut across the hills until we came to a trail that was going our way and follow that one as far as it went. We would make camp and leave a man or two with the wagon while the others

looked the country over for outlaws. At night we made our beds in places where we could be near the wagons in the safest places we could find.

We went disguised all the time; I wore dresses a lot of the time.[24]

To comprehend the challenges then facing federal deputies in Oklahoma is difficult. They enjoyed no local public support and, apart from the army, could anticipate little assistance from other officers. Dew M. Wisdom, superintendent of the Union Agency in 1895, recognized the following problems to be overcome by lawmen of the time:

The dangers which confront officers in running down and capturing outlaws have not been fully appreciated by the powers that be. The outlaw is a dangerous fellow to meet. He goes well armed and well mounted, and is a crack shot, and enters upon his business with the avowed purpose of dying with his boots on. It is, therefore, not to be wondered at that officers are often chary to encounter him, since it means little less than death to the one party or the other, and perhaps to both.[25]

To the deputies their dangerous occupation only amounted to work. They demonstrated more concern with bureaucratic regulation and regular pay than fear of personal attack. The early marshals created new rules and regulations with which to operate; they had to invent systems for keeping books, devise printed forms, and sign individual contracts with private parties providing services. Their field deputies meanwhile sought supplementary income. Rewards offered an opportunity, but such often proved difficult to collect or divide. As a consequence the lawmen entered into formal agreements among themselves and with their sources of information. A typical handwritten contract between William "Bill" Tilghman and James D. Ford, signed at Guthrie in 1897, concerned the standing reward of $300 for each offender involved in Wells Fargo robberies. In formal language the agreement specified that Ford would receive $80 for every offender whom Tilghman, as a result of information supplied, could bring in for reward.[26]

Deputy marshals enforced many unpopular laws reaching into

the home. In addition to preventing gaming and dispensation of contraband alcohol they conducted investigations of sexual impropriety, including charges of adultery and fornication. Indians might be forced to marry, while white settlers also resented interference in personal affairs. The federal government even forbade the cutting of timber in much of the territory. This created a nearly intolerable housing situation and did nothing to better the image of the deputies.

Early settlers in Oklahoma developed a strong and often reasonable antipathy to the methods used by federal officers. Most unpopular were searches for illegal whisky. Some deputies employed operatives to seek out and implicate innocent parties. Other officers arrested individuals against whom no real case might be made in order to collect fees. In certain instances the lawmen resorted to clear entrapment by encouraging violations or engaged in other highly suspicious techniques.[27] Such conditions naturally led to opposition from the public. Elijah Conger held views quite common at the time. He said,

The U.S. Marshals were the most uncanny and unliked humans in the Indian Territory, and no method was left out that they would not resort to to arrest some immigrant, usually for whiskey. While one man was searching the outfit another would be planting whiskey someplace on it . . . I have seen them wait until they had ten or twelve chained up before taking them to Fort Smith. Sometimes it would be a week before they could catch, I suppose, what they called their bag limit . . . I guess we kept them supplied was the reason they never bothered us. They would drink with us and did not have a squak coming.[28]

There is a tendency to assume that frontier justice was quick and sure. Popular representations of early western courts and magistrates leave an image of those accused being subjected to procedures far different from today's involved criminal actions. Such a common comparative impression is quite inaccurate, as frontier Oklahoma clearly indicates.

In a span of more than twenty years the federal court for Western Arkansas, under the famous "Hanging Judge" Isaac

Parker, tried some 13,000 major criminal cases. Many of these arose in the Indian Territory and involved the deputy marshals, for no other state or federal court had jurisdiction during most of the period. While Parker pronounced 172 death sentences, only 88 of which actually took place, approximately 4,000 defendants were acquitted.[29] The typical modern court hearing similar cases convicts approximately 90 per cent of the time. In short, an accused party enjoyed a better chance of being released in the most feared court on the frontier than in today's ordinary criminal tribunal of primary and original record.

Lesser charges went before grand juries and United States commissioners within the territory itself. Defendants in early Oklahoma possessed most of the rights now in effect with the added benefit of an ordinarily sympathetic public. The grand jury for the Second Judicial District of the Indian Territory had 66 routine cases presented for indictment in its April Term, 1893. Charges included 29 for introducing liquor, thirteen for larceny, five for gaming, five for dispensing alcohol to minors and lesser numbers for slander, assault, carrying weapons, burglary, fornication, disturbing the peace, and false pretenses. Of all indictments sought the grand jury returned only 47 true bills, nineteen charges being dismissed.[30]

At the trial stage, before commissioners, approximately 30 per cent of indictments resulted in *nolle prosequi*, judicial dismissal, or findings of not guilty.[31] These lesser courts in the Indian Territory could and did give sentence of several years' imprisonment, but most successful prosecutions resulted in fines. Gaming and simple disturbances of the peace ordinarily received punishments of less than $20, while more serious offenses such as introducing liquor and possession of illegal weapons might require payment of $100 or more.[32] By today's standards, considering general inflation, the fines seem heavy; but overall administration of criminal justice has, nonetheless, seen no major changes. Disorderly conduct and petty larceny constituted very high proportions of the frontier dockets, as is true in current lower courts throughout the nation.

In 1907 the federal role in Oklahoma law enforcement under-went total change. Statehood ended the long rule of United States officers and terminated the most colorful era of deputy marshals. The number of federal lawmen dwindled quickly, with most of those released finding employment with county, city, or railroad police forces. Former lawmen organized the Ex-Deputy United States Marshals Association to demand monthly pensions from the government. They held meetings for many years but were frustrated in their financial efforts. As old functions of the mar-shals came to an end throughout the West, federal law enforce-ment moved into new and more specialized fields.

Customs duties originally provided the United States govern-ment with its primary source of income. As the boundaries of the nation extended westward, collectors were appointed to in-sure adequate revenues. By the middle of the nineteenth century it had become obvious that the Mexican border would be a sensitive area for smuggling. In 1854 the first collector of customs at El Paso received authorization to employ mounted inspectors to search for items imported illegally. Few men served in such capacity during the next generation, but they formed the first true border patrol in United States history. In 1869 only Edmund Stine in Arizona and J. M. Lujan in Texas' Big Bend were at work along the entire frontier.[33] Between 1884 and 1894 the number of mounted inspectors increased from four to twelve; they averaged monthly salaries of slightly more than $100. Three years later the small force entered civil service and, until a respite in 1906, ap-pointments were made by examination, "open to all citizens of the United States without regard to race or to political or religious affiliations."[34] Applicants had to be twenty years of age with preference given legal residents of the district. The 25-point writ-ten examination for 1899 equated third-grade skills in spelling, arithmetic, letter writing, penmanship, and copying. But 75 points could be gained from "Experience and Special Qualifi-cations":

. . . determined from the evidence furnished by supplementary state-ments and vouchers which the applicant must submit, showing his record for honesty, great physical endurance, bravery, horsemanship, and marksmanship; his knowledge and experience in the management of cattle; and his ability as a brand reader.[35]

In 1862 Congress placed a new burden on federal border patrolmen when it forbade the "coolie" trade—men could themselves be contraband. Twenty years later the first of several Chinese exclusion acts went into effect. Customs officials assumed responsibility for enforcing immigration restrictions and appointed "Chinese Inspectors" along the Mexican boundary. Between 1891 and 1913 the district federal court at El Paso heard 1,236 cases under the Chinese exclusion statutes. Most involved pathetic individuals trying to slip through the customs and immigration stations along the border. When Inspector George B. Duvall caught Ah Lee wandering through at El Paso wearing a Mexican blanket in 1892, the Chinese claimed he simply did not know of the international line. Suspects ordinarily asserted legal residence in the United States and temporary absence from the country to visit relatives.[36]

Although Chinese aliens posed little overt danger, considerable numbers persisted in crossing the Mexican border. In 1904 the government appointed a roving immigration inspector with no specific station. For a district extending from Texas to California a man of unique qualifications seemed required and Jeff Davis Milton appeared a logical selection. A former Texas Ranger, deputy marshal, town policeman, and agent for Wells Fargo, Milton knew the Southwest thoroughly and combined self-reliance with humanity. The mounted immigration guard, as first of his kind, had to battle smuggling gangs and then pull the teeth or set the bones of injured aliens. Most Chinese were innocent pawns of organized criminals who would sometimes leave their human cargo to die in the desert. Milton rescued as much as he arrested; for these services he received $5 a day with $3.50 for expenses. During World War I the inspector acquired an automobile for use in parts of the Southwest and he sometimes had special assignments far from Arizona and New Mexico. Milton remained in federal employ until 1932; at the age of seventy he retired on an annuity of $100 a month.[37]

During Jeff Milton's long tour of duty the border patrol underwent many changes. The Mexican revolution dramatically altered conditions of federal law enforcement in the Southwest. Great numbers of refugees fled north to the United States. For a brief while the National Guard helped patrol the border, but their withdrawal left the region without sufficient forces in the field. Then, in the 1920s, new laws on prohibition of alcohol and additional categories of restricted immigrants further increased the difficulties of protecting international boundaries.

In 1924 Congress authorized formation of a new land border patrol under the Bureau of Immigration. For many years this force operated parallel to mounted customs guards, although their functions frequently overlapped. Both units underwent rapid expansion. By 1929 the immigration watchmen numbered 670; their counterparts in customs totaled 504. These were the largest federal police agencies then in operation.[38]

Between World War I and World War II the twin border patrols performed some of the most dangerous law enforcement work to be found within the country. The officers usually moved in pairs, heavily armed. Many districts could be best covered on horseback, and pack animals were trained to follow without a lead rope so the riders would have no encumbrances in case of sudden attack. Patrolmen used informants and might themselves lie in wait for days to trap smugglers or illegal immigrants. A successful raid or stake-out sometimes suddenly advanced into violence. After the traditional warning cry, *"¡Alto, Federales!,"* a fusillade of shots might always be anticipated.

The old customs border patrol continued on active duty until 1948. With discontinuance of the original force of mobile inspectors and watchmen the Immigration and Naturalization Service received additional responsibilities. The modern United States Border Patrol, with some 1,500 authorized positions, constitutes a tightly knit and largely self-sufficient organization with its own intelligence network. Basic operations continue to emphasize line watch on the Mexican border, but officers possess authority to enter private land, summon citizen aid, and conduct investigations within reasonable distances of international boundaries.[39]

On the closing western frontier many federal law enforcement agencies played active roles. The Secret Service, which received its first formal appropriation in 1860, became the country's "national detectives." While the suppression of counterfeiting remained the primary task, agents performed all sorts of special investigations for various departments of government. But since the force was small, with less than sixty agents in 1907 for the entire nation, it had to call upon deputy marshals or territorial officers for assistance in the West.[40]

In 1908 Congress restricted operations of the Secret Service and created the United States Bureau of Investigation. In the next sixteen years the new federal agency earned a reputation for corruption and arbitrary action. Opposition culminated after highly disputed federal raids against "subversives" in 1917 and 1920. Hundreds of suspects were subjected to unconscionable handling and held in very poor facilities at Wichita, Sacramento, and Chicago for many months.[41] In 1924 the government belatedly reorganized its controversial detective force as the Federal Bureau of Investigation under J. Edgar Hoover.

Postal law enforcement officers appeared early in the nineteenth century with a heritage extending into colonial days. In the West protection of the mails from outright robbery or destruction constituted a major and continuing problem. Before the Civil War officials took special precautions with postal shipments in the Southwest. As reported in 1857, "The U.S. mail train [from Fort Duncan to Santa Fe] is attended by a mounted guard of six men, armed with Sharp's rifles and Colt's repeaters. Their pay is forty dollars a month. A man is lost on nearly every trip out and back, but usually through his own indiscretion."[42] In later years federal guards rode the mail cars on trains and even carried special revolvers designed for use at close quarters.

By the twentieth century two new units for United States law enforcement emerged. The vast national forests and parks demanded a specialized police; the military could not be expected to provide all necessary protection. In 1905 employees of both the forest and national park services received concurrent authority to make arrests for violations of laws and regulations.[43] The small number of men available for assignment caused many problems in the West. Seasonal work with no general standards for employment and a common lack of co-ordination in the reserved areas proved major handicaps. Yet the lonely life of the early rangers attracted individuals of unusual courage and dedication. Captain C. C. Smith, on detached service from the 14th Cavalry, described them in his report from Sequoia National Park in 1908. Requirements for ranger service were numerous:

He must be an experienced mountaineer and woodsman, familiar with camp life, a good horseman and packer, capable of dealing with all classes of people; should know the history of the parks and their topography, something of forestry, zoology, and ornithology, and be capable of handling laboring parties on road, trail, telephone, bridge, and building construction. These men, in the performance of their duties, travel on horseback from 3,000 to 6,000 miles a year, must face dangers, exposure, and the risk of being sworn into the penitentiary through the evil designs of others.[44]

Acting Superintendent Smith also commented on the park visitors as follows:

The tourists in general are inclined to observe the park rules and regulations, but now and then there are some exceptions. During the present season there have been 3 ejectments—two of individuals and one of a family, and 2 rifles were taken up for retention until the end of the season, the owners having tampered with the seals.[45]

The rangers performed many tasks. They had to combat fires, remove trespassers, and face occasional threats of personal attack. In some instances they obtained special commissions from local police agencies to assist in investigations and patrol. S. B. M. Young, superintendent at Yellowstone in 1907, pointed out the diverse problems confronting his few available men:

Evidence of poaching in former unfrequented portions of the park difficult of access have been found, particularly in the northwest corner, where within the last fortnight a trapper's cabin, supplied with provisions, cooking utensils, and bedding, was found. The contents were burned and the cabin destroyed. . . .

. . .

One woman pled guilty through the telephone to writing her name on the hot water formation and was fined $10.50, including costs.[46]

During World War I rangers assumed greatly expanded law enforcement functions. The soaring numbers of travelers in following decades have placed ever-growing demands on park and forest police. Isolated conditions in the West sometimes also require federal officers to provide emergency assistance beyond their formal jurisdictions. Today, with annual visits by millions of visitors, emphasis is placed upon public safety as well as simple protection of natural resources. Rangers frequently undertake extremely hazardous rescues and now deal with involved traffic situations. To some extent law enforcement in a national reserve resembles any community police operation complicated by truly unique geographical settings. In 1969 the National Park Service had approximately 775 authorized ranger positions, supplemented seasonally with assistants. During 1968 it reported 2,585 major crimes and 20,504 minor violations, with about 80 per cent occurring in the West. Driving and parking transgressions now constitute the most frequent offenses, but "feeding/molesting bears" still accounted for 1,330 investigations in one year. While rangers ordinarily deal with minor infractions they occasionally must handle charges of rape, robbery, murder, child abandonment, burglary, and other serious crimes.[47]

Within a century the number and specialization of federal police agencies increased markedly. In the parks and forests, along the borders, and servicing the courts may be found thousands of national officers. Although no federal force has ever possessed general police power, the United States government has long furnished an underpinning to law enforcement in the American West. Vast areas of sparse population and a continuing involvement of central power would seem to indicate no reduction in scale or propriety. Current deputies, patrolmen, agents, and rangers merely carry on the tradition established by territorial officers of generations past.

EPILOGUE. "Do Not Forsake Me"

The western peace officer is better known through fiction than fact. America responded to conditions of frontier law enforcement by establishing a legend of lasting significance. Popular images sometimes took on tangible aspects with effects quite as pronounced as those occurring in reality. Such has been the story of the western lawman. Neither gone nor forgotten, he has been transformed, while the fiction of yesterday displays a tendency to alter the fact of today. The history of peace officers on the frontier is totally intertwined with popular though frequently mistaken concepts. It is possible to divide but no longer to separate truth from myth. The two have most assuredly not become one, but they have blended to such a degree that an analysis of the former cannot approach completion without mention of the latter.

Americans displayed great interest in stories of the West, its reputed lawlessness, and those who worked to control disorder. The frontier still remained in flux when enterprising writers discovered the basic material and wide appeal of stories on sheriffs, marshals, and rangers. Early tales started a distorted image of western lawlessness and prepared a foundation for mistaken concepts of a later time.

Some of the legends on frontier peace officers originated before the Civil War, with fiction preceding written history. The Texas Rangers achieved notoriety for their campaigns against various factions attempting to undermine public order. Within a few years another tendency developed in the form of popularized personalities. George Ward Nichols initiated one cult with an 1867 magazine article on "Wild Bill." A probably imaginary hotel interview with James Butler Hickok, miscalled Hitchcock at the time, supposedly produced a colorful scene:

> "I would like to see you shoot."
> "Would yer?" replied the scout, drawing his revolver; and approaching the window, he pointed to a letter O in a sign board which was fixed to the stonewall of a building on the other side of the way.
> "That sign is more than fifty yards away. I will put these six balls into the inside of a circle, which isn't bigger than a man's heart."
> In an off-hand way, and without sighting the pistol with his eye, he discharged the six shots of his revolver. I afterwards saw that all the six bullets had entered the circle.[1]

Such fantastic misrepresentations became the main element in a great stream of magazine articles and "dime novels" of the later nineteenth century.

Edward Z. C. Judson (Ned Buntline), an imaginative writer of adventure stories, ventured West to search for characters after the Civil War. He found numerous personalities who have subsequently become part of the popular American heritage. Buntline wrote scores of pieces, only a few of which dealt directly with peace officers, but he transformed the marshals of Kansas trail towns into enduring national heroes. Wyatt Earp and Hickok became known throughout the country; the latter even appeared in several plays but soon discovered his limitations as a thespian.

Writers of Western fiction in the late nineteenth and early twentieth centuries tended to present peace officers in a rather rigid mold. Alfred Henry Lewis, George Pattulo, Emerson

Hough, Zane Grey, and others portrayed lawmen as gallant young men chosen in time of desperate need on the basis of personal bravery. They usually required their heroes to undertake involved secret investigations concluding with dramatic gunbattles. But other authors presented conditions in different and somewhat more realistic form. In Owen Wister's precedent-setting *The Virginian* of 1902, formal law enforcement played no significant part with emphasis accorded vigilantism. Hamlin Garland made his sheriffs (for such office holders became dominant in Western fiction) more palpable personalities with problems apart from those of duty. The novels and short stories of Eugene Manlove Rhodes took still another approach, frequently casting the lawman as a villain and secret member of an organized gang of criminals. Despite the authenticity of his settings, he routinely showed fugitives as heroes and helped initiate a peculiar but popular pattern of good-badmen.

Before 1900 many western peace officers acquired a clear awareness of their popular image and they sometimes added to the evolving mystique. No figure serves as a better illustration than Francis Joseph Wattron of Arizona. Born and orphaned in Missouri, he undertook early training for the priesthood but made his way west in his early twenties. Wattron served as sheriff of Navajo County, Arizona Territory, from 1897 to 1900. He maintained a drugstore and bar while generally allowing his chief deputy to perform the routine functions of office. But Wattron also knew how to do his work with showmanship; he kept a giant bloodhound and wore a diamond encrusted badge of solid gold. The chief deputy, as befitted his position, had to manage with one of solid silver. Prior to his death in 1905—from an overdose of laudanum—Frank Wattron lived the role of a frontier sheriff, generous and gregarious by nature with a colorful and somewhat unusual sense of humor.[2] The latter quality became obvious in a furor over a hanging at the turn of the century. When Wattron had to perform an execution, a task commonly assigned to county sheriffs, he issued many formal invitations on white stationery, as follows:

You are hereby cordially invited to attend the hanging of one: George Smiley, Murderer.

His soul will be swung into eternity on December 8, 1899 at 2 o'clock P.M. sharp.

The latest improved methods in the art of scientific strangulation will be done to make the surroundings cheerful and the execution a success.[3]

Reaction to the invitation, which Wattron also wired throughout the nation and to prominent personalities in Europe, led to gubernatorial intervention, strong official rebuke, and a temporary stay of execution. When the disgusted sheriff sent his second invitation, he used paper with heavy black borders and took care to mail the governor's too late for a response.

Revised Statutes of Arizona, Penal Code, Title X, Section 1849, Page 807, makes it obligatory upon Sheriff to issue invitations to executions, form (unfortunately) not prescribed.

With feelings of profound sorrow and regret, I hereby invite you to attend the private, decent and humane execution of a human being; name George Smiley; crime, murder.

The said George Smiley will be executed on January 8, 1900, at 2 o'clock, P.M.

You are expected to deport yourself in a respectful manner, and any "flippant" or "unseemly" language or conduct on your part will not be allowed. Conduct, on anyone's part, bordering on ribaldry and tending to mar the solemnity of the occasion will not be tolerated.[4]

Western lawmen began to play the role expected of them and have, in many instances, continued to do so. Thousands of current peace officers who never ride a horse still wear cowboy boots and wide-brimmed hats as part of their uniforms. Low-slung, outward pitched, long-barreled revolvers are much in evidence despite obvious awkwardness in modern settings. Many agencies also cater to public and political interest by maintaining volunteer citizens' mounted posses. Wyoming even dispensed honorary "ranger" badges during the 1920s.[5]

Individual peace officers directly contributed to the expanding legend in their autobiographies. A natural tendency to emphasize dramatic incidents became the dominant element in many books written by actual lawmen. Bill Tilghman, a former deputy marshal in the Oklahoma Territory, capitalized on his past by touring the country giving performances and lectures. He even produced a film entitled *The Passing of the Oklahoma Outlaws* (1914) and made a living by showing it for most of a decade.[6]

Over the years a public image of the western peace officer became intermingled with a greatly distorted image of the gunfighter. Without doubt the frontier produced men quite proficient with firearms, but the now classic duel decided by speed of the draw leaped from the imaginations of later writers. Lawmen and outlaws alike knew the dangers and limitations of the revolvers they sometimes carried but rarely displayed. Shooting would be avoided whenever possible, and when demanded it would often be done from cover or concealment. A rifle or shotgun offered clear advantages and several nearby friends produced still more favorable odds. The fantasy picture is that of killers, good and bad, facing one another on deserted streets or in crowded saloons. Real battles normally occurred in the course of crimes or simple arrests, just as they do in every modern American community, with appalling regularity.

Public fascination with frontier violence continues, with imaginary codes of the past becoming significant images in modern minds. The public commonly visualizes the western peace officer as a quiet but quick-shooting figure who killed outlaws in fair fights and brought order to troubled areas. This gross distortion arose largely through exaggeration of true events and endless retelling in popular form. Actual incidents took place in prosaic ways, as indicated by one New Mexican newspaper report of 1882 entitled "Riddling a Rowdy: Three Brave Deputy Sheriffs at Pascal Murder a Drunken Man":

Deputy Marshal James Baines of Pascal, Grant County, was shot last night by Marshal Moore, Deputy Sheriff Tucker of Deming, and Deputy Sheriff McCellan of Central City. He had fired off his revolver during the evening and Marshal Moore went to arrest him, but he resisted and pulled his revolver. Then the three officers of the law fired at him and he fell, pierced with six bullets. The coroner's inquest is now going on.[7]

With hindsight former lawmen tended to exaggerate the problems of slow transportation, poor communication, difficulty of identification, and possible violence. And, strangely, they increasingly remembered outlaws as likable fellows with courage and an unwritten code of honor. Contemporary accounts rarely displayed such generosity and actually indicate an absence of significant innovation in basic police operations. Modern methods of law enforcement are only a response to problems created by advancing technology and social complexity; human nature displays no changes to alter the ultimate basis of police work.

Between World Wars I and II an avalanche of histories dealing with western peace officers reached a receptive market. Varying greatly in quality they elevated the image of frontier law enforcement from fiction to apparent fact. In truth, most of these popular historical works contained more myth than reality with repetition of dimly remembered or even imaginary events. Glorification of prominent peace officers, along with famous outlaws, became something of a cliché in Western writing. Walter Noble Burns, Stuart N. Lake, William MacLeod Raine, and others presented colorful but oversimplified histories for an expanding audience of frontier fans. Such authors demonstrated romanticism rather than realism in deepening the image of lawmen. But they seldom reached significant conclusions even in regard to legendary personalities. "Wild Bill" Hickok might be described as a homicidal maniac or a dauntless defender of justice, depending on the point of view adopted.[8]

Writers of history produced incorrect impressions of western law enforcement by emphasis on violence and private conflict. Some indicated that communities faced desperate problems of disorder and had difficulty in finding men to serve as a police. In fact, most areas enjoyed peace and quiet while local politicians had merely to choose from a surplus of applicants for office. Popular historians promulgated many legends about lawmen on the early frontier. One author even attributed Southwestern pecan groves to the Texas Rangers by stating that they rode about scattering nuts along streambeds![9]

Fiction continued the pattern of dramatic misrepresentation initiated in the nineteenth century. Dozens of periodicals devoted to the West routinely included stories of sheriffs, marshals, and rangers battling cattle thieves and murderers. These tales began to include a heavy dosage of romance, with scores of novels portraying peace officers as noble heroes bringing justice to a wild frontier and winning their ladies in a sea of adversity. A few authors patterned their creations after actual lawmen. Frank H. Spearman's famous railroad detective Whispering Smith was based upon Wyoming's very real Joe LeFors. William Sydney Porter (O. Henry) took Texas Ranger Captain Lee Hall as his model. And William MacLeod Raine surely and unabashedly turned Sheriff Bucky O'Neill of Yavapai County (who died in the Spanish-American War) into the fictional Arizona Ranger Lieutenant Bucky O'Connor.

Business also recognized a possible profit in the frontier lawman. During the 1920s the Studebaker company produced an automobile for general sale called "The Sheriff." Named in honor of Southwestern peace officers, it consisted of a five-passenger "Sport Phaeton" equipped with a powerful bus engine and listed at $1,575. Studebaker publicized in 1925 that twelve of Arizona's fourteen counties furnished their sheriffs with a car and each man so provided selected the company's product for his transport.[10]

Although written material certainly spawned popular images of western peace officers, modern concepts are primarily the product of mass media. Depiction more than plot has been crucial in recent generations. Frontier conditions became well established as the background for tales of violence and adventure. The first truly successful film to contain visually a complete story was *The Great Train Robbery* (1903), a Western made in Delaware which prepared the way for at least 20,000 subsequent imitations. Early motion pictures usually avoided formal law enforcement; William S. Hart, for example, normally appeared as a gambler, cowboy, or badman. The two most influential western films of the 1920s, *The Covered Wagon* (1923) and *The Iron Horse*

(1924), dealt with development of the West rather than peace officers.

With the introduction of sound in 1927 motion pictures underwent significant change. Scores of inexpensive Western series with singing heroes and "cowboy stars" reached the market. Occasionally the leading man portrayed a lawman, but very frequently the sheriff finally revealed himself as a secret member of the criminal gang. The advent of more serious films, with themes that became symbolic of the frontier, eventually changed artificiality into a more direct approach to realism. John Ford's *Stagecoach* (1939), probably the finest Western ever made, placed a lawman in a supporting but quite sympathetic role. *The Ox-Bow Incident* (1942), closely based on Walter Van Tilburg Clark's impressive novel, pictured a deputy as instrumental in a lynch mob, although the sheriff finally arrived to at least give hope of organized society's eventual triumph.

After World War II the peace officer emerged as the dominant Western figure in mass media. One motion picture which achieved remarkable distinction engraved a portrait of the town marshal into the American culture. Stanley Kramer's *High Noon* (1952), based upon a short story entitled "The Tin Star" by John W. Cunningham, graphically portrayed the struggle of an individual against evil. The film not only gave new stature and dimension to the Western but crystallized the quality of a strange morality play which the frontier lawman has come to represent. *High Noon* relied almost entirely upon visual impact and included ten full minutes in the climatic battle scene without a word of dialogue. Like the best of all Westerns it did not depend upon conversation but relied upon Dimitri Tiompkin's symbolic title song "Do Not Forsake Me" for dramatic effect. The plot of *High Noon* simply revolved around the refusal of a local marshal (Gary Cooper) to run when confronted by four killers. The solution concerned personal courage rather than actual duty, for the townspeople would significantly provide no assistance. By staying to meet his fate, killing the evildoers, and riding away with a new bride (Grace Kelly) after throwing his badge in the dust, the lawman may have drifted far from reality, but he culminated a popular image. The western peace officer is portrayed as beyond requirements of either written or customary law. He is not limited by socially recognized need; he is a primary manifestation of good in the timeless and unchanging picture of the last frontier. And he wins.

In recent years television has displaced motion pictures as the mass medium paying most attention to the lawman. It is very difficult to sustain a logical basis for violence and adventure in the Western by focusing upon an ordinary cowboy. This problem has necessitated television's reliance upon families, which can spread the action among several characters, or, more reasonably, upon the peace officer. One series, which first enjoyed several years of success on radio in the 1950s, easily exemplifies the formalization of the lawman myth—*Gunsmoke*. In more than a decade the indomitable Marshal Matt Dillon (James Arness) has killed hundreds of badmen but apparently failed to bring any degree of order to television's changeless Dodge City. It is quite impossible to conceive the cultural imagery which *Gunsmoke* and its dozens of imitators have created. Impact must be measured in tens of billions of viewer hours on an international scope, for such series are broadcast throughout the world in many languages. Yet it is here rather than in fact that the American derives his typical impression of the West and its law enforcers, both past and present.

Time and truth blur when subjected to the requirements of mass media. Dramatic license and technical considerations become fully as significant as historical bases, and so the myth comes to rule the reality. One film, *True Grit* (1969), was taken by most observers as a caricature of well-developed fictional patterns and thereupon accorded high honors. In truth, the motion picture contained a more factual representation of conditions and probable personalities, despite considerable liberty with geography, than most Westerns. It also included a dramatic final battle sequence of single good defeating multiple evil which marked a new but classic illustration of a major frontier legend.

If the fact and fiction of the western lawman can ever be conjoined it must be through the supremacy of the individual, a rather strange basis for those charged with responsibility for social order. The basic myth of isolated personalities winning out against seemingly insuperable odds is quite obvious. In reality the unfortunate result of rampant individualism has been a general continuation of poor administration, private interest, low standards, and political involvement. Modern police officers know almost nothing of their true heritage; they tend to believe as much of the past's fiction as do other citizens. With little true perspective it is difficult to accept the changeless form of fundamental law enforcement. In America, furthermore, most policemen are still expected to accomplish their challenging task largely on the basis of personal will. Little or no training, lax or actually detrimental supervision, inferior pay, inadequate facilities—this is the lot of many modern lawmen. The public somehow expects a legend founded on few original truths to flourish unattended in the midst of rapid social and technological change.

The history of the western peace officer reveals a surprising absence of fundamental alteration. Police work today is very similar to that of a century ago. Urban expansion, improvements in communications and transportation, development of various industries—such trends have affected the lawman peripherally. Equipment changes but the ultimate problems endure. The majority of agency organizations and related operations resemble closely those of four generations past. Legislation and administration permit or encourage few marked advances in modern law enforcement. Probably general quality of personnel has improved slightly, with some related betterment in public regard. But progress of this type is mixed and not subject to quantitative analysis.

Frontier lawmen did not bring peace and order to the American West; modern conditions, especially in larger cities, reflect more violence and crime than existed in the days of original settlement. An incredible variety of peace officers attempted to control disorder with a lasting residue of outdated statutes and customs. Communities in the West developed quite sophisticated and fully structured police agencies while the frontier still remained in flux. County law enforcement principally relied upon traditional positions of yet pronounced political natures. Perhaps most underestimated and ignored were the great numbers of varied private officers, including many with quasi-public authority. Also often forgotten are the police services of Indian and military forces on the changing frontier. The only significant alterations in law enforcement organizational form occurred in the creation of diverse state and specialized federal agencies. In the main, however, history reveals a direct continuation of frequently outmoded structural and procedural concepts.

In retrospect it may be noted that police systems in the West still follow patterns which should have been discarded a century ago. Many agencies retain deplorable standards for personnel, have little training, and serve as feeding grounds for corruption and waste. Gross political involvement, particularly in departments not covered by forms of civil service, exists in obvious and widespread form. Recent years have witnessed an expansion of inefficient bureaucracy in the guise of reform or dispensation of federal funds. Not infrequently, a larger urban area may contain a score or more of independent local police agencies with considerable duplication of effort by additional governmental units of wide jurisdiction. Thus chaotic conditions result in the primary stage of criminal justice. And lessons of the past, while obvious for generations, are ignored by an unwilling and involved political leadership.

Solutions to enduring problems of law enforcement organization have been known for many decades. High standards for recruitment, thorough training, and an unfaltering demand for proper conduct constitute the bases of progress. Salaries commensurate with ability and adequate means of advancement must be insured, but related status in the community remains of equal importance. These goals in the fragmented American political system are extremely difficult to realize. Several fine police agencies exist within the western United States, but they tend to be lost in a sea of administrative disorder and strongly influenced by deeply embedded interests.

Centralized communications, officer standards, and staff services have been in order but avoided for more than a century. The real threats of militarism and diminution of local autonomy pose the greatest apparent obstacles to law enforcement on a regional or state basis. But the fundamental obstruction is neither of these admitted dangers—organized control by involved political groups and individuals has prevented significant improvement in police service for generations. A balance can be obtained between central regulation and community needs to gain the benefits of both, and such an effort could directly serve the vast majority of citizens. Response to local conditions and desires must remain a basic tenet of law enforcement within a democracy; such a requirement, however, does not demand retention of outmoded systems and overt political manipulation of office.

Any significant and widespread improvement of governmental agencies will necessarily involve sacrifice by incompetents and those enjoying privileged positions. No drastic changes can occur with wholesale retention of present personnel or operations; too frequently piecemeal efforts at reform devolve to a repetition of existing practices and procedures. Better law enforcement ultimately requires better men, and they cannot be expected to rise slowly above a generation of continued inefficiency and disorder. Lastly, it must be recalled that the police are but one link in the complex chain of American criminal justice. Isolated improvement of law enforcement remains an ephemeral goal; prosecution, courts, corrections, and other units exist in a disjointed and frequently contradictory scheme. Any positive modifications require direct involvement and major alteration in all related agencies toward the general aim of prevention.

The solution of improved law enforcement requires an ultimate decision on the primary role of the police. Is the individual peace officer to be a protector of fundamental rights and freedoms, or is he merely to suppress discontent and social unrest? Surprisingly the actual duty of lawmen in the American West has never been made clear. Police personnel and organizations of past and present remain in limbo, with resultant rifts in the primary structure

255

of the culture. Conflicting experiences, attitudes, and analyses leave the query unanswered, for it must be solved not through isolated observation but by the entire American society. The peace officer may be viewed in perspective as the very embodiment of oppression, the primary tool of tyranny. But he may also be treated as a concrete manifestation of collective conscience and a basic stabilizing element within the community. His Western history and legend gives credence to either supposition. The choice remains.

Appendices

A. Tables

Table 1
Social Conditions of Cities, 1880[a]

City	Population	Bordellos	Saloons
New York, New York	1,206,299	183	9,067
Chicago, Illinois	503,185	200	3,141
Boston, Massachusetts	362,839	100	2,347
San Francisco, California	233,959	0[b]	8,694
New Orleans, Louisiana	216,040	365	429
San Antonio, Texas	20,550	6	70
Elmira, New York	20,541	3	145
Portland, Oregon	17,577	30	110
Wilmington, North Carolina	17,350	4	65
Leadville, Colorado	14,820	100	150
Norwalk, Connecticut	13,956	3	20
Burlington, Vermont	11,365	8	40
Los Angeles, California	11,183	12	70
Dallas, Texas	10,358	5	52
Alameda, California	5,708	0	28
Sharon, Pennsylvania	5,659	2	0

[a] Based upon "Report on the Defective, Dependent, and Delinquent Classes [1880]," Serial No. 2151 (1888), 566–74.

[b] Police statistics in 1880 were as questionable as those of modern times.

Table 2
Crime in Cities, 1880[a]

City	Population	Arrests	Homicides
New York, New York	1,206,299	66,703	9,067
St. Louis, Missouri	350,518	14,036	0[c]
Cincinnati, Ohio	255,139	13,329	17
San Francisco, California	233,959	21,063	0[c]
Atlanta, Georgia	37,409	4,291	5
Oakland, California	34,555	2,063	10
Galveston, Texas	22,248	4,285	2
Norfolk, Virginia	21,966	1,461	0
Auburn, New York	21,924	1,052	0
Salt Lake City, Utah	20,768	616	0
San Antonio, Texas	20,550	1,563	6
Elmira, New York	20,541	1,340	0
Chester, Pennsylvania	14,997	250	1
Leadville, Colorado	14,820	0 [4,320][b]	0
Virginia City, Nevada	10,917	76	0
Watertown, New York	10,697	167	0
New London, Connecticut	10,537	1,351	0
Dallas, Texas	10,358	1,668	0
Cape Elizabeth, Maine	5,302	36	0
Silver City, Colorado	5,040	500	0

[a] Based upon "Report on the Defective, Dependent, and Delinquent Classes [1880]," Serial No. 2151 (1888), 566–74.

[b] Corrected through "Social Statistics of Cities [1880]," Serial No. 2149 (1887), 777–78.

[c] None reported.

Table 3
Inmates of Correctional Institutions
(expressed in a ratio of prisoners to 1,000 population)

	1850[a]	1860[a]	1870[a]	1880[a]	1960[b]
United States (total)	.29	.61	.85	1.17	1.19
California	.67	2.32	2.81	3.06	1.64
Colorado	—	—	.48	1.96	1.41
Dakota	—	—	.21	.44	.70[c]
Florida	.13	.11	.95	1.00	1.48
Idaho	—	—	1.87	.98	.76
Kansas	—	.03	.33	1.30	2.44[d]
New York	.42	1.77	1.07	1.72	1.04
Texas	.07	.17	.89	1.98	1.34
Washington	—	1.29	.79	1.08	1.44

[a] Based upon "Report on the Defective, Dependent, and Delinquent Classes [1880]," Serial No. 2151 (1888), 480–83.

[b] Based upon *Inmates of Institutions: U.S. Census of Population, 1960*, 67–82.

[c] Includes both North and South Dakota.

[d] The apparently high ratio is primarily accounted for by the presence of the federal penitentiary at Leavenworth.

Table 4
City Police, 1890[a]

City	Population	Commander's Title	Stations	Arrests	Force Size[b]	Police Ratio 1890[c]	Police Ratio 1967[d]
New York, N.Y.	1,515,301	Board of Police	35	82,200	3,342	2.2	3.6
Chicago, Ill.	1,099,850	General Superintendent	34	48,119	1,622	1.5	3.3
San Francisco, Cal.	298,997	Chief	9	23,462	406	1.4	2.5
New Orleans, La.	242,039	Superintendent	1	20,150	224	0.9	1.9
Omaha, Neb.	140,452	Superintendent	1	10,872	88	0.6	1.3
Rochester, N.Y.	133,896	Superintendent	1	4,584	108	0.8	1.8
Denver, Colo.	106,713	Chief	1	9,706	91	0.9	1.5
Indianapolis, Ind.	105,436	Superintendent	2	3,851	96	0.9	1.8
Lincoln, Neb.	55,154	Marshal	1	1,600	16	0.3	1.0
Charleston, S.C.	54,955	Chief	1	3,452	89	1.6	2.4
Los Angeles, Cal.	50,395	Chief	2	3,407	81	1.6	1.8
Portland, Ore.	46,385	Chief	1	3,349	41	0.9	1.9
San Antonio, Tex.	37,673	Marshal	2	3,000	60	1.6	0.9
San Diego, Cal.	16,159	Chief	1	489	13	0.8	1.1
Austin, Tex.	14,575	Marshal	1	529	15	1.0	1.1
Easton, Pa.	14,481	Chief	2	452	11	0.8	1.9
Laredo, Tex.	11,319	Marshal	[1]	1,302	20	1.8	0.8
Hutchinson, Kan.	8,682	Marshal	1	370	6	0.7	1.0
Athens, Ga.	8,639	Chief	1	321	7	0.8	1.5
Paris, Tex.	8,254	Marshal	1	554	8	1.0	1.5

[a] Based upon "Police Statistics for 1890 of Cities of the U.S." Serial No. 3029 (1895), 1023–35.

[b] Force sizes in 1890 are highly misleading as some cities reported authorized strength instead of the number of officers actually employed. Such distortion, of course, inflates the police ratio accordingly.

[c] Number of officers to 1,000 population.

[d] Estimated from *Uniform Crime Reports for the United States* [1967], 160–76.

Table 5
Indian Police, 1912[a]

State	Officers	Salaries
Arizona	106	$22,860
California	46	10,152
Colorado	6	1,980
Idaho	20	4,416
Kansas	1	300
Minnesota	40	9,972
Montana	74	17,052
Nebraska	7	2,220
Nevada	24	5,292
New Mexico	44	11,352
North Carolina	2	600
North Dakota	59	12,804
Oklahoma	40	13,560
Five Civilized Tribes	36	9,900
Oregon	29	6,996
South Dakota	133	59,640
Utah	12	2,904
Washington	47	9,456
Wisconsin	21	6,128
Wyoming	14	3,480
United States (total)	766	$183,976

[a] Based upon *Report of the Commissioner of Indian Affairs for the Fiscal Year Ended June 30, 1912,* 297–305.

B. Sheriff's Fees

Sheriff's Fees*

Section 34. The Sheriff shall receive for his services the following fees, to-wit:

Serving Summons, for each person therein named	$0.25
Writ of Mandamus	0.50
Subpoena, for each person therein named	0.12½
Serving Writ of Attachment	0.75
Serving Writ of Replevin	0.75
Serving Writ of Order or notice of Court	0.25
Executing order of Arrest	0.25
Taking each bond	0.25
All copies necessary to complete the service, for each hundred words or fraction over, or less number of words	0.10
Summoning each Juror	0.25
Summoning each Talesman	0.07½
Serving in criminal cases	0.50
Attending Prisoner before court or jury	0.50
For each mile travel, computed each way	0.05
Appraisement of Property	0.75

---

* Independent District, Gilpin County [Colorado], "Laws of Independent District [1861]" (University of Colorado Archives, Boulder).

Advertising Property for Sale, besides actual expenses	0.75
Levying Execution	0.50
Selling Property on Execution or order of Sale	0.50
Making Deed for Property sold upon Execution	1.50
Attending court, per day	1.00
Bringing up Prisoner on writ of habeas corpus, besides actual expenses	0.75

For all sums made by sale on execution or order of sale, not exceeding five hundred dollars, $2\frac{1}{2}$ per cent

On all sums over five hundred dollars, one per cent

If made without sale, on all sums under five hundred dollars, $1\frac{1}{2}$ per cent, and over five hundred dollars $\frac{1}{2}$ per cent

All fees not enumerated to be in proportion to those enumerated

WITNESS' and JUROR'S FEES, per day	2.50

C. Thiel's Detective Service

Thiel's Detective Service[*]

Sir:

One year ago a very large convention of range cattlemen was held in Denver, Colorado. This convention organized itself into the International Range Association. They came together to discuss three subjects, each of which was considered of paramount importance to the industry they represented:

1. Contagious Diseases.
2. Detection and punishment of crime.
3. Transportation.

In each they recognized there was danger and evil. To protect against this danger and to rid themselves of these evils, they organized, made their convention permanent, elected an Executive Committee, representing one member from each State and Territory lying west of the 100th Meridian, and as president, they elected one of the most active, intelligent and progressive men in the entire range country. It was believed these dangers and evils were of vital importance, and that the dangers, evils and losses the business was threatened with and suffered could be controlled and overcome by intelligent and concerted action.

[*] Peace Officers, Manuscript File (Western History Research Center, University of Wyoming, Laramie).

The Executive Committee met, organized and very carefully and fully went over these several matters. Comprehensive plans of action were submitted and discussed. The detection and punishment of depredators on the range was recognized as all important. From the evidence submitted at that time it was shown that these depredations were of more common occurrence than any believed could be possible; that in every portion of the range country brands were being defaced, cattle were run out of the country, calves were separated from their mothers and beef was killed. That to a very limited extent these things were being done was believed by all, but no one believed it was carried on to the extent that it was there shown to be the case.

It was further established, that to stop these thefts—and it was essential they should be stopped—skilled detectives must be put in the field, officered by men who were professionals and who could properly direct and manage them. To do this would require large outlays of money, a thorough organization, and an army of drilled men. The Committee decided the task was too great, the country to be covered too broad, the cost too large, and so they concluded to leave this all-important work to the local associations. Thus the matter stands to-day.

On several occasions I have done important work in different portions of the range country. This work showed me the immense capital that is invested in range cattle: it also disclosed to me that there was no species of property that had so little protection and that was so much at the mercy of bad men. It was therefore no surprise to me to learn that ingenious thieves were taking advantage of the situation and were plying their illegal trade on almost every range in the country.

Upon learning of the determination of the Executive Committee of the Range Association to not undertake this branch of the business, I determined to enter the field. Accordingly I began the organization of a new department to my business, whose duty it should be to work exclusively in this field. I made careful preliminary examinations of the country, of the kind and manner of men now employed by outfits to work their cattle, of the way in which they were worked, of the men that hang round cow-outfits and live no one knows how, and in that way gained an exact knowledge of the situation. From this knowledge I could see plainly that to successfully detect the "rustlers" on the range it was essential to do it with men who were skillful cow men and skillful detectives, and they must be under the supervision of a man thoroughly acquainted with both callings. In order to get a foothold for the operative it is essential that he shall be able to do any work on the range he may be called on to do, and be sufficiently well

267

up in his profession to be able to do his work effectively. To supply myself with these men I have found a very difficult task, but have finally succeeded, and I am now ready to do any range work offered.

Each operative will report daily in writing, or as often as is practicable, to the Superintendent in charge of the work, whose headquarters will be at my Denver office; and he in turn will advise our clients fully of all facts that will be of value or interest to them.

I never work for a reward, or for a gratuity, or for a contingent fee. I have fixed charges, and these I adhere to in all cases and under all circumstances. For each operative engaged I shall charge $5 per day and his actual expenses from the time he leaves the Denver office until his return. Any reward that may be due by reason of my work will be placed to the credit of my employer; and this is true as to all wages earned and paid to the operative by outsiders while engaged on an operation.

Should there be at any time any work in any portion of your jurisdiction that you would like done, I shall be glad to do it. In writing it will be necessary to advise me of your suspicions, of the depredations you fear are being committed and the place where committed, as near as you can, so that I may make an intelligent selection of an operative to put on the ground.

I wish to impress upon you the fact that no successful detective work can be done without secrecy. The operative must not be known, the fact of his employment must not be known, and the fact that you suspect that depredations are being committed ought not to be known. It is unwise to put thieves on their guard. When the work is completed, then it may be advertised to the extent you may see fit.

Any communications received from you will receive my careful attention, and to this end correspondence is solicited. Please direct all communications to me at my Denver office.

Respectfully,

[signed]
John F. Farley
Manager
Denver Colo [1883]

D. New Mexico Mounted Police

New Mexico Mounted Police*

BE IT ENACTED BY THE LEGISLATIVE ASSEMBLY OF THE TERRITORY OF
NEW MEXICO [February, 1905]:

Section 1. That the Governor of this Territory is hereby authorized
to raise and muster into service of this territory, for the protection
of the frontier of this territory, and for the preservation of the peace
and the capture of persons charged with crime, one company of New
Mexico Mounted Police, to be raised as hereinafter prescribed, and to
consist of one captain, one lieutenant, one sergeant, and not more
than eight privates, each entitled to pay as follows: Captain to receive
Two Thousand ($2,000.00) Dollars per annum, Lieutenant to receive
Fifteen Hundred ($1,500.00) Dollars per annum and privates to re-
ceive Nine Hundred ($900.00) Dollars per annum each, and the pay
herein provided shall be full compensation in lieu of all other pay
and compensation, including clothing and all other expenses for officers and men.

Section 2. That the Governor is authorized and empowered, within
sixty days after the passage of this act, to appoint competent persons
as captain, lieutenant, and sergeant, and to enroll, as set forth in this
act, the requisite number of men for the company; the captain shall

* New Mexico Territorial Mounted Police Correspondence, 1906–12 (University of New Mexico Archives, Albuquerque).

return to the Governor the muster roll and the report of the condition of the company, and the Governor shall thereupon commission the officers of the said company, supply said company as under the provisions of this act, he may deem proper and necessary, and order them upon duty in accordance with the provisions of this act.

Section 3. Said men shall be furnished by the Territory with the most effective and approved breechloading rifles, and for this purpose the Governor is hereby authorized to contract in behalf of the territory for eleven stands of arms, together with a full supply of ammunition, the same to be all of the same make and calibre, and each member of the company to be furnished with the arms to be used by him at the price the same shall cost the territory, which sum shall be retained out of the first money due him.

Section 4. Each member of said company shall be required to furnish himself with a suitable horse, six-shooting pistol (army size) and all necessary accoutrements and camp equipage, the same to be passed upon and approved by the enrolling officer before enlisted; and should any member fail to keep himself furnished as above required, then the officer in command shall be authorized and required to purchase the articles of which he may be deficient, and charge the cost of the same to the person for whom the same shall be provided: Provided, that all horses killed in action shall be replaced by the Territory, and the cost of horses so killed in action shall be determined by the captain.

Section 5. The men shall be enrolled for twelve months, unless sooner discharged and at the expiration of their term of service they shall be again enrolled, or others shall be enrolled to supply their places.

Section 6. The captain of such company has authority to suspend any member for cause and shall immediately report his action in writing to the Governor for his consideration.

Section 7. No member of said company shall dispose of or exchange his or their horses or arms without the consent of the commanding officer of the company while in the service of the territory.

Section 8. That the captain of the company shall use his own discretion as to the manner of operations, selecting as his base the most unprotected and exposed settlement of the territory.

Section 9. That the troops raised under and by virtue of this act shall be governed by the rules and regulations of the army of the United States, as far as the same may be applicable, but shall always be and remain subject to the authority of the Territory of New Mexico for frontier service.

Section 10. The captain of such company shall have authority to concentrate all of such company, or divide it into squads for the purpose of following and capturing any outlaws, law breakers, marauding Indians or bands of hostile Indians or for the purpose of carrying out any measure that may contribute to the better security of the frontier, but the entire force raised under the provisions of this act shall be at all times during their employment, as aforesaid, under and subject to the orders of the Governor, and shall be exempt from all military, jury and other service, except that for which they shall be appointed or controlled as aforesaid, and that the Governor shall direct all the arrangements necessary to carry out the intentions of this act, with full power to remove any officer or man thereof for incompetency, neglect of duty or disobedience of orders.

Section 11. Members of said company shall have full power to make arrests of criminals in any part of the territory, and upon the arrest of any criminal, shall deliver the same over to some peace officer in the county where the crime is committed.

Section 12. It shall be the duty of the Auditor of this Territory to draw his warrant on the Territorial Treasurer at the end of each month for the pay of each officer and man in said company, and to forward the same to the captain of said company; and it shall be the duty of the Territorial Treasurer to pay such warrants out of the fund for mounted police, as other warrants are paid.

Section 13. There shall be annually levied and collected in addition to all other taxes authorized by law, a tax of one-half mill on taxable property in this territory, to be placed in a fund by the Territorial Treasurer, to be known as the New Mexico Mounted Police Fund, and upon which fund all warrants and payments made under any of the provisions of this act, shall be drawn and made. Said tax shall be levied and collected in the same manner, and at the same time and by the same officers as other territorial taxes; Provided, that until collections shall have been made under the provisions of the levy herein authorized for the payment of such mounted police that the territorial treasurer shall pay the same out of any funds, except the interest and sinking funds in the Territorial Treasury.

Section 14. That no portion of said troops shall become a charge against this territory until organized and placed under orders, and the total cost and expense of the organization, equipment and support of said company shall not exceed the sum of Thirteen Thousand Dollars for any one year.

Section 15. The captain of said company shall provide and issue to each member of said company, a badge, uniform in size and shape with the words "New Mexico Mounted Police" inscribed thereon in plain, legible letters, which said badge shall belong to, and be returned to this territory, and be returned to it by the possessor thereof, when any members of such company shall cease to be a member thereof; a sum not exceeding twelve hundred dollars per annum is hereby appropriated for the contingent expense of such company which shall be paid in the same manner as heretofore provided in this act, and out of which shall be bought and paid for the arms hereinbefore provided and such other incidental expenses as shall be necessary for the carrying out of the provisions provided for in this act. All such incidental expenses or contingent expense shall be accounted for by itemized voucher duly certified to by the captain of such mounted police and approved by the Territorial Auditor but no expense of any kind shall be incurred or allowed in any one year in excess of the sum of Twelve hundred dollars.

Section 16. This act shall take effect and be in full force from and after its passage.

Notes

With some exceptions the form of citation utilized corresponds to that of standard academic research. However, in certain instances involving legal materials it has been necessary both to expand and simplify the style of notation. Case decisions in federal and state courts are usually cited with the standard legal form, and to regional reports. Therefore, "109 S.W.2d 53 (Texas, 1937)" would indicate reference to a 1937 Texas decision found in volume 109 of the *South Western Reporter, Second Series*, beginning on page 53. Abbreviations of early state and other reports are normally self-explanatory.

Statutory references, other than national, are given in a slightly modified legal form. "Oklahoma Statutes, 21–1274 (1890)" would indicate an Oklahoma provision currently in effect, namely Section 1274 of Title 21. Because of the different state schemes in use, a wide variation in numbering systems will be encountered; the date following shows the year of original passage of the statute. Of course, the particular section usually first appeared under a different codification number than that now used. Statutes no longer in effect are cited in normal academic form to a specific publication.

Throughout the book the method of notation utilized is designed to facilitate the easiest location of references. Consequently, it will not directly correspond in every instance to either regular academic or to specialized legal forms. The use of certain government publications, for example, has prompted reference by United States document title, standard Serial Set number, date, and pagination. This identification, in most instances, should quickly lead to the finding of material given in reference regardless of site.

A great deal of knowledge was imparted to the writer during the course of scores of interviews conducted with present and former peace officers throughout the western states. While these are at times noted, items relating to identifiable individuals and agencies were also included. Because of the confidence with which certain matters of this nature must continue to be treated, there are occasional but deliberate instances of omitted citation.

Although actual police records have often been destroyed, lost, or closed for purposes of academic investigation, a wealth of diverse material on law enforcement and criminal justice remains available throughout the West. Perhaps most encouraging is the general accessibility of long untouched government documents, manuscripts, court reports, and even statutory items. The bibliography includes the major sources utilized in preparation of this book. It is by no means meant to constitute a definitive listing of possible materials, but may, nevertheless, indicate significant primary and secondary items for further inquiry.

CHAPTER I:

"Wild and Unsettled Portions of Our Territories"

1. Jack D. Forbes, *Apache, Navaho, and Spaniard*, 135–36, 166.

2. *Report of the Acting Governor of Arizona Made to the Secretary of the Interior for the Year 1881*, 5.

3. Charles H. Howard to William Steel, October 25, 1877, "El Paso Troubles in Texas," Serial No. 1809 (1878), 154.

4. James Truslow Adams, "Our Lawless Heritage," *Atlantic Monthly*, Vol. CXLII, No. 6 (December, 1928), 733–36; Mabel A. Elliott, *Crime in Modern Society*, 272.

5. Alexis de Tocqueville, *Democracy in America*, I, 46.

6. R. W. Mondy, "Analysis of Frontier Social Instability," *Southwestern Social Science Quarterly*, Vol. XXIV, No. 2 (September, 1943), 172–73.

7. Oliver Wendell Holmes, Jr., *The Common Law*, 41.

8. J. J. Sheridan to Fred Fornoff, May 7, 1909, New Mexico Territorial Mounted Police Correspondence, 1906–12 (University of New Mexico Archives, Albuquerque).

9. Frederic M. Thrasher, *The Gang*, 33–34, 144–49, 289.

10. Wayne Gard, *Frontier Justice*, 117–18.

11. Philip D. Jordan, "Lady Luck and Her Knights of the Royal Flush," *Southwestern Historical Quarterly*, Vol. LXXII, No. 3 (January, 1969), 299–300.

12. Hubert Howe Bancroft, *Popular Tribunals*, I, 121.

13. Robert Thomas Pritchett, "Impeachment Proceedings in Congress Against John Charles Watrous of Texas: 1851–1861" (M.A. thesis, University of Texas, 1925).

14. Hubert Howe Bancroft, *Popular Tribunals*, II, 332.

15. Sam Howe Scrapbook, Vol. 6, item 1259 (Colorado Historical Society Archives, Denver).

16. William Ransom Hogan, *The Texas Republic*, 274.

17. Criminal Dockets, First Judicial District, New Mexico Territory, 1882–1912 (Federal Records Center, Denver).

18. Benjamin F. Wright, "Political Institutions and the Frontier," in Dixon Ryan Fox (ed.), *Sources of Culture in the Middle West*, 27.

19. *The Book of the States, 1968–1969*, 110–11.

20. "Statutory Structures for Sentencing Felons to Prison," *Columbia Law Review*, Vol. LX, No. 8 (December, 1960), 1154–55.

21. Duane A. Smith, "Colorado and Judicial Recall," *The American Journal of Legal History*, Vol. VII, No. 3 (July, 1963), 198–209.

22. Roberts *v.* State, 158 N.W. 930 (Nebraska, 1916).

23. *The Challenge of Crime in a Free Society*, 22–27.

24. *Uniform Crime Reports for the United States* [1967], 62–67.

25. *Ibid.*, 100.

26. *Ibid.*, 64–66.

27. Sam Howe Scrapbook, Vol. 4, item 917 (Colorado Historical Society Archives, Denver).

28. *Uniform Crime Reports for the United States* [1967], 121, 124.

29. Territorial Secretary, Extradition Papers for Fugitives from New Mexico, 1900–1905 (University of New Mexico Archives, Albuquerque).

30. Police Docket, Denver, 1873 (Colorado State Archives, Denver).

31. U.S. Court Docket, Central District, Indian Territory, 1898–1904 [criminal cases] (Federal Records Center, Fort Worth).

32. Records of the U.S. District Court, Territory of New Mexico, Fifth Judicial District, 1890–1911 [cases 1–26] (Federal Records Center, Denver).

33. Records of the U.S. District Court, Territory of New Mexico, First Judicial District, 1896–1909 (Federal Records Center, Denver).

34. Sam Howe Scrapbook, Vol. 1, item 137 (Colorado Historical Society Archives, Denver).

35. *The Challenge of Crime in a Free Society*, 18.

36. "Report on the Defective, Dependent, and Delinquent Classes [1880]," Serial No. 2151 (1888), 479.

37. *Oklahoma Gazette* (Oklahoma City, Oklahoma Territory), May 21, 1889–May 5, 1890.

38. Lynn I. Perrigo, "Law and Order in Early Colorado Mining Camps," *Mississippi Valley Historical Review*, Vol. XXVIII, No. 1 (June, 1941), 54.

39. "Tijerina Wins Acquittal," *Express and Evening News* (San Antonio, Texas), December 14, 1968.

40. Hubert Howe Bancroft, *Popular Tribunals*, I, 71.

CHAPTER II:

"A Duty to Maintain Public Order"

1. John P. Manguson, "The Private Person's Duty to Assist the Police in Arrest," *Wyoming Law Journal*, Vol. XIII, No. 1 (Fall, 1958), 72.

2. Edward Eldefonso, Alan Coffey, and Richard C. Grace, *Principles of Law Enforcement*, 277.

3. Independent District, Gilpin County [Colorado], "Minutes of Miners' Meeting [May, 1860]" (University of Colorado Archives, Boulder).

4. *Laws of the Territory of Idaho, First Session*, ch. 2, sec. 17 (1864).

5. Utah Code, 77–10–6 (1898); Idaho Code, 19–510 (1864).

6. *The General Statutes of the State of Nevada*, sec. 3994 (1861).

7. Nevada Revised Statutes, 171.155 (1861).

8. Revised Codes of Montana, 95–210 (1967).

9. Jacob Walter Feigenbaum, William B. Blanchet, and J. B. Arnold, *The Texas Peace Officer's Manual*, 158–59.

10. California Penal Code, 817 (1872).

11. Revised Code of Washington, 68.48.080 (1943); Nevada Revised Statutes, 574.040 (1873); California Education Code, 15832 (1961); Oklahoma Statutes, 45–476 (1907), 21–1398 (1951).

12. Harrison Grant Williams, "The Peace Officer in California: Concept and Development" (M. Crim. thesis, University of California at Berkeley, 1964), 80.

13. *Task Force Report: The Police*, 7–9.

14. Walter F. Sibley, *Peace Officers of the State of California*, 10–11.

15. Harry De Winton and L. D. La Tourette, *Peace Officers of Arizona, 1917–1918*, 3–15, 18–19.

16. Walter Prescott Webb, *The Texas Rangers*, 521.

17. California Government Code, 1029 (1949).

18. Fred Fornoff to George Curry, March 20, 1908, New Mexico Territorial Mounted Police Correspondence, 1906–12 (University of New Mexico Archives, Albuquerque).

19. *Uniform Crime Reports for the United States* [1967], 47.

20. *Proceedings of the Sheriffs' Association of Texas* [First Annual Meeting], 4–8.

21. *Uniform Crime Reports for the United States* [1967], 47.

22. Woodrow Carlton Whitten, "Criminal Syndicalism and the Law in California: 1919–1927" (Ph.D. dissertation, University of California at Berkeley, 1946), 271–73.

23. Utah Code, 76–57–1 to 76–57–5 (1919); Oklahoma Statutes, 21–1266 (1919).

24. Nevada Revised Statutes, 527.250 (1961); Oregon Revised Statutes, 483.472 (1955); Oklahoma Statutes, 21–1336 (1890).

25. North Dakota Century Code, 19–06–07 (1931).

26. Colorado Revised Statutes, 40–23–6 (1919), 66–10–11 (1947), 105–2–4 (1897).

27. Revised Codes of Montana, 94–2413 (1907).

28. Revised Statutes of Nebraska, 28–932 (1891).

29. New Mexico Statutes, 39–1–7 (1850–51).

30. Oregon Revised Statutes, 166.260 (1953).

31. *Ibid.*, 166.140 (1953).

32. Wyoming Statutes, 18–304 (1876).

33. Texas Revised Civil Statutes, 4001 (1927).

34. Oklahoma Statutes, 21–1274 (1890).

35. Texas Code of Criminal Procedure, 14.04 (1895); Wright *v.* State, 44 Tex. 645 (1876); Texas Penal Code, 1222 (1879), 609 (1909).

36. New Mexico Statutes, 3–8–28 (1935), 3–3–39 (1935), 64–22–16 (1953).

CHAPTER III:
"The Marshal Shall Be Chief of Police"

1. Eugene C. Barker (ed.), "Minutes of the Ayuntamiento of San Felipe de Austin, 1828–1832, Part XII," *Southwestern Historical Quarterly*, Vol. XXIV, No. 2 (October, 1920), 155.

2. *Laws of the Territory of Kansas, 1857–1858*, ch. 42, sec. 182 (1857–58).

3. *Daily Territorial Enterprise* (Virginia City, Nevada), May–September, 1866.

4. Kansas Statutes, 80–702 (1868); Utah Code, 10–6–67 (1898).

5. Oklahoma Statutes, 11–574 (1890).

6. "Social Statistics of Cities [1880]," Serial No. 2149 (1887), 777–78.

7. Robert R. Dykstra, *The Cattle Towns*, 142–47.

8. *Meldrum v. State*, 146 P. 596 (Wyoming, 1915).

9. Frank Brown, "Annals of Travis County and the City of Austin: From the Earliest Times to the Close of 1875," ch. XXVI [1867] (Texas State Archives, Austin).

10. Paul Adams, "The Unsolved Murder of Ben Thompson, Pistoleer Extraordinary,"· *Southwestern Historical Quarterly*, Vol. XLVIII, No. 3 (January, 1945), 322–29; Owen Payne White, *Lead and Likker*, 253–56.

11. Sam Howe Scrapbook, Vol. 3, item 449, Vol. 8, item 2355 (Colorado Historical Society Archives, Denver); William R. Schnitger, Manuscript File (Western History Research Center, University of Wyoming, Laramie).

12. Texas Revised Civil Statutes, 999 (1911).

13. Revised Codes of Montana, 11–1814 (1907), 11–1832 (1935).

14. Leon Radzinowicz, *A History of English Criminal Law and Its Administration from 1750: The Clash Between Private Initiative and Public Interest in the Enforcement of the Law*, 188, 198.

15. Metropolitan Police Act of 1829, 10 Geo. 4, c.44 (England).

16. Charles Reith, *A New Study of Police History*, 136–43.

17. Roger Lane, *Policing the City: Boston 1822–1885*, 29–35.

18. *Laws, Joint Resolutions, and Memorials of the State of Nebraska*, ch. 13, sec. 48 (1889); *Leyes de la Asamblea Legislativa del Territorio de Nuevo Mexico*, "Una Acta Relativa a Ciudades y Villas Incorporadas," sec. 4 (1891); North Dakota Century Code, 40–20–05 (1887).

19. "Social Statistics of Cities [1880]," Serial No. 2149 (1887), 748.

20. Kansas Statutes, 13–508 (1862), 13–2124 (1945).

21. Texas Revised Civil Statutes, 995 (1875).

22. North Dakota Century Code, 58–15–01 (1905); Oregon Revised Statutes, 449.315 (1953).

23. John P. Young, *San Francisco, A History of the Pacific Coast Metropolis*, I, 182, 201.

24. *Daily Alta California* (San Francisco), January 10, 1881.

25. *Ibid.*, November 26, 1850.

26. Hubert Howe Bancroft, *Popular Tribunals*, I, 223.

27. *Daily Alta California* (San Francisco), February 24, 1854.

28. B. S. Brooks, "A Detective Police," *The Pioneer or California Monthly Magazine*, Vol. II, No. 6 (December, 1854), 321, 327.

29. Hubert Howe Bancroft, *Popular Tribunals*, II, 92–93.

30. *Ibid.*, 649–50.

31. *Daily Alta California* (San Francisco), May 17, 1875; Harrison Grant

Williams, "The Peace Officer in California: Concept and Development," (M. Crim. thesis, University of California at Berkeley, 1964), 24.

32. *San Francisco Municipal Reports for the Fiscal Year 1894–1895*, 489.

33. *Ibid.*, 469–78, 490, 512.

34. *Ibid.*, 467–68.

35. John P. Young, *San Francisco, A History of the Pacific Coast Metropolis*, II, 890–91.

36. Sam Howe Scrapbook, Vol. 5, item 1179 (Colorado Historical Society Archives, Denver).

37. Police Docket, Denver, 1873 (Colorado State Archives, Denver).

38. "Relics of Local Criminals," *Colorado Sun* (Denver), April 17, 1892; "Pets of the Department," *Ibid.*, April 3, 1892.

39. Sam Howe Scrapbook, Vol. 2, item 311 (Colorado Historical Society Archives, Denver).

40. "Art of Making Arrests," Denver *Tribune*, April 18, 1886.

41. Sam Howe Scrapbook, Vol. 12, item 4493 (Colorado Historical Society Archives, Denver).

42. *Daily News* (Denver), October 15, 1890.

43. Edward P. Costigan Papers (University of Colorado Archives, Boulder).

44. "Judge Lindsey Says Cops and Sheriff Are Worst Offenders Against Laws," Denver *Express*, May 25, 1906; Denver *Post*, February 10, 1906.

45. Phillip N. Spiller, "A Short History of the San Antonio Police Department" (M.S. thesis, Trinity University, 1954), 32–37.

46. *San Antonio Police Department Annual Report: 1966*, 14.

47. "The Present City Government," San Antonio *Express*, December 2, 1868.

48. Phillip N. Spiller, "A Short History of the San Antonio Police Department" (M.S. thesis, Trinity University, 1954), 40.

49. San Antonio *Express*, December 3, 1868; *San Antonio Police Department Annual Report: 1966*, 26–27.

50. "How the Police Operated Before Patrol Wagon Was Put into Service," San Antonio *Express*, May 3, 1936.

51. "The Servants of the People," San Antonio *Express*, February 19, 1885.

52. *Annual Message of Hon. Marshall Hicks, Mayor of the City of San Antonio*, xxiii–xxv.

53. *Annual Message of Bryan Callaghan, Mayor of the City of San Antonio*, 264–68.

54. Phillip N. Spiller, "A Short History of the San Antonio Police Department" (M.S. thesis, Trinity University, 1954), 45–47.

55. Sergeant's Record of Arrest: 1913–14; Sergeants' Record of Arrest: 1924 (San Antonio Police Department Property Room).

56. Hubert Howe Bancroft, *Popular Tribunals*, II, 646.

57. City of Houston *v.* Estes, 79 S.W. 848 (Texas, 1904).

58. City of Galveston *v.* Brown, 67 S.W. 156 (Texas, 1902).

59. State *v.* Anselmo, 148 P. 1071 (Utah, 1915).

60. Joseph G. Rosa, *The Gunfighter: Man or Myth*, 63.

61. Sam Howe Scrapbook, Vol. 12, item 4493 (Colorado Historical Society Archives, Denver).

62. *Annual Message of Hon. Marshall Hicks, Mayor of the City of San Antonio*, xxiii–xxv.

63. "Social Statistics of Cities [1880]," Serial No. 2149 (1887), 748.

64. LaClef *v.* City of Concordia, 21 P. 272 (Kansas, 1889).

65. Hubert Howe Bancroft, *Popular Tribunals*, I, 160.

CHAPTER IV:
Posse Comitatus

1. Eugene C. Barker, "The Government of Austin's Colony, 1821–1831," *Southwestern Historical Quarterly*, Vol. XXI, No. 3 (January, 1918), 227–29; Clarence Wharton, "Early Judicial History of Texas," *Texas Law Review*, Vol. XII, No. 3 (April, 1934), 315.

2. Constitution of the Republic of Texas (1836), art. 4, sec. 12.

3. "Texas' First Sheriff," *Sheriffs' Association of Texas Magazine*, Vol. I, No. 11 (September, 1932), 15.

4. Constitution of the State of Texas (1845), art. 14, sec. 13.

5. Constitution of the State of Texas (1866), art. 4, sec. 18; Constitution of the State of Texas (1869), art. 5, secs. 18, 21.

6. Constitution of the State of Texas (1876), art. 5, sec. 23.

7. Texas Revised Civil Statutes, 6865 (1846); Constitution of the State of Texas (1876), art. 5, sec. 18.

8. Independent District, Gilpin County [Colorado], "Laws of Independent District [1861]" (University of Colorado Archives, Boulder).

9. Nathaniel K. Boswell, Manuscript File (Western History Research Center, University of Wyoming, Laramie).

10. Oregon Revised Statutes, 565–240 (1953).

11. Texas Revised Civil Statutes, 7652a(3) (1917), 7880–7(c) (1925), 7930–4(5) (1941), 1581b (1943).

12. *Ibid.*, 6699 (1919); Jones *v.* State, 238 S.W. 661, 663 (Texas, 1922); Texas Penal Code, 827a (1937).

13. California Government Code, 31904 (1931), 31904.5 (1947).

14. Colorado Revised Statutes, 39–2–2 (1861).

15. New Mexico Statutes, 15–40–10 (1905).

16. Arizona Revised Statutes, 11–442 (1901).

17. State *v.* Wilson, 243 P. 359 (Idaho, 1925); Lyle *v.* State, 17 S.W. 425 (Texas, 1886); Weatherford *v.* State, 21 S.W. 251 (Texas, 1893).

18. Patton *v.* State, 86 S.W.2d 774 (Texas, 1935).

19. New Mexico Statutes, 15–40–14 (1868–69); Wyoming Statutes, 18–175 (1876).

20. Texas Penal Code, 803b (1931).

21. *The General Statutes of the State of Nevada*, "An Act Relating to Sheriffs," sec. 5 (1861).

22. John Sinclair to George McKinstry, May 2, 1847, George McKinstry Documents (Bancroft Library, University of California at Berkeley).

23. George Brown to John Morrison, September 26, 1852, David Jacks Papers (Stanford University Archives, Stanford, California); "Administration of Justice in California, Illustrated in the Trial, Conviction, and Punishments of Delinquents" [1850], *California Pamphlets*, Vol. XXVI, No. 1 (n.d.), 356.

24. Utah Code, 4–12–1 (1949); Colorado Revised Statutes, 35–5–13 (1903), 36–12–2 (1931); Texas Revised Civil Statutes, 191 (1915).

25. Frank Soulé, John H. Gihon, and James Nisbet, *The Annals of San Francisco*, 271.

26. Thomas Jefferson Carr, Manuscript File (Western History Research Center, University of Wyoming, Laramie); "Wyoming Sheriffs," *Annals of Wyoming*, Vol. XV, No. 3 (July, 1943), 247; "Index to Names of United States Marshals, 1789–1960" (Washington: National Archives, 1961); "Thomas Jeffer-

son Carr—A Frontier Sheriff," *Annals of Wyoming*, Vol. XX, No. 2 (July, 1948), 165–76.

27. *Evening Review* (Albuquerque), July 26, 1882.

28. [John] Slaughter, Manuscript File (University of Arizona Archives, Tucson); Frederick Ritchie Bechdolt, *When the West Was Young*, 160–90.

29. Harold Preece, *Lone Star Man*, 47–56; Reeves v. State, 258 S.W. 577 (Texas, 1924); Jones v. State, 109 S.W.2d 244 (Texas, 1937).

30. Steinicke v. Harr, 240 P. 66, 69 (Oklahoma, 1925).

31. Denver *World*, December 14, 1887.

32. *Evening Review* (Albuquerque), March 6, 1882.

33. McLain v. Arnold, 174 P. 563 (Oklahoma, 1918).

34. In the Matter of the Inquest over the Bodies of Robert F. McBride, Martin R. Kempton, and Thomas K. Wootan, Deceased, Transcript (Arizona State Archives, Phoenix).

35. Cortez v. State, 66 S.W. 453 (Texas, 1902); Cortez v. State, 69 S.W. 536 (Texas, 1902); John Oliver West, "To Die Like a Man: The 'Good' Outlaw Tradition in the American Southwest" (Ph.D. dissertation, University of Texas, 1964), 174–90.

36. Robert R. Maiden, "Colorado Sheriffs Who Failed to Complete Terms of Office" in Law Enforcement—Sheriffs, Manuscript File (Colorado State Archives, Denver).

37. Payroll of Sheriff's Department, Denver, 1904–1905 (Colorado State Archives, Denver).

38. George McKinstry Documents (Bancroft Library, University of California at Berkeley).

39. "The Ticket," Atchison *Daily Champion and Press* (Kansas), October 9, 1869.

40. Broadside, 1907, William Tilghman Manuscript File (University of Oklahoma Archives, Norman).

41. Hubert Howe Bancroft, *Popular Tribunals*, II, 650.

42. *San Francisco Municipal Reports for the Fiscal Year 1863–1864*, 296.

43. Payroll of Sheriff's Department, Denver, 1904–1905 (Colorado State Archives, Denver).

44. William M. Breakenridge, *Helldorado*, 102; Allen A. Erwin, *The Southwest of John H. Slaughter*, 252–53.

45. Maxine Frances Benson, "Labor and the Law in Colorado 1915–1917" (M.A. thesis, University of Colorado, 1962), 38–44.

46. Harry Wheeler, Manuscript File (Arizona Pioneers Historical Society Archives, Tucson); "Fear Gripped Bisbee 50 Years Ago Today," Tucson *Daily Citizen* (Arizona), July 12, 1967; Dane Coolidge, *Fighting Men of the West*, 295–99.

47. *One Big Union Monthly* (Chicago), August, 1919.

48. Con P. Cronin, "Arizona's Six Gun Classic," *Arizona Historical Review*, Vol. III, No. 2 (July, 1930), 7–11; "Deputies Up in Arms," San Antonio *Daily Express*, October 4, 1891.

49. *Proceedings of the Sheriffs' Association of Texas* [1879], 4–7.

50. Interview with Inspector Ron Cassingham, Nevada Highway Patrol, Carson City, August 6, 1968; Colorado Revised Statutes, 49–2–8 (1964), 79–1–2 (1964).

51. *The General Statutes of the State of Nevada*, "An Act in Relation to County Jails" (1861).

52. Texas Revised Civil Statutes, 5116 (1846).

53. "Prisoners in County Jails [1890]," Serial No. 3028, Part 2 (1896), 25–27.

54. San Francisco Municipal Reports for the Fiscal Year 1894–1895, 665.

55. San Francisco Municipal Reports for the Fiscal Year 1863–1864, 297–98.

56. Ann Patton Baenziger, "The Texas State Police During Reconstruction: A Reexamination," Southwestern Historical Quarterly, Vol. LXXII, No. 4 (April, 1969), 473.

57. Sam Howe Scrapbook, Vol. 4, item 945 (Colorado Historical Society Archives, Denver).

58. Statutes of the Territory of Washington, "An Act Relative to Crimes and Punishments, and Proceedings in Criminal Cases," sec. 77 (1854).

59. Bracken v. Cato, 54 F.2d 457 (5th Cir., 1931).

60. Leyes de la Asamblea Legislativa del Territorio de Nuevo Mexico, "Una Acta Para Abrogar el Capitulo 100 de las Leyes de Sesion de la Asamblea 28 a," sec. 1 (1891).

61. Utah Code, 17–22–5 (1898).

62. Wyoming Statutes, 18–300 (1876); Revised Statutes of Nebraska, 47–114 (1913); Oklahoma Statutes, 57–53 (1890).

63. The Statutes of California, ch. 23, sec. 17 (1851).

64. The General Statutes of the State of Nevada, "An Act in Relation to County Jails," sec. 7 (1861).

65. Ibid., "An Act to Authorize the Employment of Criminals Confined in the Several Jails throughout this State," sec. 4 (1879); Oklahoma Statutes, 57–10 (1890).

CHAPTER V:

"A Private Person May Arrest Another"

1. Leon Radzinowicz, A History of English Criminal Law and Its Administration from 1750: The Clash Between Private Initiative and Public Interest in the Enforcement of the Law, 112–37.

2. Barbara Julia Hansen, "Wagon Train Government" (M.A. thesis, University of Colorado, 1962), 35–37, 97–117; Wallace E. Stegner, The Gathering of Zion, 90–92, 103–104.

3. Fitz Hugh Ludlow, The Heart of the Continent, 286.

4. Idaho Code, 19–604 (1864).

5. Harrison Grant Williams, "The Peace Officer in California: Concept and Development" (M. Crim. thesis, University of California at Berkeley, 1964), 16–33.

6. Record of Deputy Sheriffs, Arapahoe County, 1892–1894 (Colorado State Archives, Denver).

7. Report of the Governor of Arizona to the Secretary of the Interior, 1885, 19; California Penal Code, 13601 (1965).

8. Hubert Howe Bancroft, Popular Tribunals, I, 10.

9. William A. Bell, New Tracks in North America, I, 92.

10. Independent District, Gilpin County [Colorado], "Laws of Independent District [1861]" (University of Colorado Archives, Boulder).

11. Tom Bailey to Eleanor B. Sloan, June 12 and 26, 1958, Tom (Seth) Bailey, Manuscript File (Arizona Pioneers' Historical Society Archives, Tucson); R. H. Williams, With the Border Ruffians, 230–303.

12. Helen Fitzgerald Sanders (ed.), X. Biedler, 80–94; James A. B. Scherer, The Lion of the Vigilantes, 235–43, 301–10.

13. Chester H. Rowell Papers (Bancroft Library, University of California at Berkeley).

14. Bruce Smith, *Police Systems in the United States*, 94–95.

15. Utah Code, 67–12–1 through 67–12–18 (1941); Harrison Grant Williams, "The Peace Officer in California: Concept and Development" (M. Crim. thesis, University of California at Berkeley, 1964), 30–31.

16. Record of Deputy Sheriffs, Arapahoe County, 1892–1894 (Colorado State Archives, Denver).

17. *The American Detective*, Vol. I, No. 1 (March, 1893), 6–7.

18. Charles Howard Shinn, *Graphic Descriptions of Pacific Coast Outlaws*, 97–102.

19. James D. Horan and Howard Swiggett, *The Pinkerton Story*, 4–12, 243–44, 289–308; "Keep Them Out," *Daily News* (Denver), July 12, 1892.

20. Tom Horn, *Life of Tom Horn*, 222–25; Charles A. Siringo, *Two Evil Isms*, 44–48.

21. Constitution of the State of Wyoming (1889), art. 19, sec. 6.

22. Constitution of North Dakota (1889), art. 13, sec. 190; Constitution of Montana (1889), art. 3, sec. 31; Constitution of the State of Idaho (1890), art. 14, sec. 6.

23. Constitution of Utah (1895), art. 12, sec. 16; Constitution of the State of Arizona (1910), art. 2, sec. 26; Revised Statutes of Nebraska, 28–727 (1893).

24. Constitution of the Commonwealth of Kentucky (1891), sec. 225; Constitution of the State of South Carolina (1895), art. 8, sec. 9.

25. William Ross Collier and Edwin Victor Westrate, *Dave Cook of the Rockies*, 39–45, 64–67, 113–34, 214–18; David J. Cook, *Hands Up*, ix–x, 8–9, 253–56.

26. James Otey Bradford Papers (Stanford University Archives, Stanford, California); William Banning and George Hugh Banning, *Six Horses*, 257–61.

27. Neill Compton Wilson, *Treasure Express*, 225–51; George David Hendricks, "The Bad Man of the West" (M.A. thesis, University of Texas, 1938), 23–24; Lucius Beebe and Charles Clegg, *U.S. West, the Saga of Wells Fargo*, 180–94.

28. Henry Stephen Dewhurst, *The Railroad Police*, 9, 21–32, 167; Jeremiah P. Shalloo, "The Private Police of Pennsylvania," *Annals of the American Academy of Political and Social Science*, Vol. CXLVI (November, 1929), 58.

29. Wyoming Statutes, 6–209 (1876), 7–79 (1917); North Dakota Century Code, 49–17–12 (1887), 49–17–10 (1889).

30. Oklahoma Statutes, 66–183 (1890).

31. Interview with Special Agent Jerry J. Guidry (S.P.R.R.), San Antonio, Texas, September 16, 1969.

32. James B. Gillett, *Six Years with the Texas Rangers*, 325–26.

33. Eugene Cunningham, *Triggernometry*, 75–77.

34. Thomas Furlong, *Fifty Years a Detective*, 306–27.

35. New Mexico Statutes, 69–2–20 (1921).

36. Presley *v.* Ft. Worth and D. C. Ry. Co., 145 S.W. 669 (Texas, 1912).

37. Barry B. Combs (U.P.R.R.) to Frank R. Prassel, July 24, 1968.

38. John L. McCarty, *Maverick Town*, 129–50, 238–39; Dulcie Sullivan, *The LS Brand*, 87–88; J. Evetts Haley, *The XIT Ranch of Texas and the Early Days of the Llano Estacado*, 114–28; Harold Preece, *Lone Star Man*, 229–35.

39. Minnie M. Brashear, "The Anti-Horse Thief Association of Northeast Missouri," *Missouri Historical Review*, Vol. XLV, No. 4 (July, 1951), 342–47.

40. *Constitution for State and Subordinate Orders of the Anti-Horse Thief Association, Missouri Division,* 3.

41. *Proceedings of the Eleventh Annual Session of the Anti-Horse Thief Association, I. T. Division,* 14, 17.

42. Oklahoma Statutes, 542 (1910).

43. Minnie M. Brashear, "The Anti-Horse Thief Association of Northeast Missouri," *Missouri Historical Review,* Vol. XLV, No. 4 (July, 1951), 347.

44. J. Frank Dobie, "Detectives of the Cattle Ranges," *The Country Gentleman,* Vol. XCII, No. 2 (February, 1927), 30, 176; Rebecca Bailey, "Wyoming Stock Inspectors and Detectives, 1873–1890" (M.A. thesis, University of Wyoming, 1948), 4–5, 135–36.

45. *Compiled Statutes of Montana,* Fifth Division—General Laws (1885).

46. Rebecca Bailey, "Wyoming Stock Inspectors and Detectives, 1873–1890" (M.A. thesis, University of Wyoming, 1948), 9, 35, 105–109, 145–47.

47. Frank M. Canton, Manuscript File (Western History Research Center, University of Wyoming, Laramie); Frank M. Canton, *Frontier Trails,* Edward Everett Dale (ed.), xii, 28–35.

48. Horn v. State, 73 P. 705, 709 (Wyoming, 1903).

49. Oscar O. Mueller, "The Central Montana Vigilante Raid of 1884," *Montana Magazine of History,* Vol. I, No. 1 (January, 1951), 27–34.

50. Asa Shinn Mercer, *The Banditti of the Plains,* 20; T. A. Larson, *History of Wyoming,* 268–84; Malcom Campbell, *Malcom Campbell, Sheriff,* 157, 344.

CHAPTER VI:
"There Shall Be a Corps of Rangers"

1. Plans and Powers of the Provisional Government of Texas (1835), "Of the Military," art. IX.

2. John S. Ford, "Memoirs," 655–57 (Texas State Archives, Austin).

3. Frederick Law Olmstead, *A Journey Through Texas,* 300–302.

4. James Pike, *Scout and Ranger,* xiv–xv; William C. Holden, "Frontier Problems and Movements in West Texas, 1846–1900" (Ph.D. dissertation, University of Texas, 1928), 61–63.

5. Frank Brown, "Annals of Travis County and the City of Austin: From the Earliest Times to the Close of 1875," Ch. XXIV [1865] (Texas State Archives, Austin).

6. Ann Patton Baenziger, "The Texas State Police During Reconstruction: A Reexamination," *Southwestern Historical Quarterly,* Vol. LXXII, No. 4 (April, 1969), 477–78.

7. A. J. Sowell, *Rangers and Pioneers of Texas,* 234–35.

8. Walter Prescott Webb, *The Texas Rangers,* 82, 238–44.

9. N. A. Jennings, *A Texas Ranger,* 229.

10. J. B. John Dunn, *Perilous Trails of Texas,* 86–87, 106; Ringer v. State, 26 S.W. 69 (Texas, 1894).

11. N. A. Jennings, *A Texas Ranger,* 89–90, 93, 111–12; Dora Neill Raymond, *Captain Lee Hall of Texas,* 37, 45; George Durham, *Taming the Nueces Strip, The Story of McNelly's Rangers,* 8.

12. Rufus Rockwell Wilson, *A Notable Company of Adventurers,* 94–96.

13. J. Frank Dobie, *A Vaquero of the Brush Country,* 82–83; Albert Bigelow Paine, *Captain Bill McDonald, Texas Ranger,* 221–42.

14. Walter Prescott Webb, *The Texas Rangers*, 513.

15. Stephen W. Schuster, "The Modernization of the Texas Rangers: 1933–1936," *West Texas Historical Association Year Book*, Vol. XLIII (October, 1967), 67–70.

16. Fagan *v.* State, 14 S.W.2d 838 (Texas, 1929).

17. Walter Prescott Webb, "Oil Town Cleaned Up," *The State Trooper*, Vol. VIII, No. 4 (December, 1926), 11; "Texas Rangers Praised," *The State Trooper*, Vol. IX, No. 1 (September, 1927), 15; Neff *v.* Elgin, 270 S.W. 873 (Texas, 1925).

18. Texas Revised Civil Statutes, 4413 (11) (1935).

19. Jill Lillie Emma Cossley-Batt, *The Last of the California Rangers*, xvii, 180–94; Horace Bell, *Reminiscences of a Ranger, or Early Times in Southern California*, 165–71.

20. Roger Lane, *Policing the City: Boston 1822–1885*, 136–37, 162–63.

21. *Report of the Acting Governor of Arizona Made to the Secretary of the Interior for the Year 1881*, 9; Stuart N. Lake, *Wyatt Earp*, 315–16.

22. *Report of the Governor of Arizona Made to the Secretary of the Interior for the Year 1883*, 12.

23. *Report of the Governor of Arizona Made to the Secretary of the Interior for the Year 1884*, 10.

24. Arizona Rangers, Governor's Report, Manuscript File (Arizona Pioneers' Historical Society Archives, Tucson); *Report of the Governor of Arizona to the Secretary of the Interior for the Year Ended June 30, 1902*, 88, 172.

25. Arizona Rangers: Good History and Records, Manuscript File (Arizona Pioneers' Historical Society Archives, Tucson).

26. *Report of the Governor of Arizona to the Secretary of the Interior for the Year Ended June 30, 1904*, 78; *Report of the Governor of Arizona to the Secretary of the Interior, 1905*, 69; *Report of the Governor of Arizona to the Secretary of the Interior, 1906*, 21; *Report of the Governor of Arizona to the Secretary of the Interior for the fiscal year ended June 30, 1907*, 13–14.

27. Carl M. Rathbun, "Keeping Peace Along the Mexican Border," *Harper's Weekly*, Vol. L, No. 2604 (November 17, 1906), 1632.

28. *Report of the Governor of Arizona to the Secretary of the Interior for the Year Ended June 30, 1904*, 79.

29. *Ibid.*, 78.

30. Arizona Rangers, Jeff Kidder, Manuscript File (Arizona Pioneers' Historical Society Archives, Tucson); Thomas H. Rynning, *Gun Notches*, 286–89.

31. *Report of the Governor of Arizona to the Secretary of the Interior, 1905*, 68.

32. New Mexico Territory, Secretary, Oaths of Office and Bonds: Territorial Officials, Inspector of Cattle, Mounted Police (University of New Mexico Archives, Albuquerque).

33. William Jackson to Fred Fornof [Fornoff], March 29, 1908, New Mexico Territorial Mounted Police Applications, 1907–1913 (University of New Mexico Archives, Albuquerque).

34. P. B. Estes to John Collier, May 6, 1907, New Mexico Territorial Mounted Police Applications, 1907–1913 (University of New Mexico Archives, Albuquerque).

35. List dated April 3, 1906, New Mexico Territorial Mounted Police Correspondence, 1906–1912 (University of New Mexico Archives, Albuquerque).

36. George Curry to Fred Fornoff, June 14, 1909, New Mexico Territorial

Mounted Police Correspondence, 1906–1912 (University of New Mexico Archives, Albuquerque).

37. W. T. Dufur to Fred Fornoff, September, 1909, New Mexico Territorial Mounted Police Correspondence, 1906–1912 (University of New Mexico Archives, Albuquerque).

38. J. M. Henderson to Fred Fornoff, November, 1909, New Mexico Territorial Mounted Police Correspondence, 1906–1912 (University of New Mexico Archives, Albuquerque).

39. Fred Fornoff to John Collier, June 4, 1910, New Mexico Territorial Mounted Police Correspondence, 1906–1912 (University of New Mexico Archives, Albuquerque).

40. "Report of the Governor of New Mexico [1907]," Serial No. 5296 (1907), 606.

41. New Mexico Territorial Mounted Police Case Records, 1906–1912 (University of New Mexico Archives, Albuquerque).

42. *Statutes of the State of Nevada, Passed at the Special Session of the Legislature, 1908*, ch. 4.

43. *Ibid.*

44. *Ibid.*, sec. 14.

45. Nevada State Police, Criminal Identification Bureau (Nevada State Archives, Carson City).

46. G. A. Raymer to E. D. Boyle, May 16, 1918, Nevada State Police Applications (Nevada State Archives, Carson City).

47. Thomas J. Salter to Delworth S. Woolley, April 2, 1923, Nevada State Police, Misc., 1923 (Nevada State Archives, Carson City).

48. "Labor Record of Governor William E. Sweet," Pamphlet File (University of Colorado Archives, Boulder); J. Frank Norfleet, *Norfleet*, 335–69.

49. Richard Deich to E. D. Boyle, September 14, 1918, Nevada State Police, Miscellaneous (Nevada State Archives, Carson City).

50. California Penal Code, 11103 (1905); Utah Code, 77–59–1.1 (1927); Robert M. Gray, "A History of the Utah State Bureau of Criminal Identification and Investigation," *Utah Historical Quarterly*, Vol. XXIV, No. 2 (April, 1956), 173–76.

51. South Dakota Code of 1939, 55.16 (1935); Kansas Statutes, 75–711 (1939).

52. Frederick S. Warren, "Colorado Legislative Committee Urges State Police Organization," *The State Trooper*, Vol. XII, No. 4 (December, 1930), 14.

53. Revised Statutes of Nebraska, 60–401 (1937).

54. *Thirteenth Annual Report of the State Sheriff* [Fred S. Miner, South Dakota], 4–21.

55. South Dakota Code of 1939, 55.16a (1943).

56. Texas Revised Civil Statutes, 907–10 (1920).

57. J. R. Underwood, "Texas Pleased with Its Expanding Force of Trained Highway Patrolmen," *The State Trooper*, Vol. XIII, No. 2 (October, 1931), 11–12; Texas Penal Code 827a (1931); Texas Revised Civil Statutes, 4413 (12) (4) (1935).

58. Dorotha B. Kelsay (Oregon State Library) to Frank R. Prassel, November 14, 1968; Frank W. Barton, "Gen. Butler Begins His Work of Organizing Oregon State Police," *The State Trooper*, Vol. XII, No. 10 (June, 1931), 7–8.

59. *Rules Governing State Highway Patrol*, 6–8.

60. Alva Ray Stephens, "History of the Oklahoma Highway Patrol" (M.A. thesis, University of Oklahoma, 1957), 15–19.

61. *Acts, Resolutions and Memorials of the Regular Session, Tenth Legislature of the State of Arizona,* ch. 104 (1931).

62. California Vehicle Code, 2409 (1959).

63. Revised Statutes of Nebraska, 60–435 (1937), 60–437 (1937); North Dakota Century Code, 39–03–03 (1935), 39–03–09 (1967); Kansas Statutes, 74–20a02 and 74–20a03 (1937); State v. Bishop, 160 P.2d 658 (Kansas, 1945).

64. Interview with Sergeant Tom Lindquist, Colorado State Patrol, Denver, June 19, 1968; Frederick S. Warren, "Colorado's New State Highway Courtesy Patrol Is Now in Effective Operation," *The State Trooper,* Vol. XVII, No. 4 (December, 1935), 5.

65. Colorado Revised Statutes, 120–10–15 (1949).

66. Revised Codes of Montana, 31–110 (1965); Arizona Revised Statutes, 28–231 (1931).

67. Utah Code, 27–10–5 (1941); Wyoming Statutes, 31–10 (1935).

68. Idaho Code, 19–4810 (1939).

69. Arizona Revised Statutes, 28–252 (1956).

70. New Mexico Statutes, 9–11–5 (1941), 39–2–16 (1941).

71. *New Mexico State Police, 1967, Annual Report;* Interview with Lieutenant Don W. Moberly, New Mexico State Police, Santa Fe, June 13, 1968.

CHAPTER VII:

Ex Parte Crow Dog

1. Karl N. Llewellyn and E. Adamson Hoebel, *The Cheyenne Way,* 99–100, 107–19.

2. Carolyn Thomas Foreman, "The Light-Horse in the Indian Territory," *Chronicles of Oklahoma,* Vol. XXXIV, No. 1 (Spring, 1956), 17–24.

3. Laws of the Choctaw Nation: Act of 1860 (Federal Records Center, Fort Worth, Texas).

4. Laws of the Choctaw Nation: Appropriation Act of 1867 (Federal Records Center, Fort Worth, Texas).

5. John P. Clum, "The San Carlos Police," *New Mexico Historical Review,* Vol. IV, No. 3 (July, 1929), 203–10.

6. William T. Hagan, *Indian Police and Judges,* 45–47.

7. "Police for Indian Reservations," Serial No. 1935 (1880), 2.

8. Ex parte Crow Dog, 109 U.S. 556 (1883); William T. Hagan, *Indian Police and Judges,* 87–89, 98, 145.

9. U.S. v. Clapox, 35 F. 575 (Oregon, 1888).

10. Indian-Pioneer History, Vol. C, 489–90 (Oklahoma Historical Society Archives, Oklahoma City).

11. Paul McKennon to R. L. Kidd, 1940, Hiram Impson, Manuscript File (University of Oklahoma Archives, Norman).

12. *Ibid.*

13. *Sixty-First Annual Report of the Commissioner of Indian Affairs to the Secretary of the Interior, 1892,* 258.

14. *Annual Report of the Commissioner of Indian Affairs, 1895,* 126.

15. *Annual Reports of the Department of the Interior: 1906. Indian Affairs: Report of the Commissioner and Appendixes,* 254.

16. *Sixty-First Annual Report of the Commissioner of Indian Affairs to the Secretary of the Interior, 1892,* 351.

17. *Annual Reports of the Department of the Interior, for the Fiscal Year ended June 30, 1897: Report of the Commissioner of Indian Affairs,* 290.

18. *Annual Reports of the Department of the Interior, 1906. Indian Affairs: Report of the Commissioner and Appendixes,* 294.

19. *Annual Report of the Commissioner of Indian Affairs, 1895,* 283.

20. *Ibid.,* 157–58.

21. *Annual Reports of the Department of the Interior, 1901. Indian Affairs,* 353.

22. "Report of the Commissioner of Indian Affairs," Serial No. 5296 (1907), 10–11.

23. *Ibid.,* 26–31.

24. *Ibid.,* 30.

25. "Report of the Commissioner of Indian Affairs," Serial No. 5453 (1908), 37; 18 U.S.C. 3055 (1912).

26. *Report of the Commissioner to the Five Civilized Tribes, 1911,* 6.

27. *Report of the Commissioner of Indian Affairs for the Fiscal Year Ended June 30, 1912,* 47.

28. *Report of the Commissioner of Indian Affairs for the Fiscal Year Ended June 30, 1913,* 185.

29. *Report of the Commissioner of Indian Affairs for the Fiscal Year Ended June 30, 1911,* 35.

30. *Annual Report of the Secretary of the Interior, 1941,* 420–21.

31. K. W. Rayborn (Special Officer, Window Rock, Arizona) to Frank R. Prassel, October 14, 1968; Interview with Lieutenant Don W. Moberly, New Mexico State Police, Santa Fe, June 13, 1968.

32. 18 U.S.C. 1153 (1948); William B. Benge, "Law and Order on Indian Reservations," *Federal Bar Journal,* Vol. XX, No. 3 (Summer, 1960), 228–29; State v. Begay, 320 P.2d 1017 (New Mexico, 1958).

33. Dean Tidwell, "The Indian Career Officer," *Police Chief,* Vol. XXXVI, No. 11 (November, 1969), 30–31.

34. Barbara Julia Hansen, "Wagon Train Government" (M.A. thesis, University of Colorado, 1962), 101–103.

35. Hubert Howe Bancroft, *Popular Tribunals,* I, 719–20.

36. N. A. Jennings, *A Texas Ranger,* 108.

37. *Report of the Acting Governor of Arizona Made to the Secretary of the Interior for the Year 1881,* 9.

38. James D. Richardson (ed.), *A Compilation of the Messages and Papers of the Presidents, 1789–1902,* VIII, 53–54.

39. 16 U.S.C. 23 (1883).

40. "Report of the Acting Superintendent of the Yosemite National Park," Serial No. 5295 (1907), 557–58.

41. Joyce L. Kornbluh (ed.), *Rebel Voices,* 251–57.

42. Sydney G. Pettit, "Judge Begbie in Action: The Establishment of Law and Preservation of Order in British Columbia," *British Columbia Historical Quarterly,* Vol. XI, No. 2 (April, 1947), 128–29, 146.

43. *The Consolidated Statutes of Canada,* "An Act respecting Riots near Public Works" (1845).

44. An Act respecting the Administration of Justice, and for the establishment of a Police Force in the North West Territories (1873), 36 Vict., c. 35 (Canada).

45. *Ibid.*

46. John Peter Turner, *The North-West Mounted Police, 1873–1893*, I, 92–107.

47. Thomas H. Rynning, *Gun Notches*, 70, 127, 309–20; Dane Coolidge, *Fighting Men of the West*, 225–28, 242–44.

CHAPTER VIII:

"¡Alto, Federales!"

1. Organic Act of the Territory of Idaho (1863), sec. 10.

2. *Evening Review* (Albuquerque, New Mexico), March 6, 1882.

3. *Ibid.*, March 18, 1882.

4. "Index to Names of United States Marshals, 1789–1960" (Washington: National Archives, 1961); Charles E. Calvert, "United States Marshals: Territorial and State" (Colorado State Archives, Denver).

5. *Instructions to United States Marshals, Attorneys, Clerks, and Commissioners: January 1, 1899*, 25.

6. *Report of the Governor of Arizona to the Secretary of the Interior, 1894*, 65.

7. "Earnings of United States Marshals, Attorneys, Etc. Per Annum," Serial No. 2206 (1884), 2–10; *Annual Report of the Attorney-General of the United States for the Year 1881*, 9–10, 15.

8. *Instructions to United States Marshals, Attorneys, Clerks, and Commissioners: January 1, 1899*, 20, 25.

9. "Compensation of District Attorneys, Marshals, and Circuit Court Commissioners," Serial No. 2030 (1882), 6.

10. "Instructions to United States Marshals, Attorneys, Clerks, and Commissioners," Serial No. 5084 (1907), 119.

11. *Instructions to United States Marshals, Attorneys, Clerks, and Commissioners: January 1, 1899*, 18; Office Records, 1884, U.S. Marshal's Office, Arizona Territory (Arizona Pioneers' Historical Society Archives, Tucson).

12. Cunningham *v.* Neagle, 135 U.S. 1 (1890).

13. "Tragedy on a Train!," "The Capture," San Antonio *Daily Express*, February 22, 1885.

14. Asher *v.* Cabell, 50 F. 818 (5th Cir., 1892); William MacLeod Raine, *Famous Sheriffs and Western Outlaws*, 27–44.

15. "Index to Names of United States Marshals, 1789–1960" (Washington, National Archives, 1961).

16. Grant Foreman—U.S. Marshal, Vertical File (Oklahoma Historical Society Archives, Oklahoma City); Evett Dumas Nix, *Oklahombres*, 71–73, 83–85; Richard S. Graves, *Oklahoma Outlaws*, i.

17. "Annual Report of the Attorney-General of the United States for the Year 1903," Serial No. 4657 (1903), 334–36.

18. Indian-Pioneer History, Vol. XCIII, 165–66 (Oklahoma Historical Society Archives, Oklahoma City).

19. *Ibid.*, Vol. II, 336.

20. Charles B. Rhodes, Manuscript File (University of Oklahoma Archives, Norman); Grant Foreman—U.S. Marshal, Vertical File (Oklahoma Historical Society Archives, Oklahoma City); *Annual Report of the Commissioner of Indian Affairs, 1895*, 158.

21. Indian-Pioneer History, Vol. XV, 349 (Oklahoma Historical Society Archives, Oklahoma City).

22. Chris Madsen, "United States Deputy Marshals," Manuscript File (Oklahoma Historical Society Archives, Oklahoma City).

23. Indian-Pioneer History, Vol. XXIX, 306–307 (Oklahoma Historical Society Archives, Oklahoma City).

24. *Ibid.*, Vol. XXXIV, 30.

25. *Annual Report of the Commissioner of Indian Affairs, 1895*, 158.

26. Agreement between Wm. Tilghman and James D. Ford, William Tilghman, Manuscript File (University of Oklahoma Archives, Norman).

27. William Frank Jones, *The Experiences of a Deputy U.S. Marshal of the Indian Territory*, 27; Kiowa-Courts, Vertical File (Oklahoma Historical Society Archives, Oklahoma City).

28. Indian-Pioneer History, Vol. II, 199 (Oklahoma Historical Society Archives, Oklahoma City).

29. Wayne Gard, *Frontier Justice*, 280–89.

30. Grand Jury Docket, U.S. Court, 2nd Judicial Division, Indian Territory, 1893–1897 (Federal Records Center, Fort Worth, Texas).

31. U.S. Commissioner's Docket [criminal cases], 2nd Judicial Division, Indian Territory, 1895–1899 (Federal Records Center, Fort Worth, Texas).

32. Docket of Fines, U.S. Court, 1st Judicial Division, Indian Territory, 1893–1895 (Federal Records Center, Fort Worth, Texas).

33. Employees in the District of Paso del Norte, 1869, Records of the Bureau of Customs—El Paso District (Federal Records Center, Fort Worth, Texas).

34. Records of Payments, Salaries, Collectors Office, Customs House, June, 1884–September, 1899, Records of the Bureau of Customs—El Paso District (Federal Records Center, Fort Worth, Texas).

35. Scrapbook—Department of the Interior, Records of the Bureau of Customs—El Paso District (Federal Records Center, Fort Worth, Texas).

36. Records of the U.S. District Court, El Paso, Texas, Chinese Exclusion Act (Federal Records Center, Fort Worth, Texas).

37. J. Evetts Haley, *Jeff Milton*, 340–402; Jeff Milton, Manuscript File (Arizona Pioneers' Historical Society Archives, Tucson).

38. Albert Langeluttig, "Federal Police," *Annals of the American Academy of Political and Social Science*, Vol. CXLVI (November, 1929), 54.

39. 8 U.S.C. 1357 (1952); 19 U.S.C. 507 (1866).

40. Norman Ansley, "The United States Secret Service: An Administrative History," *Journal of Criminal Law, Criminology and Police Science*, Vol. XLVII, No. 1 (May–June, 1956), 93–95; "Secret Service Work," *Colorado Sun* (Denver), December 31, 1893.

41. Joyce L. Kornbluh (ed.), *Rebel Voices*, 318–24.

42. Frederick Law Olmstead, *A Journey Through Texas*, 287.

43. 16 U.S.C. 10 (1905); 16 U.S.C. 559 (1905).

44. "Report of the Acting Superintendent of the Sequoia and General Grant National Parks," Serial No. 5452 (1908), 457–58.

45. *Ibid.*, 451.

46. "Annual Report of the Superintendent of the Yellowstone National Park," Serial No. 5295 (1907), 551–52.

47. Robert F. Gibbs (National Park Service) to Frank R. Prassel, October 30, 1969.

EPILOGUE:
"Do Not Forsake Me"

1. George Ward Nichols, "Wild Bill," *Harper's New Monthly Magazine*, Vol. XXXIV, No. 201 (February, 1867), 285.

2. Lloyd C. Henning, "Sheriff, Scholar and Gentleman: Frank J. Wattron," Manuscript File (University of Arizona Archives, Tucson).

3. Frank J. Wattron, Manuscript File (Arizona Pioneers' Historical Society Archives, Tucson).

4. *Ibid.*

5. Ron Donoho to Neal E. Miller, August 4, 1967 (Wyoming State Archives, Cheyenne).

6. Zoe A. Tilghman, *Marshal of the Last Frontier*, 312–30; Ex parte Tilghman, 177 P. 9 (Kansas, 1918).

7. Albuquerque *Review*, September 2, 1882.

8. George W. Hansen, "True Story of Wild Bill–McCanles Affray in Jefferson County, Nebraska," *Nebraska History Magazine*, Vol. X, No. 2 (April–June, 1927), 84; O. W. Coursey, *Wild Bill*, 80.

9. Thomas H. Rynning, *Gun Notches*, 44–45.

10. Grover F. Sexton, *The Arizona Sheriff*, 3, 24.

Bibliography

Personal Interviews and Correspondence

Benge, William B. (Chief of Law and Order, Bureau of Indian Affairs) to Frank R. Prassel; October 2, 1968.

Boyd, N. C. (Captain, Wyoming Highway Patrol), Cheyenne, Wyoming; June 20, 1968, Interview.

Cassingham, Ron (Inspector, Nevada Highway Patrol), Carson City, Nevada; August 6, 1968, Interview.

Combs, Barry B. (Union Pacific Railroad) to Frank R. Prassel; July 24, 1968.

Gaffney, Merrill S. (Executive Secretary, California Peace Officers Association), Sacramento, California; August 8, 1968, Interview.

Gibbs, Robert F. (National Park Service) to Frank R. Prassel; October 30, 1969.

Guidry, Jerry J. (Special Agent, Southern Pacific Railroad), San Antonio, Texas; September 16, 1969, Interview.

Hoffman, E. H. (Senior Inspector, United States Border Patrol), El Paso, Texas; January 24, 1970, Interview.

Jenkins, Myra Ellen (New Mexico State Archives) to Frank R. Prassel; July 30, 1968.

Kelsay, Dorotha B. (Oregon State Library) to Frank R. Prassel; November 14, 1968.

Lindquist, Tom (Sergeant, Colorado State Patrol), Denver, Colorado; June 19, 1968, Interview.

Maiden, Robert R. (Colorado Peace Officers Association) to Frank R. Prassel; July 11, 1968.

Moberly, Don W. (Lieutenant, New Mexico State Police), Santa Fe, New Mexico; June 13, 1968, Interview.

Nimmo, George M. (Director, Wyoming Law Enforcement Academy), Laramie, Wyoming; June 21, 1968, Interview.

Nuñez, Peter E. (Former Inspector, Guanajuato State Police), San Antonio, Texas; December 19, 1969, Interview.

Petty, Dale (Lieutenant, Oklahoma Highway Patrol), Oklahoma City, Oklahoma; June 26, 1968, Interview.

Rayborn, K. W. (Special Officer, Window Rock, Arizona) to Frank R. Prassel; October 14, 1968.

Settel, Arthur (Bureau of Customs) to Frank R. Prassel; August 28, 1968.

Stratton, George (Lieutenant, Oklahoma Highway Patrol), Oklahoma City, Oklahoma; June 26, 1968, Interview.

Archival Materials

Arizona Pioneers' Historical Society, Tucson, Arizona:
    Arizona Rangers: Good History and Records, Manuscript File.
    Arizona Rangers, Governor's Report: Organization of Rangers, Manuscript File.
    Arizona Rangers, Jeff Kidder: Politics, Shooting and Burial, Manuscript File.
    Bailey, Tom (Seth), Manuscript File.
    Daily Journal, March 17, 1890–June 19, 1890, U.S. Marshal R. H. Paul, Arizona Territory.
    Milton, Jeff, Manuscript File.
    Mossman, Burton C., Manuscript File.
    Office Records, 1884, U.S. Marshal's Office, Arizona Territory.
    Wattron, Frank J., Manuscript File.
    Wheeler, Harry, Manuscript File.
Arizona State Archives, Phoenix, Arizona:
    Hayes, Jess, "Gila County Sheriffs," Manuscript File.
    In the Matter of the Inquest Over the Bodies of Robert F. McBride, Martin R. Kempton, and Thomas K. Wootan, Deceased, Transcript.
Colorado Historical Society, Denver, Colorado:
    Dawson, T. F., Scrapbooks.
    Howe, Sam, Scrapbooks.
Colorado State Archives, Denver, Colorado:
    Calvert, Charles E., "United States Marshals: Territorial and State."

Maiden, Robert R., "Colorado Sheriffs Who Failed to Complete Terms of Office."

Payroll of Sheriff's Department, Denver, 1904–1905.

Police Docket, Denver, 1873.

Record of Deputy Sheriffs, Arapahoe County, 1892–1894.

Federal Records Center, Denver, Colorado:

Criminal Dockets, First Judicial District, New Mexico Territory, August 1, 1882–March 26, 1912.

Records of the U.S. District Court, Territory of New Mexico. Fifth Judicial District, 1890–1911.

Records of the U.S. District Court, Territory of New Mexico. First Judicial District, 1896–1909.

Records of the U.S. District Court, Territory of New Mexico. Seventh Judicial District, 1909–1911.

Federal Records Center, Fort Worth, Texas:

Docket of Fines, U.S. Court, 1st Judicial Division, Indian Territory, 1893–1895.

Employees in the District of Paso del Norte, 1869. Records of the Bureau of Customs—El Paso District.

Grand Jury Docket, U.S. Court, 2nd Judicial Division, Indian Territory, 1893–1897.

Laws of the Choctaw Nation.

Records of the U.S. District Court, El Paso, Texas, Chinese Exclusion Act.

Records of Payments, Salaries, Collectors Office, Customs House, June, 1884–September, 1899. Records of the Bureau of Customs—El Paso District.

Scrapbook—Department of the Interior. Records of the Bureau of Customs—El Paso District.

U.S. Commissioner's Docket [criminal cases], 2nd Judicial Division, Indian Territory, 1895–1899.

U.S. Court Docket, Central District, Indian Territory [criminal cases], 1898–1904.

Nevada State Archives, Carson City, Nevada:

Letters of Recognition to Registrars.

Nevada State Police, Files:

Applications.

Captain Dickerson.

Criminal Identification Bureau.

General.

Inspector [D. B. Renear], 1924.

293

      Miscellaneous.

      Miscellaneous, 1923.

      Miscellaneous Reports, 1923.

      Payrolls, Etc.

      Payrolls, 1923.

      Reports, 1923.

   State Detectives, File.

   State Police and Highway Patrol, File.

   State Police (Miscellaneous), File.

Oklahoma Historical Society, Oklahoma City, Oklahoma:

   Foreman, Grant—U.S. Marshal, Vertical File.

   Indian-Pioneer History (W.P.A. Project, 1937).

   Kiowa-Courts, Vertical File.

   Kiowa-Employee, Vertical File.

   Madsen, Chris, "United States Deputy Marshals," Manuscript File.

San Antonio Police Department, San Antonio, Texas:

   Sergeant's Record of Arrest: 1913–1914.

   Sergeants' Record of Arrest: 1924.

San Francisco Public Library, San Francisco, California:

   Police, Chiefs and Marshals, Photo File.

   Police, China Town Squad, Photo File.

Stanford University Archives, Stanford, California:

   Bradford, James Otey, Papers.

   Jacks, David, Papers.

Texas State Archives, Austin, Texas:

   Brown, Frank, "Annals of Travis County and the City of Austin: From the Earliest Times to the Close of 1875."

   Ford, John S., "Memoirs."

University of Arizona Archives, Tucson, Arizona:

   Henning, Lloyd C., "Sheriff, Scholar and Gentleman: Frank J. Wattron," Manuscript File.

   McKinney, Joseph Thomas, Papers.

   Slaughter, [John], Manuscript File.

University of California at Berkeley, Bancroft Library, Berkeley, California:

   McKinstry, George, Documents.

   Pierce, Elisha H., Letters to, 1862–1863.

   Rowell, Chester H., Papers.

University of Colorado Archives, Boulder, Colorado:

   Costigan, Edward P., Papers.

   Independent District, Gilpin County, [Colorado], "Laws of Independent District [1861]."

Independent District, Gilpin County, [Colorado], "Minutes of Miners' Meeting [May, 1860]."

"Labor Record of Governor William E. Sweet," Pamphlet File.

University of New Mexico Archives, Albuquerque, New Mexico:

New Mexico Territorial Mounted Police Applications, 1907–1913.

New Mexico Territorial Mounted Police Case Records, 1906–1912.

New Mexico Territorial Mounted Police Correspondence, 1906–1912.

New Mexico Territorial Mounted Police Description Cards, 1906–1910.

New Mexico Territory, Secretary, Oaths of Office and Bonds: Territorial Officials, Inspector of Cattle, Mounted Police.

Territorial Secretary. Extradition papers for fugitives from New Mexico, 1900–1905.

Thompson, Albert W., "Clay Allison, Extinguisher of Bad Men."

University of Oklahoma Archives, Norman, Oklahoma:

Impson, Hiram, Manuscript File.

Lee, Mrs. Ottie, Manuscript File.

Rhodes, Charles B., Manuscript File.

Tilghman, [Mr. and Mrs.] William, Manuscript File.

University of Wyoming, Western History Research Center, Laramie, Wyoming:

Boswell, Nathaniel K., Manuscript File.

Canton, Frank M., Manuscript File.

Carr, Thomas Jefferson, Manuscript File.

Cook, Alfred, Manuscript File.

Le Fors, Joe, Manuscript File.

Loomis, William H., Manuscript File.

Peace Officers, Manuscript File.

Schnitger, William R., Manuscript File.

Wyoming State Archives and Historical Department, Cheyenne, Wyoming:

Donoho, Ron, to Miller, Neal E., August 4, 1967, Letter File.

Theses and Dissertations

Bailey, Rebecca. "Wyoming Stock Inspectors and Detectives, 1873–1890." Unpublished M.A. thesis, University of Wyoming, 1948.

Benson, Maxine Frances. "Labor and the Law in Colorado 1915–1917: The People vs. John R. Lawson." Unpublished M.A. thesis, University of Colorado, 1962.

Cheng, Teh-Show. "Police Systems in California." Unpublished M.A. thesis, University of California at Berkeley, 1948.

Gunn, Jack Winton. "Life of Ben McCulloch." Unpublished M.A. thesis, University of Texas, 1947.

Hansen, Barbara Julia. "Wagon Train Government." Unpublished M.A. thesis, University of Colorado, 1962.

Hendricks, George David. "The Bad Man of the West." Unpublished M.A. thesis, University of Texas, 1938.

Holden, William C. "Frontier Problems and Movements in West Texas, 1846–1900." Unpublished Ph.D. dissertation, University of Texas, 1928.

Hollister, Charles A. "The Organization and Administration of the Sheriff's Office in Arizona." Unpublished M.A. thesis, University of Arizona, 1946.

Nunn, William Curtis. "A Study of the State Police During the E. J. Davis Administration." Unpublished M.A. thesis, University of Texas, 1931.

Prassel, Frank R. "Leisure Time Activities in San Antonio, 1877–1917." Unpublished M.A. thesis, Trinity University, 1961.

Pritchett, Robert Thomas. "Impeachment Proceedings in Congress Against John Charles Watrous of Texas: 1851–1861." Unpublished M.A. thesis, University of Texas, 1925.

Spiller, Phillip N. "A Short History of the San Antonio Police Department." Unpublished M.S. thesis, Trinity University, 1954.

Steakley, Dan Lewis. "The Border Patrol of the San Antonio Collection District." Unpublished M.A. thesis, University of Texas, 1936.

Stephens, Alva Ray. "History of the Oklahoma Highway Patrol." Unpublished M.A. thesis, University of Oklahoma, 1957.

Thomson, George. "The History of Penal Institutions in the Rocky Mountain West." Unpublished Ph.D. dissertation, University of Colorado, 1965.

Ward, Charles F. "The Salt War of San Elizario, 1877." Unpublished M.A. thesis, University of Texas, 1932.

West, John Oliver. "To Die Like a Man: The 'Good' Outlaw Tradition in the American Southwest." Unpublished Ph.D. dissertation, University of Texas, 1964.

Whitten, Woodrow Carlton. "Criminal Syndicalism and the Law in California: 1919–1927." Unpublished Ph.D. dissertation, University of California at Berkeley, 1946.

Williams, Harrison Grant. "The Peace Officer in California: Concept and Development." Unpublished M.Crim. thesis, University of California at Berkeley, 1964.

Woo, Tao Fu. "State Police and State Highway Patrols." Unpublished M.S. thesis, University of Colorado, 1949.

Government Documents

Annual Message of Bryan Callaghan, Mayor of the City of San Antonio and Review of Reports of City Officers for Fiscal Year Ending May 31, 1910. San Antonio, J. A. Appler Press, 1910.

Annual Message of Hon. Marshall Hicks, Mayor of the City of San Antonio and Reports of City Officers for Fiscal Year Ending June, 1900. San Antonio, Buckeye Printing Co., 1900.

Annual Report of the Attorney-General of the United States for the Year 1881. Washington, Government Printing Office, 1881.

"Annual Report of the Attorney-General of the United States for the Year 1897," Serial No. 3655, 1897.

"Annual Report of the Attorney-General of the United States for the Year 1903," Serial No. 4657, 1903.

Annual Report of the Commissioner of Indian Affairs, 1895. Washington, Government Printing Office, 1896.

Annual Report of the Secretary of the Interior, 1941. Washington, U.S. Government Printing Office, 1941.

"Annual Report of the Superintendent of the Yellowstone National Park," Serial No. 5295, 1907.

Annual Reports of the Department of the Interior for the Fiscal Year Ended June 30, 1897: Report of the Commissioner of Indian Affairs. Washington, Government Printing Office, 1897.

Annual Reports of the Department of the Interior, 1901. Indian Affairs. Washington, Government Printing Office, 1902.

Annual Reports of the Department of the Interior, 1906. Indian Affairs: Report of the Commissioner and Appendixes. Washington, Government Printing Office, 1906.

Arizona Highway Patrol. Annual Report. Phoenix, n.p., 1934.

The Border Patrol: Its Origin and Work. Washington, U.S. Government Printing Office, 1967.

The Challenge of Crime in a Free Society: A Report by the President's Commission on Law Enforcement and Administration of Justice. Washington, U.S. Government Printing Office, 1967.

"Compensation of District Attorneys, Marshals, and Circuit Court Commissioners," Serial No. 2030, 1882.

Comprehensive Law Enforcement Planning in the Alamo Area Council of Governments Region. San Antonio, Alamo Area Council of Governments, 1969.

"Earnings of United States Marshals, Attorneys, Etc. Per Annum," Serial No. 2206, 1884.

"El Paso Troubles in Texas," Serial No. 1809, 1878.

"Families of Certain Indian Policemen," Serial No. 4573, 1904.

"Female Prisoners in County Jails [1890]," Serial No. 3028, 1896.

"Index to Names of United States Marshals, 1789–1960." Washington, National Archives, 1961 (Microcopy T–577).

Inmates of Institutions: U.S. Census of Population, 1960. Washington, U.S. Government Printing Office, 1961.

Instructions to United States Marshals, Attorneys, Clerks, and Commissioners: January 1, 1899. Washington, Government Printing Office, 1898.

"Instructions to United States Marshals, Attorneys, Clerks, and Commissioners," Serial No. 5084, 1907.

"Letter from The Assistant Secretary of War," Serial No. 3414, 1895.

"Medals for the Captors of Sitting Bull," Serial No. 6071, 1911.

New Mexico State Police, 1967, Annual Report. Santa Fe, New Mexico State Police, 1968.

"Police for Indian Reservations," Serial No. 1935, 1880.

"Police Statistics for 1890 of Cities of the U.S.," Serial No. 3029, 1895.

"Prisoners in County Jails [1890]," Serial No. 3028, Part 2, 1896.

Report of the Acting Governor of Arizona Made to the Secretary of the Interior for the Year 1881. Washington, Government Printing Office, 1881.

"Report of the Acting Superintendent of the Sequoia and General Grant National Parks," Serial No. 5452, 1908.

"Report of the Acting Superintendent of the Yosemite National Park," Serial No. 5295, 1907.

"Report of the Commissioner of Indian Affairs," Serial No. 5296, 1907.

"Report of the Commissioner of Indian Affairs, " Serial No. 5453, 1908.

Report of the Commissioner of Indian Affairs for the Fiscal Year Ended June 30, 1911. Washington, Government Printing Office, 1912.

Report of the Commissioner of Indian Affairs for the Fiscal Year Ended June 30, 1912. Washington, Government Printing Office, 1912.

Report of the Commissioner of Indian Affairs for the Fiscal Year Ended June 30, 1913. Washington, Government Printing Office, 1914.

Report of the Commissioner to the Five Civilized Tribes, 1911. Washington, Government Printing Office, 1911.

Report of the Governor of Arizona Made to the Secretary of the Interior for the Year 1883. Washington, Government Printing Office, 1883.

Report of the Governor of Arizona Made to the Secretary of the In-

terior for the Year 1884. Washington, Government Printing Office, 1884.

Report of the Governor of Arizona to the Secretary of the Interior, 1885. Washington, Government Printing Office, 1885.

Report of the Governor of Arizona to the Secretary of the Interior, 1894. Washington, Government Printing Office, 1894.

Report of the Governor of Arizona to the Secretary of the Interior, for the Year Ended June 30, 1902. Washington, Government Printing Office, 1903.

Report of the Governor of Arizona to the Secretary of the Interior, for the Year Ended June 30, 1904. Washington, Government Printing Office, 1904.

Report of the Governor of Arizona to the Secretary of the Interior, 1905. Washington, Government Printing Office, 1905.

Report of the Governor of Arizona to the Secretary of the Interior, 1906. Washington, Government Printing Office, 1906.

Report of the Governor of Arizona to the Secretary of the Interior for the fiscal year ended June 30, 1907. Washington, Government Printing Office, 1907.

"Report of the Governor of New Mexico [1907]," Serial No. 5296, 1907.

Report of the Superintendent for the Five Civilized Tribes of Oklahoma, 1919. Washington, Government Printing Office, 1919.

"Report on the Defective, Dependent and Delinquent Classes [1880]," Serial No. 2151, 1888.

Rules Governing State Highway Patrol. State of Arizona, n.p., 1933.

San Antonio Police Department Annual Report: 1966. San Antonio, San Antonio Police Department, 1967.

San Francisco Municipal Reports for the Fiscal Year 1863–1864. San Francisco, William P. Harrison, 1864.

San Francisco Municipal Reports for the Fiscal Year 1894–1895. San Francisco, Hilton Printing Co., 1895.

Sixty-First Annual Report of the Commissioner of Indian Affairs to the Secretary of the Interior, 1892. Washington, Government Printing Office, 1892.

"Social Statistics of Cities [1880]," Serial No. 2149, 1887.

Task Force Report: The Police. Washington, U.S. Government Printing Office, 1967.

Thirteenth Annual Report of the State Sheriff [Fred S. Miner, South Dakota]. Pierre, n.p., 1930.

Uniform Crime Reports for the United States [1967]. Washington, U.S. Government Printing Office, 1968.

Uniform Crime Reports for the United States [1968]. Washington, U.S. Government Printing Office, 1969.
Wyoming Highway Patrol. Wyoming Highway Patrol, n.p., n.d.

Cases

Allen *v.* State, 419 S.W.2d 852 (Texas, 1967).
Asher *v.* Cabell, 50 F. 818 (5th Cir., 1892).
Baker *v.* Hines, 213 P. 313 (Oklahoma, 1923).
Bracken *v.* Cato, 54 F.2d 457 (5th Cir., 1931).
Browning *v.* Graves, 152 S.W.2d 515 (Texas, 1941).
Burton *v.* State, 101 S.W. 226 (Texas, 1907).
Caldwell *v.* State, 41 Tex. 86 (1874).
City of Galveston *v.* Brown, 67 S.W. 156 (Texas, 1902).
City of Houston *v.* Estes, 79 S.W. 848 (Texas, 1904).
Corder *v.* People, 287 P. 85 (Colorado, 1930).
Cortez *v.* State, 66 S.W. 453 (Texas, 1902).
Cortez *v.* State, 69 S.W. 536 (Texas, 1902).
Cunningham *v.* Neagle, 135 U.S. 1 (1890).
Ex parte Abbey, 237 P. 179 (Arizona, 1925).
Ex parte Crow Dog, 109 U.S. 556 (1883).
Ex parte Tilghman, 177 P. 9 (Kansas, 1918).
Ex parte Tracey, 93 S.W. 538 (Texas, 1905).
Fagan *v.* State, 14 S.W.2d 838 (Texas, 1929).
Grafft *v.* State, 113 S.W.2d 546 (Texas, 1938).
Helgeson *v.* Powell, 34 P.2d 957 (Idaho, 1934).
Hixon *v.* Cupp, 49 P. 927 (Oklahoma, 1897).
Horn *v.* State, 73 P. 705 (Wyoming, 1903).
In re Boyle, 57 P. 706 (Idaho, 1899).
Jacobs *v.* State, 12 S.W. 408 (Texas, 1889).
James *v.* State, 44 Tex. 314 (Texas, 1875).
Jones *v.* State, 9 S.W. 53 (Texas, 1888).
Jones *v.* State, 65 S.W. 92 (Texas, 1901).
Jones *v.* State, 238 S.W. 661 (Texas, 1922).
Jones *v.* State, 109 S.W.2d 244 (Texas, 1937).
Kasling *v.* Morris, 9 S.W. 739 (Texas, 1888).
King *v.* Brown, 94 S.W. 328 (Texas, 1906).
Kinnomen *v.* Great Northern Ry. Co., 158 N.W. 1058 (North Dakota, 1916).
Kusah *v.* McCorkle, 170 P. 1023 (Washington, 1918).
LaClef *v.* City of Concordia, 21 P. 272 (Kansas, 1889).
Lasater *v.* Waits, 68 S.W. 500 (Texas, 1902).

Lyle v. State, 17 S.W. 425 (Texas, 1886).

McCasland v. Board of Commissioners of Adair County, 258 P. 750 (Oklahoma, 1927).

McLain v. Arnold, 174 P. 563 (Oklahoma, 1918).

Meek v. Tilghman, 154 P. 1190 (Oklahoma, 1916).

Meldrum v. State, 146 P. 596 (Wyoming, 1915).

Miles v. Wright, 194 P. 88 (Arizona, 1920).

Miller v. Ouray Electric Light and Power Company, 70 P. 447 (Colorado, 1902).

Moyer v. Peabody, 212 U.S. 78 (1909).

Neff v. Elgin, 270 S.W. 873 (Texas, 1925).

Nolen v. State, 9 Tex. Ct. App. R. 419 (1880).

O'Neal v. State, 22 S.W. 25 (Texas, 1893).

Paris v. State, 31 S.W. 855 (Texas, 1895).

Patton v. State, 86 S.W.2d 774 (Texas, 1935).

Presley v. Ft. Worth & D. C. Ry. Co., 145 S.W. 669 (Texas, 1912).

Ray v. State, 70 S.W. 23 (Texas, 1902).

Reeves v. State, 258 S.W. 577 (Texas, 1924).

Ringer v. State, 26 S.W. 69 (Texas, 1894).

Roberts v. State, 158 N.W. 930 (Nebraska, 1916).

Serrato v. State, 171 S.W. 1133 (Texas, 1914).

Sima v. Skaggs Payless Drug Center, 353 P.2d 1085 (Idaho, 1960).

Simmerman v. State, 17 N.W. 115 (Nebraska, 1883).

State v. Anselmo, 148 P. 1071 (Utah, 1915).

State v. Autheman, 274 P. 805 (Idaho, 1929).

State v. Begay, 320 P.2d 1017 (New Mexico, 1958).

State v. Bishop, 160 P.2d 658 (Kansas, 1945).

State v. Bradshaw, 161 P. 710 (Montana, 1916).

State v. Dreiling, 12 P.2d 735 (Kansas, 1932).

State v. Hum Quock, 300 P. 220 (Montana, 1931).

State v. Neely, 300 P. 561 (Montana, 1931).

State v. Middleton, 192 P. 483 (New Mexico, 1920).

State v. Wilson, 243 P. 359 (Idaho, 1925).

State Bank of Monte Vista v. Brennan, 43 P. 1050 (Colorado, 1896).

Steinicke v. Harr, 240 P. 66 (Oklahoma, 1925).

Stephenson v. State, 249 S.W. 492 (Texas, 1923).

Sterling v. Constantin, 287 U.S. 378 (1932).

Taylor v. Slaughter, 42 P.2d 235 (Oklahoma, 1935).

Tuttle v. Short, 288 P. 524 (Wyoming, 1930).

U.S. v. Clapox, 35 F. 575 (Oregon, 1888).

Weatherford v. State, 21 S.W. 251 (Texas, 1893).

White v. Texas, 310 U.S. 530 (1940).

Wiley *v.* State, 170 P. 869 (Arizona, 1918).
Wright *v.* State, 44 Tex. 645 (1876).

Constitutions

Constitution of the State of Arizona (1910), art. 2, sec. 26.
Organic Act of the Territory of Idaho (1863), sec. 10.
Constitution of the State of Idaho (1890), art. 14, sec. 6.
Constitution of the Commonwealth of Kentucky (1891), sec. 225.
Constitution of Montana (1889), art. 3, sec. 31.
Constitution of North Dakota (1889), art. 13, sec. 190.
Constitution of the State of South Carolina (1895), art. 8, sec. 9.
Plans and Powers of the Provisional Government of Texas (1835), "Of the Military," art. IX.
Constitution of the Republic of Texas (1836), art. 4, sec. 12.
Constitution of the State of Texas (1845), art. 14, sec. 13.
Constitution of the State of Texas (1866), art. 4, sec. 18.
Constitution of the State of Texas (1869), art. 5, secs. 18, 21.
Constitution of the State of Texas (1876), art. 5, secs. 18, 23.
Constitution of Utah (1895), art. 12, sec. 16.
Constitution of the State of Wyoming (1889), art. 19, sec. 6.

Statutory Materials

United States:
   Code, Title 8. St. Paul, Minnesota, West Publishing Co.
   Code, Title 16. St. Paul, Minnesota, West Publishing Co.
   Code, Title 18. St. Paul, Minnesota, West Publishing Co.
   Code, Title 19. St. Paul, Minnesota, West Publishing Co.
Arizona:
   Revised Statutes. St. Paul, Minnesota, West Publishing Co.
   Acts, Resolutions, and Memorials of the Regular Session, Tenth Legislature of the State of Arizona. N.p., Arizona Printers, 1931.
California:
   Education Code. San Francisco, Bancroft-Whitney Co.
   Government Code. San Francisco, Bancroft-Whitney Co.
   Penal Code. San Francisco, Bancroft-Whitney Co.
   Vehicle Code. San Francisco, Bancroft-Whitney Co.
   The Statutes of California. N.p., Eugene Casserly, State Printer, 1851.
Colorado:
   Revised Statutes. Denver, Bradford-Robinson Printing Co.

Idaho:
  Code. Indianapolis, Bobbs-Merrill Co.
  Laws of the Territory of Idaho, First Session. Lewiston, Idaho,
    James A. Glasscock, Territorial Printer, 1864.
Kansas:
  Statutes. Topeka, Kansas, Harry "Bud" Timberlake, State Printer.
  Laws of the Territory of Kansas, 1857–1858. Lecompton, Kansas
    Territory, R. H. Bennet, Public Printer, n.d.
Montana:
  Revised Codes. Indianapolis, Allen Smith Co.
  *Compiled Statutes of Montana, Embracing the Laws of a General
    and Permanent Nature, in Force at the Expiration of the Fifteenth
    Regular Session of the Legislative Assembly.* Helena, Montana,
    Journal Publishing Co., 1888.
Nebraska:
  Revised Statutes. Lincoln, Nebraska, George H. Turner, State Li-
    brarian.
  Laws, Joint Resolutions, and Memorials of the State of Nebraska.
    Omaha, Nebraska, Henry Gibson, State Printer, 1889.
Nevada:
  Revised Statutes. Carson City, Nevada, Legislative Counsel Bureau.
  *The General Statutes of the State of Nevada: In force from 1861 to
    1885, inclusive.* Carson City, Nevada, Superintendent of State
    Printing, 1885.
  *Statutes of the State of Nevada, Passed at the Special Session of the
    Legislature, 1908.* Carson City, Nevada, State Printing Office,
    1908.
New Mexico:
  Statutes. Indianapolis, Allen Smith Co.
  *Leyes de la Asamblea Legislativa del Territorio de Nuevo Mexico,
    1891.* Santa Fe, New Mexico, Compania Impresoria del Nuevo
    Mexicano, 1891.
North Dakota:
  Century Code. Indianapolis, Allen Smith Co.
  *Laws Passed at the Seventeenth Session of the Legislative Assembly
    of the Territory of Dakota.* Bismarck, Dakota, Tribune Printers
    and Binders, 1887.
Oklahoma:
  Statutes. St. Paul, Minnesota, West Publishing Co.
Oregon:
  Revised Statutes. Portland, Oregon, Legislative Counsel Committee.
  The Statutes of Oregon. N.p., Asahel Bush, Public Printer, 1854.

South Dakota:

Code of 1939. Pierre, South Dakota, State Publishing Co.

Laws of the Legislative Assembly of the Territory of Dakota. Yankton, Dakota Territory, Bowen and Kingsbury, Public Printers, 1879.

Texas:

Code of Criminal Procedure. Kansas City, Missouri, Vernon Law Book Co.

Penal Code. Kansas City, Missouri, Vernon Law Book Co.

Revised Civil Statutes. Kansas City, Missouri, Vernon Law Book Co.

Utah:

Code. Indianapolis, Allen Smith Co.

Acts, Resolutions and Memorials of the Legislative Assembly of the Territory of Utah from 1851 to 1870 Inclusive. Salt Lake City, Utah, Joseph Bull, Public Printer, 1870.

Washington:

Revised Code. San Francisco, Bancroft-Whitney Co.

Statutes of the Territory of Washington. Olympia, Washington, George B. Goudy, Public Printer, 1855.

Wyoming:

Statutes. Charlottesville, Virginia, Michie Co.

Session Laws of the State of Wyoming. Laramie, Wyoming, n.p., 1901.

Canada:

Acts of the Parliament of the Dominion of Canada, Passed in the Thirty-sixth Year of the Reign of Her Majesty Queen Victoria. Ottawa, Brown Chamberlin, 1873.

The Consolidated Statutes of Canada. Toronto, Stewart Derbishire and George Desbarats, 1859.

England:

Chitty's Statutes of Practical Utility, 6th ed. London, Sweet and Maxwell, 1912.

The Laws of England: Being a Complete Statement of the Whole Law of England. London, Butterworth and Co., 1912.

Newspapers

Albuquerque *Review* (New Mexico), 1882.

Atchison *Daily Champion and Press* (Kansas), 1869–1870.

Boulder County News (Colorado), 1871–1873.

Colorado Banner (Denver), 1875–1876.

Colorado Sun (Denver), 1892–1893.

Daily Alta California (San Francisco), 1850–1881.
Daily News (Denver, Colorado), 1882–1892.
Daily Territorial Enterprise (Virginia City, Nevada), 1859–1866.
Denver *Express* (Colorado), 1906.
Denver *Post* (Colorado), 1906.
Denver *Tribune* (Colorado), 1886.
Denver *World* (Colorado), 1887.
Evening Review (Albuquerque, New Mexico), 1882.
Galveston *Daily News* (Texas), 1899.
Gateway Times (Sierra Vista, Arizona), 1960.
Mediator (Portland, Oregon), 1918.
One Big Union Monthly (Chicago, Illinois), 1919.
Oklahoma Gazette (Oklahoma City, Oklahoma), 1889–1890.
San Antonio *Daily Express* (Texas), 1885–1891.
San Antonio *Express* (Texas), 1868–1936.
San Antonio *Express and Evening News* (Texas), 1968–1969.
San Francisco *Chronicle* (California), 1940.
Sequoyah County Times (Oklahoma), 1937.
Taos *News* (New Mexico), 1968.
Tucson *Daily Citizen* (Arizona), 1967.
Weekly Oregonian (Portland), 1850–1854.
Wyoming Eagle (Cheyenne), 1931–1932.

General Works

Adamic, Louis. *Dynamite: The Story of Class Violence in America.* New York, Viking Press, 1935.
Bancroft, Hubert Howe. *Popular Tribunals.* 2 vols. San Francisco, History Co., 1887.
Banning, William, and George Hugh Banning. *Six Horses.* New York, Century Co., 1930.
Bartholomew, Ed. *Western Hard-Cases, or Gunfighters Named Smith.* Ruidoso, New Mexico, Frontier Book Co., 1960.
Beard, Frances Birkhead (ed.). *Wyoming: From Territorial Days to the Present.* Chicago and New York, American Historical Society, 1933.
Bechdolt, Frederick Ritchie. *When the West Was Young.* New York, Century Co., 1922.
Beebe, Lucius, and Charles Clegg. *The American West: The Pictorial Epic of a Continent.* New York, E. P. Dutton and Co., 1955.
———. *U.S. West, the Saga of Wells Fargo.* New York, E. P. Dutton and Co., 1949.

Bell, Daniel. *The End of Ideology.* Glencoe, Illinois, Free Press, 1960.

Bell, Horace. *Reminiscences of a Ranger; or Early Times in Southern California.* Santa Barbara, William Hebberd, 1927.

Bell, William A. *New Tracks in North America, A Journal of Travel and Adventure Whilst Engaged in the Survey for a Southern Railroad to the Pacific Ocean during 1867–8.* 2 vols. London, Chapman and Hall, 1869.

Bolton, Herbert E. *The Spanish Borderlands: A Chronicle of Old Florida and the Southwest.* New Haven, Yale University Press, 1921.

The Book of the States, 1968–1969. Vol. 17. Chicago, Council of State Governments, 1968.

Breakenridge, William M. *Helldorado: Bringing the Law to the Mesquite.* New York and Boston, Houghton Mifflin, 1928.

Brooks, Juanita. *The Mountain Meadows Massacre.* Norman, University of Oklahoma Press, 1962.

Brown, Richard Maxwell. "The American Vigilante Tradition," in Graham, Hugh Davis and Ted Robert Gurr (eds.), *Violence in America: Historical and Comparative Perspectives.* New York, Signet, 1969.

Burns, Walter Noble. *The Saga of Billy the Kid.* Garden City, New York, Garden City Publishing Co., 1926.

———. *Tombstone: An Iliad of the Southwest.* Garden City, New York, Doubleday, Page and Co., 1927.

Bush, Ira Jefferson. *Gringo Doctor.* Caldwell, Idaho, Caxton Printers, 1939.

Campbell, Malcom. *Malcom Campbell, Sheriff.* Casper, Wyoming, Wyomingana, 1932.

Canton, Frank M. *Frontier Trails, The Autobiography of Frank M. Canton.* Edited by Edward Everett Dale. Boston, Houghton Mifflin, 1930.

Carey, Robert J. *The Texas Border and Some Borderlines: A Chronicle and a Guide.* Indianapolis and New York, Bobbs-Merrill, 1950.

Carlisle, William. *Bill Carlisle, Lone Bandit, An Autobiography.* Pasadena, California, Trail's End Publishing Co., 1946.

Castleman, Harvey N. *The Texas Rangers: The Story of an Organization That Is Unique, Like Nothing Else in America.* Girard, Kansas, E. Haldeman-Julius, 1944.

Caughey, John W. *Their Majesties the Mob.* Chicago, University of Chicago Press, 1960.

Chapman, Samuel G., and T. Eric St. Johnston. *The Police Heritage in England and America: A Developmental Survey.* East Lansing, Michigan, Michigan State University, 1962.

Cleveland, Agnes Morley. *Satan's Paradise, from Lucien Maxwell to Fred Lambert.* Boston, Houghton Mifflin, 1952.

Cloward, Richard A., and Lloyd E. Ohlin. *Delinquency and Opportunity: A Theory of Delinquent Gangs.* New York, Free Press, 1960.

Collier, William Ross, and Edwin Victor Westrate. *Dave Cook of the Rockies, Frontier General, Fighting Sheriff, and Leader of Men.* New York, Rufus Rockwell Wilson, 1936.

Constitution for State and Subordinate Orders of the Anti-Horse Thief Association, Missouri Division. St. Paul, Kansas, Press of the News, 1908.

Cook, David J. *Hands Up; or Twenty Years of Detective Life in the Mountains and on the Plains.* Norman, University of Oklahoma Press, 1958.

Cook, James H. *Fifty Years on the Old Frontier As Cowboy, Hunter, Guide, Scout and Ranchman.* New Haven, Yale University Press, 1925.

Coolidge, Dane. *Fighting Men of the West.* New York, E. P. Dutton, 1932.

Cossley-Batt, Jill Lillie Emma. *The Last of the California Rangers.* New York and London, Funk and Wagnalls Co., 1928.

Coursey, O. W. *Wild Bill: James Butler Hickok.* Mitchell, South Dakota, Educator Supply Co., 1924.

Cox, William R. *Luke Short and His Era.* Garden City, New York, Doubleday, 1961.

Cunningham, Eugene. *Triggernometry: A Gallery of Gunfighters with Technical Notes on Leather Slapping As a Fine Art Gathered from Many a Loose Holstered Expert over the Years.* Caldwell, Idaho, Caxton Printers, 1947.

De Toqueville, Alexis. *Democracy in America.* Translated by Henry Reeve. 2 vols. New York, P. F. Collier and Son, 1900.

Dewhurst, Henry Stephen. *The Railroad Police.* Springfield, Illinois, Charles C. Thomas, 1955.

De Winton, Harry, and L. D. La Tourette. *Peace Officers of Arizona, 1917–1918.* N.p., W. H. Wilky, n.d.

Dick, Everett. *The Sod House Frontier 1854–1890: A Social History of the Northern Plains from the Creation of Kansas and Nebraska to the Admission of the Dakotas.* Lincoln, Nebraska, Jensen Publishing Co., 1954.

Dimsdale, Thomas J. *The Vigilantes of Montana.* Norman, University of Oklahoma Press, 1953.

Dixon, Olive K. *Life of "Billy" Dixon: Plainsman, Scout and Pioneer, A Narrative in Which Are Described Many Things Relating to the*

Early Southwest, with an Account of the Fights Between Indians and Buffalo Hunters at Adobe Walls and at Buffalo Wallow, for Which Congress Voted the Medal of Honor to the Survivors. Dallas, P. L. Turner Co., 1927.

Dobie, J. Frank. *A Vaquero of the Brush Country: Partly from the Reminiscences of John Young.* Boston, Little, Brown and Co., 1949.

Douglas, C. L. *The Gentlemen in the White Hats, Dramatic Episodes in the History of the Texas Rangers.* Dallas, Southwest Press, 1934.

Dunn, J. B. John. *Perilous Trails of Texas.* Dallas, Southwest Press, 1932.

Durham, George. *Taming the Nueces Strip, The Story of McNelly's Rangers.* Austin, University of Texas Press, 1962.

Dykstra, Robert R. *The Cattle Towns.* New York, Alfred A. Knopf, 1968.

Eldefonso, Edward, Alan Coffey, and Richard C. Grace. *Principles of Law Enforcement.* New York, John Wiley and Sons, 1968.

Elliott, Mabel A. *Crime in Modern Society.* New York, Harper and Bros., 1952.

Erwin, Allen A. *The Southwest of John H. Slaughter, 1841–1922: Pioneer Cattleman and Traildriver of Texas, the Pecos, and Arizona and Sheriff of Tombstone.* Glendale, California, Arthur H. Clark Co., 1965.

Feigenbaum, Jacob Walter, William B. Blanchet, and J. B. Arnold. *The Texas Peace Officers Manual.* San Antonio, the authors, 1937.

Fenin, George N., and William K. Everson. *The Western: From Silents to Cinerama.* New York, Orion Press, 1962.

Forbes, Jack D. *Apache, Navaho, and Spaniard.* Norman, University of Oklahoma Press, 1960.

Fox, Dixon Ryan (ed.). *Sources of Culture in the Middle West: Backgrounds Versus Frontier.* New York, D. Appleton-Century Co., 1934.

Furlong, Thomas. *Fifty Years a Detective.* St. Louis, C. E. Barnett, [1912].

Gard, Wayne. *Frontier Justice.* Norman, University of Oklahoma Press, 1949.

———. *Sam Bass.* Boston and New York, Houghton Mifflin, 1936.

Garland, Hamlin. *They of the High Trails.* New York, Harper and Bros., 1916.

Garrett, Patrick F. *The Authentic Life of Billy, the Kid: The Noted Desperado of the Southwest, Whose Deeds of Daring and Blood Made His Name a Terror in New Mexico, Arizona, and Northern Mexico.* Norman, University of Oklahoma Press, 1954.

Germann, A. C., Frank D. Day, and Robert R. J. Gallati. *Introduction to Law Enforcement and Criminal Justice.* Springfield, Illinois, Charles C. Thomas, 1968.

Gillett, James B. *Six Years with the Texas Rangers: 1875 to 1881.* Edited by Milo Milton Quaife. Chicago, R. R. Donnelly & Sons, 1943.

Graves, Richard S. *Oklahoma Outlaws: A Graphic History of the Early Days of Oklahoma.* Oklahoma City, State Printing Co., 1915.

Greer, James Kimmins. *Colonel Jack Hays: Texas Frontier Leader and California Builder.* New York, E. P. Dutton & Co., 1952.

Grey, Zane. *The Lone Star Ranger: A Romance of the Border.* New York, Grosset and Dunlap, 1915.

Hagan, William T. *American Indians.* Chicago, University of Chicago Press, 1961.

———. *Indian Police and Judges: Experiments in Acculturation and Control.* New Haven, Yale University Press, 1966.

Haley, J. Evetts. *Jeff Milton: A Good Man with a Gun.* Norman, University of Oklahoma Press, 1948.

———. *The XIT Ranch of Texas and the Early Days of the Llano Estacado.* Chicago, Lakeside Press, 1929.

Hicks, John D. *The Populist Revolt: A History of the Farmers' Alliance and the People's Party.* N.p., University of Nebraska Press, 1961.

Hogan, William Ransom. *The Texas Republic: A Social and Economic History.* Norman, University of Oklahoma Press, 1946.

Holmes, Oliver Wendell, Jr. *The Common Law.* Boston, Little Brown, 1881.

Hopping, Richard Coke. *A Sheriff-Ranger in Chuckwagon Days.* New York, Pageant Press, 1952.

Horan, James D., and Howard Swiggett. *The Pinkerton Story.* New York, G. P. Putnam's Sons, 1951.

Horn, Tom. *Life of Tom Horn, Government Scout and Interpreter, Written by Himself, Together with His Letters and Statements by His Friends.* Norman, University of Oklahoma Press, 1964.

Hough, Emerson. *The Girl at Halfway House: A Story of the Plains.* New York, D. Appleton, 1900.

———. *The Story of the Outlaw: A Study of the Western Desperado.* New York, Grosset and Dunlap, 1905.

Hunter, John Marvin, and Noah H. Rose. *The Album of Gunfighters.* Bandera, Texas, Rose and Hunter, 1951.

James, Vinton Lee. *Frontier and Pioneer Recollections of Early Days in San Antonio and West Texas.* San Antonio, Vinton Lee James, 1938.

Jenkins, John H., and H. Gordon Frost. *I'm Frank Hamer.* Austin, Texas, Pemberton Press, 1968.

Jennings, N. A. *A Texas Ranger.* New York, Charles Scribner's Sons, 1899.

Jones, William Frank. *The Experiences of a Deputy U.S. Marshal of the Indian Territory.* N.p., 1937.

Journal and Debates of the Constitutional Convention of the State of Wyoming. Cheyenne, Daily Sun, 1893.

Kornbluh, Joyce L. (ed.). *Rebel Voices: An I.W.W. Anthology.* Ann Arbor, University of Michigan Press, 1964.

Krakel, Dean F. *The Saga of Tom Horn: The Story of a Cattlemen's War.* Laramie, Wyoming, Powder River Publishers, 1954.

Lake, Stuart N. *Wyatt Earp: Frontier Marshal.* Boston and New York, Houghton Mifflin, 1931.

Lane, Roger. *Policing the City: Boston 1822–1885.* Cambridge, Harvard University Press, 1967.

Langford, Nathaniel Pitt. *Vigilante Days and Ways, The Pioneers of the Rockies, The Makers and Making of Montana, Idaho, Oregon, Washington, and Wyoming.* 2 vols. New York and St. Paul, D. D. Merrill Co., 1893.

Larson, T. A. *History of Wyoming.* Lincoln, University of Nebraska Press, 1965.

LeFors, Joe. *Wyoming Peace Officer, An Autobiography.* Laramie, Wyoming, Laramie Printing Co., 1953.

Lewis, Alfred Henry. *Wolfville.* New York, Grosset and Dunlap, 1897.

Llewellyn, Karl N., and E. Adamson Hoebel. *The Cheyenne Way: Conflict and Case Law in Primitive Jurisprudence.* Norman, University of Oklahoma Press, 1941.

Ludlow, Fitz Hugh. *The Heart of the Continent: A Record of Travel Across the Plains and in Oregon.* New York, Hurd and Houghton, 1870.

Martin, Douglas D. *Tombstone's Epitaph.* Albuquerque, University of New Mexico Press, 1951.

McCarty, John L. *Maverick Town: The Story of Old Tascosa.* Norman, University of Oklahoma Press, 1946.

Mercer, Asa Shinn. *The Banditti of the Plains: Or the Cattlemen's Invasion of Wyoming in 1892.* San Francisco, George Fields, 1935.

Metz, Leon Claire. *Dallas Stoudenmire: El Paso Marshal.* Austin, Texas, Pemberton Press, 1969.

Monaghan, Jay. *The Great Rascal: The Life and Adventures of Ned Buntline.* Boston, Little Brown, 1951.

Nix, Evett Dumas. *Oklahombres: Particularly the Wilder Ones.* As told to Gordon Hines. St. Louis, E. D. Nix, 1929.

Norfleet, J. Frank. *Norfleet: The Amazing Experiences of an Intrepid*

Texas Rancher with an International Swindling Ring. As told to Gordon Hines. Sugarland, Texas, Imperial Press, 1927.

O'Connor, Richard. *Wild Bill Hickok*. Garden City, New York, Doubleday and Co., 1959.

Olmstead, Frederick Law. *A Journey Through Texas; or, a Saddle-trip on the Southwestern Frontier: with a Statistical Appendix*. New York, Dix, Edwards and Co., 1857.

Paine, Albert Bigelow. *Captain Bill McDonald, Texas Ranger: A Story of Frontier Reform*. New York, J. J. Little and Ives Co., 1909.

Paine, Lauran. *Tom Horn: Man of the West*. Barre, Massachusetts, Barre Publishing Co., 1963.

Pattulo, George. *The Sheriff of Badger: A Tale of the Southwestern Borderland*. New York, D. Appleton, 1912.

Paul, Rodman W. *California Gold: The Beginning of Mining in the Far West*. Lincoln, University of Nebraska Press, 1947.

Penfield, Thomas. *Western Sheriffs and Marshals*. New York, Grosset and Dunlap, 1955.

Pike, James. *Scout and Ranger, Being the Personal Adventures of James Pike of the Texas Rangers in 1859–60*. Princeton, Princeton University Press, 1932.

Pound, Roscoe. *Criminal Justice in America*. New York, Henry Holt, 1930.

Preece, Harold. *Lone Star Man: Ira Aten, Last of the Old Texas Rangers*. New York, Hastings House, 1960.

Pringle, Patrick. *Hue and Cry: The Story of Henry and John Fielding and Their Bow Street Runners*. New York, William Morrow and Co., 1955.

Proceedings of the Eleventh Annual Session of the Anti-Horse Thief Association, I. T. Division, Held at McAlester, Oklahoma, October 22–23, 1913. St. Paul, Kansas, Press of the A.H.T.A. News, 1913.

Proceedings of the Sheriffs' Association of Texas. Austin, Texas, Eugene Von Boeckmann Printers, 1879.

Radzinowicz, Leon. *A History of English Criminal Law and Its Administration from 1750: The Clash Between Private Initiative and Public Interest in the Enforcement of the Law*. London, Stevens and Sons, 1956.

Raine, William MacLeod. *Bucky O'Connor: A Tale of the Unfenced Border*. New York, Grosset and Dunlap, 1910.

———. *Famous Sheriffs and Western Outlaws*. Garden City, New York, Garden City Publishing Co., 1929.

———. *45-Calibre Law: The Way of Life of the Frontier Peace Officer*. Evanston, Illinois, Row, Peterson and Co., 1941.

Rak, Mary Kidder. *Border Patrol*. Boston, Houghton Mifflin, 1938.

Raymond, Dora Neill. *Captain Lee Hall of Texas*. Norman, University of Oklahoma Press, 1940.

Reith, Charles. *A New Study of Police History*. London, Oliver and Boyd, 1956.

Rhodes, Eugene Manlove. *The Best Novels and Stories of Eugene Manlove Rhodes*. Edited by Frank V. Dearing. Boston, Houghton Mifflin Co., 1949.

Richardson, Albert D. *Beyond the Mississippi*. Hartford, Connecticut, American Publishing Co., 1869.

Richardson, James D. (ed.). *A Compilation of the Messages and Papers of the Presidents, 1789–1902*. 11 vols. Vol. VIII. Washington, Bureau of National Literature and Art, 1904.

Roberts, Dan Webster. *Rangers and Sovereignty*. San Antonio, Wood Printing and Engraving Co., 1914.

Roberts, Lou Conway [Mrs. Dan W.]. *A Woman's Reminiscences of Six Years in Camp with the Texas Rangers*. Austin, Texas, Von Boeckmann-Jones [1928].

Robinson, Duncan W. *Judge Robert McAlpin Williamson: Texas' Three Legged Willie*. Austin, Texas, Texas State Historical Association, 1948.

Robinson, William Henry. *The Story of Arizona*. Phoenix, Berryhill Co., 1919.

Rosa, Joseph G. *The Gunfighter: Man or Myth?* Norman, University of Oklahoma Press, 1969.

Rynning, Thomas H. *Gun Notches: The Life Story of a Cowboy-Soldier*. As told to Al Cohn and Joe Chisholm. New York, Frederick A. Stokes, 1931.

Sanders, Helen Fitzgerald (ed.). *X. Beidler: Vigilante*. Norman, University of Oklahoma Press, 1957.

Scherer, James A. B. *The Lion of the Vigilantes: William T. Coleman and the Life of Old San Francisco*. Indianapolis and New York, Bobbs-Merrill, 1939.

Sexton, Grover F. *The Arizona Sheriff*. N.p., Studebaker Corporation of America, 1925.

Sharp, Paul F. *The Agrarian Revolt in Western Canada: A Survey Showing American Parallels*. Minneapolis, University of Minnesota Press, 1948.

Shaw, James C. *North from Texas: Incidents in the Early Life of a Range Cowman in Texas, Dakota, and Wyoming, 1852–1883*. Edited by Herbert O. Brayer. Evanston, Illinois, Branding Iron Press, 1952.

Sheffy, Lester Fields. *The Francklyn Land and Cattle Company: A Panhandle Enterprise, 1882–1957.* Austin, University of Texas Press, 1963.

Shinn, Charles Howard. *Graphic Descriptions of Pacific Coast Outlaws: Thrilling Exploits of Their Arch-enemy Sheriff Harry N. Morse.* Los Angeles, Westernlore Press, 1958.

———. *Mining Camps: A Study in American Frontier Government.* New York, Alfred A. Knopf, 1948.

Shirley, Glenn. *Heck Thomas: Frontier Marshal, The Story of a Real Gunfighter.* Philadelphia and New York, Chilton Co., 1962.

———. *Six-gun and Silver Star.* Albuquerque, University of New Mexico Press, 1955.

Shores, Cyrus Wells "Doc." *Memoirs of a Lawman.* Edited by Wilson Rockwell. Denver, Sage Books, 1962.

Sibley, Walter F. *Peace Officers of the State of California, Sheriffs of Arizona, Nevada, Oregon, Washington, State Prison Credits and Legal Distances.* N.p., 1903.

Simmons, Lee. *Assignment Huntsville: Memoirs of a Texas Prison Official.* Austin, University of Texas Press, 1957.

Siringo, Charles A. *Riata and Spurs: The Story of a Lifetime Spent in the Saddle As Cowboy and Ranger.* Boston and New York, Houghton Mifflin, 1931.

———. *A Texas Cowboy: Or Fifteen Years on the Hurricane Deck of a Spanish Pony.* New York, William Sloane, 1950.

———. *Two Evil Isms: Pinkertonism and Anarchism, by a Cowboy detective who knows, as he spent twenty-two years in the inner circle of Pinkerton's National Detective Association.* Chicago, Charles A. Siringo, 1915.

Smiley, Jerome C. (ed.). *History of Denver with Outlines of the Earlier History of the Rocky Mountain Country.* Denver, Times-Sun Publishing Co., 1901.

Smith, Bruce. *Police Systems in the United States.* New York, Harper and Row, 1960.

Smith, Henry Nash. *Virgin Land: The American West As Symbol and Myth.* New York, Vintage Books, 1950.

Smithwick, Noah. *The Evolution of a State or Recollections of Old Texas Days.* Austin, Texas, Gammel Book Co., 1900.

Sonnichsen, Charles Leland. *I'll Die Before I'll Run: The Story of the Great Feuds of Texas.* New York, Harper and Bros., 1951.

Soulé, Frank, John H. Gihon, and James Nisbet. *The Annals of San Francisco; containing A summary of the history of the first discovery, settlement, progress, and present condition of California,*

And a complete history of all the important events connected with its great city: to which are added, Biographical memoirs of some prominent citizens. New York, D. Appleton and Co., 1855.

Sowell, A. J. *Rangers and Pioneers of Texas, With A Concise Account of the Early Settlements, Hardships, Massacres, Battles, and Wars, by Which Texas Was Rescued from the Rule of the Savage and Consecrated to the Empire of Civilization.* San Antonio, Shepard Bros., 1884.

Steckmesser, Kent Ladd. *The Western Hero in History and Legend.* Norman, University of Oklahoma Press, 1965.

Stegner, Wallace E. *The Gathering of Zion: The Story of the Mormon Trail.* New York, McGraw-Hill, 1964.

Sullivan, Dulcie. *The LS Brand: The Story of a Texas Panhandle Ranch.* Austin, University of Texas Press, 1968.

Sullivan, John L. *Introduction to Police Science.* New York, McGraw-Hill, 1966.

Summerfield, Charles. [Alfred W. Arrington]. *The Desperadoes of the Southwest: containing an account of the Cane-Hill murders, together with the lives of several of the most notorious regulators and moderators of that region.* New York, W. H. Graham, 1847.

———. *The Rangers and Regulators of the Tanaha: or, Life Among the Lawless, a Tale of the Republic of Texas.* New York, Robert M. DeWitt, 1856.

Sutton, Fred Ellsworth. *Hands Up!: Stories of the Six-Gun Fighters of the Old Wild West.* As told to A. B. McDonald. Indianapolis, Bobbs-Merrill, 1927.

Thrasher, Frederick M. *The Gang: A Study of 1,313 Gangs in Chicago.* Chicago, University of Chicago Press, 1963.

Tilghman, Zoe A. *Marshal of the Last Frontier: Life and Services of William Matthew (Bill) Tilghman for 50 years one of the greatest peace officers of the West.* Glendale, California, Arthur H. Clark, 1964.

Turner, John Peter. *The North-West Mounted Police, 1873–1893.* 2 vols. Ottawa, Edmond Cloutier, 1950.

Underhill, Ruth M. *The Navajos.* Norman, University of Oklahoma Press, 1956.

Wallace, Ernest, and E. Adamson Hoebel. *The Comanches: Lords of the Plains.* Norman, University of Oklahoma Press, 1952.

Walter, William W. (comp.). *The Great Understander: True Life Story of the Last of the Wells, Fargo Shotgun Messengers.* Aurora, Illinois, William W. Walter, 1931.

Webb, Walter Prescott. *The Great Plains.* New York, Grosset and Dunlap, 1931.
——. *The Texas Rangers: A Century of Frontier Defense.* Austin, University of Texas Press, 1965.
Wells Fargo. San Francisco, Wells Fargo Bank, 1967.
Wentworth, Edward Norris. *America's Sheep Trails: History, Personalities.* Ames, Iowa, Iowa State College Press, 1948.
White, Owen Payne. *Lead and Likker.* New York, Minton, Balch, and Co., 1932.
Williams, R. H. *With the Border Ruffians: Memories of the Far West, 1852–1868.* London, John Murray, 1907.
Wilson, Neill Compton. *Treasure Express: Epic Days of the Wells Fargo.* New York, Macmillan, 1936.
Wilson, Rufus Rockwell. *A Notable Company of Adventurers.* New York, B. W. Dodge and Co., 1908.
Wister, Owen. *The Virginian: A Horseman of the Plains.* New York, Macmillan, 1930.
Young, John P. *San Francisco, A History of the Pacific Coast Metropolis.* 2 vols. San Francisco and Chicago, S. J. Clarke Publishing Co., 1912.

Periodicals

Adams, James Truslow. "Our Lawless Heritage," *The Atlantic Monthly,* Vol. CXLII, No. 6 (December, 1928), 732–40.
Adams, Lynn G. "The State Police," *Annals of the American Academy of Political and Social Science,* Vol. CXLVI (November, 1929), 34–40.
Adams, Paul. "The Unsolved Murder of Ben Thompson, Pistoleer Extraordinary," *Southwestern Historical Quarterly,* Vol. XLVIII, No. 3 (January, 1945), 321–29.
"Administration of Justice in California, Illustrated in the Trial, Conviction, and Punishment of Delinquents. Log Cabin on the North Fork, California, Feb. 16th, 1850." *California Pamphlets,* Vol. XXVI, No. 1 (n.d.), 354–56.
The American Detective, Vol. I, No. 1 (March, 1893).
Ansley, Norman. "The United States Secret Service: An Administrative History," *Journal of Criminal Law, Criminology, and Police Science,* Vol. XLVII, No. 1 (May-June, 1956), 93–109.
Arnett, R. E. "A Young Cowboy Detective," as told to Ida Drum Arnett, *Colorado Magazine,* Vol. XXIV, No. 6 (November, 1947), 250–58.

Baenziger, Ann Patton. "The Texas State Police During Reconstruction: A Reexamination," *Southwestern Historical Quarterly*, Vol. LXXII, No. 4 (April, 1969), 470–91.

Barker, Eugene C. "The Government of Austin's Colony, 1821–1831," *Southwestern Historical Quarterly*, Vol. XXI, No. 3 (January, 1918), 223–52.

——— (ed.). "Minutes of the Ayuntamiento of San Felipe de Austin, 1828–1832," *Southwestern Historical Quarterly*, "Part II," Vol. XXI, No. 4 (April, 1918), 395–423; "Part IV," Vol. XXII, No. 2 (October, 1918), 180–96; "Part X," Vol. XXIII, No. 4 (April, 1920), 302–307; "Part XII," Vol. XXIV, No. 2 (October, 1920), 154–66.

Barton, Frank W. "Gen. Butler Begins His Work of Organizing Oregon State Police," *The State Trooper*, Vol. XII, No. 10 (June, 1931), 7–8.

Benge, William B. "Law and Order on Indian Reservations," *Federal Bar Journal*, Vol. XX, No. 3 (Summer, 1960), 223–29.

"Bill Tilghman," *The Link*, Vol. XXV, No. 4 (July–August, 1960), 5–7.

Brashear, Minnie M. "The Anti-Horse Thief Association of Northeast Missouri," *Missouri Historical Review*, Vol. XLV, No. 4 (July, 1951), 341–48.

Brooks, B. S. "A Detective Police," *The Pioneer or California Monthly Magazine*, Vol. II, No. 6 (December, 1854), 321–33.

Callan, Austin. "A Sentinel of the Old Frontier," *Sheriffs' Association of Texas Magazine*, Vol. I, No. 1 (1930), 13–14.

———. "Sheriffing in the Old Days," *Sheriffs' Association of Texas Magazine*, Vol. I, No. 1 (1930), 9–10.

Canlis, Michael N. "The Evolution of Law Enforcement in California," *The Far-Westerner*, Vol. II, No. 3 (July, 1961), 1–13.

Cato, E. Raymond. "The Highway Patrol of California," *Our Sheriff and Police Journal*, Vol. XXX, No. 6 (June, 1935), 7, 28.

Cawelti, John G. "The Gunfighter and Society," *The American West*, Vol. V, No. 2 (March, 1968), 30–35, 76–78.

Clum, John P. "It All Happened in Tombstone," *Arizona Historical Review*, Vol. II, No. 3 (October, 1929), 46–72.

———. "The San Carlos Police," *New Mexico Historical Review*, Vol. IV, No. 3 (July, 1929), 203–19.

Conklin, J. J. "Forty-four Years with Mounties: No Romance, Just Plain Hard Work," *The State Trooper*, Vol. XI, No. 5 (January, 1930), 15.

Cronin, Con P. "Arizona's Six-Gun Classic, A Vivid Personal Narrative of the Historic Duel Between Pete Gabriel and Joe Phy, Famous

Old-time Peace Officers," *Arizona Historical Review*, Vol. III, No. 2 (July, 1930), 7–11.

Cunningham, J. F. "Experiences of a Pioneer District Attorney," *West Texas Historical Association Year Book*, Vol. XIII (June, 1932), 126–35.

Dobie, J. Frank. "Detectives of the Cattle Ranges: How the Texas and South-Western Cattle Raisers' Association Goes After Thieves," *The Country Gentleman*, Vol. XCII, No. 2 (February, 1927), 30–31, 176–79.

Duke, J. K. "Bad Men and Peace Officers of the Southwest," *West Texas Historical Association Year Book*, Vol. XIII (June, 1932), 51–61.

Elliott, Mabel A. "Crime and the Frontier Mores," *American Sociological Review*, Vol. IX, No. 2 (April, 1944), 185–92.

Fanger, Fred. "The Colorado Sheriffs' and Peace Officers' Association," *Colorado Magazine*, Vol. XXIII, No. 2 (March, 1946), 88–92.

Foreman, Carolyn Thomas. "The Light-Horse in the Indian Territory," *Chronicles of Oklahoma*, Vol. XXXIV, No. 1 (Spring, 1956), 17–43.

Gass, Olive. "The Vigilantes, Nebraska's First Defenders," *Nebraska History Magazine*, Vol. XIV, No. 1 (January–March, 1933), 3–18.

Gray, Robert M. "A History of the Utah State Bureau of Criminal Identification and Investigation," *Utah Historical Quarterly*, Vol. XXIV, No. 2 (April, 1956), 171–79.

Hansen, George W. "True Story of Wild Bill–McCanles Affray in Jefferson County, Nebraska, July 12, 1861," *Nebraska History Magazine*, Vol. X, No. 2 (April–June, 1927), 71–112.

Havins, T. R. "Sheepmen-Cattlemen Antagonism on the Texas Frontier," *West Texas Historical Association Year Book*, Vol. XVIII (October, 1942), 10–23.

Higgins, Lois. "Historical Background of Policewomen's Service," *Journal of Criminal Law and Criminology*, Vol. XLI, No. 6 (March–April, 1951), 822–33.

Holden, W. C. "Law and Lawlessness on the Texas Frontier, 1875–1890," *Southwestern Historical Quarterly*, Vol. XLIV, No. 2 (October, 1940), 188–203.

Holt, R. D. "The Introduction of Barbed Wire into Texas and the Fence Cutting War," *West Texas Historical Association Year Book*, Vol. VI (June, 1930), 72–88.

Hough, Emerson. "Traveling the Old Trails: The Road to Tomorrow," *Saturday Evening Post*, Vol. CXCII, No. 14 (October 4, 1919), 22–23, 133–44.

Hume, C. Ross. "Oklahoma History Embedded in the Law," *Chronicles of Oklahoma*, Vol. XXV, No. 2 (Summer, 1947), 92–101.

Jones, Oakah L., Jr. "The Origins of the Navajo Indian Police, 1872–1873," *Arizona and the West*, Vol. VIII, No. 3 (Autumn, 1966), 225–38.

Jordan, Philip D. "Lady Luck and Her Knights of the Royal Flush," *Southwestern Historical Quarterly*, Vol. LXXII, No. 3 (January, 1969), 295–312.

Julian, George W. "Land Stealing in New Mexico," *North American Review*, Vol. CXLV, No. 368 (July 1, 1887), 2–31.

Langeluttig, Albert. "Federal Police," *Annals of the American Academy of Political and Social Science*, Vol. CXLVI (November, 1929), 41–54.

McKelvey, Blake. "Penology in the Westward Movement," *Pacific Historical Review*, Vol. II (December, 1933), 418–38.

MacLeod, William Christie. "Police and Punishment Among Native Americans of the Plains," *Journal of Criminal Law and Criminology*, Vol. XXVIII, No. 2 (May–June, 1937), 181–201.

McNeil, Irving. "Indian Justice," *New Mexico Historical Review*, Vol. XIX, No. 4 (October, 1944), 261–70.

Manguson, John P. "The Private Person's Duty to Assist the Police in Arrest," *Wyoming Law Journal*, Vol. XIII, No. 1 (Fall, 1958), 72–76.

Marx, Jerry. "Pioneer Lawman, Lee Pollock," *The Peace Officer*, Vol. XXXI, No. 4 (January, 1961), 11–13.

Moley, Raymond. "The Sheriff and the Constable," *Annals of the American Academy of Political and Social Science*, Vol. CXLVI (November, 1929), 28–33.

Mondy, R. W. "Analysis of Frontier Social Instability," *Southwestern Social Science Quarterly*, Vol. XXIV, No. 2 (September, 1943), 167–77.

Mueller, Oscar O. "The Central Montana Vigilante Raids of 1884," *Montana Magazine of History*, Vol. I, No. 1 (January, 1951), 23–56.

Nichols, George Ward. "Wild Bill," *Harper's New Monthly Magazine*, Vol. XXXIV, No. 201 (February, 1867), 273–85.

Opler, Morris Edward and Catherine H. Opler. "Mescalero Apache History in the Southwest," *New Mexico Historical Review*, Vol. XXV, No. 1 (January, 1950), 1–36.

Outland, Charles F. "San Buenaventura Justice, 1870–1871," *Ventura County Historical Society Quarterly*, Vol. VII, No. 1 (November, 1961), 10–18.

Perrigo, Lynn I. "Law and Order in Early Colorado Mining Camps,"

Mississippi Valley Historical Review, Vol. XXVIII, No. 1 (June, 1941), 41–62.

Pettit, Sydney G. "Judge Begbie in Action: The Establishment of Law and Preservation of Order in British Columbia," *British Columbia Historical Quarterly*, Vol. XI, No. 2 (April, 1947), 113–48.

Pierson, George Wilson. "The Frontier and American Institutions: A Criticism of the Turner Thesis," *New England Quarterly*, Vol. XV, No. 2 (June, 1942), 224–55.

Rathburn, Carl M. "Keeping Peace Along the Mexican Border: The Unceasing Task of the Arizona Rangers, A Picturesque Body of Fighting-Men, and What They Accomplish by Coolness and Bravery," *Harper's Weekly*, Vol. L, No. 2604 (November 17, 1906), 1632–34, 1649.

Rister, Carl Coke. "Outlaws and Vigilantes of the Southern Plains: 1865–1885," *Mississippi Valley Historical Review*, Vol. XIX, No. 4 (March, 1933), 537–54.

Roosevelt, Theodore. "Sheriff's Work on a Ranch," *Century Magazine*, Vol. XXXVI, No. 1 (May, 1888), 39–51.

Sage, Walter N. "The North-West Mounted Police and British Columbia," *Pacific Historical Review*, Vol. XVIII, No. 3 (August, 1949), 345–61.

"Sam Bass, Famous Desperado Was Likable Outlaw," *Sheriffs' Association of Texas Magazine*, Vol. I, No. 3 (July, 1931), 14.

Schaefer, Jack. "Real Heroes of the West," *Holiday*, Vol. II, No. 6 (December, 1957), 76–77, 184–200.

Schuster, Stephen W. "The Modernization of the Texas Rangers: 1933–1936," *West Texas Historical Association Year Book*, Vol. XLIII (October, 1967), 65–79.

Shalloo, Jeremiah P. "The Private Police of Pennsylvania," *Annals of the American Academy of Political and Social Science*, Vol. CXLVI (November, 1929), 55–62.

Smith, Bruce. "History of State Police Organizations," *Our Sheriff and Police Journal*, Vol. XXX, No. 6 (June, 1935), 9.

Smith, Duane A. "Colorado and Judicial Recall," *The American Journal of Legal History*, Vol. VII, No. 3 (July, 1963), 198–209.

"Statutory Structures for Sentencing Felons to Prison," *Columbia Law Review*, Vol. LX, No. 8 (December, 1960), 1134–72.

"Texas' First Sheriff," *Sheriffs' Association of Texas Magazine*, Vol. I, No. 11 (September, 1932), 15.

"Texas Rangers Praised, Make Short Work of Cleaning Up Oil Boom Town, Borger," *The State Trooper*, Vol. IX, No. 1 (September, 1927), 15–17.

"Thomas Jefferson Carr—A Frontier Sheriff," *Annals of Wyoming*, Vol. XX, No. 2 (July, 1948), 165–76.

Tidwell, Dean. "The Indian Career Officer," *Police Chief*, Vol. XXXVI, No. 11 (November, 1969), 30–31.

Underwood, J. R. "Texas Pleased With Its Expanding Force of Trained Highway Patrolmen," *The State Trooper*, Vol. XIII, No. 2 (October, 1931), 11–12.

Warren, Frederick S. "Colorado Legislative Committee Urges State Police Organization," *The State Trooper*, Vol. XII, No. 4 (December, 1930), 13–14.

———. "Colorado's New State Highway Courtesy Patrol Is Now in Effective Operation," *The State Trooper*, Vol. XVII, No. 4 (December, 1935), 5–6.

Webb, Walter Prescott. "Oil Town Cleaned Up: Texas Rangers Summoned to Restore Order When Local Officials Could Not Enforce Law," *The State Trooper*, Vol. VIII, No. 4 (December, 1926), 11–12.

———. "Texas Rangers Kept Idle: Present Restraints Upon Force Brings Back Memories of Past Accomplishments of Men," *The State Trooper*, Vol. VII, No. 10 (June, 1926), 13–14.

Welty, Raymond L. "The Policing of the Frontier by the Army, 1860–1870," *Kansas Historical Quarterly*, Vol. VII, No. 3 (August, 1938), 246–57.

Wharton, Clarence. "Early Judicial History of Texas," *Texas Law Review*, Vol. XII, No. 3 (April, 1934), 311–25.

Winsor, Mulford. "The Arizona Rangers," *Our Sheriff and Police Journal*, Vol. XXXI, No. 6 (June, 1936), 49–61.

"Wyoming Sheriffs," *Annals of Wyoming*, Vol. XV, No. 3 (July, 1943), 247–48.

Index

321

330